Groups and Group Rights

An *AMINTAPHIL Volume*

Groups and Group Rights

Edited by
Christine Sistare, Larry May,
and Leslie Francis

University Press of Kansas

© 2001 by the University Press of Kansas
All rights reserved

Published by the University Press of Kansas (Lawrence, Kansas 66049), which was
organized by the Kansas Board of Regents and is operated and funded by Emporia
State University, Fort Hays State University, Kansas State University, Pittsburg State
University, the University of Kansas, and Wichita State University.

Library of Congress Cataloging-in-Publication Data

Groups and group rights / edited by Christine Sistare, Larry May, and Leslie Francis.
    p.   cm.
    "An AMINTAPHIL volume"—P. preceding t.p.
    Includes index.
    ISBN 0-7006-1041-3 (cloth : alk. paper)—ISBN 0-7006-1042-1 (pbk. : alk paper)
    1. Social groups.   2. Civil rights.   3. Democracy.   I. Sistare, C. T.
(Christine T.), 1951-   II. May, Larry.   III. Francis, Leslie, 1946-

    HM711.G76   2000
    305—dc21   00-043451

British Library Cataloguing in Publication Data is available.

Printed in the United States of America

10 9 8 7 6 5 4 3 2 1

The paper used in this publication meets the minimum requirements of the American
National Standard for Permanence of Paper for Printed Library Materials Z39.48-
1984.

This volume is dedicated to the executive committee

and membership of AMINTAPHIL

CONTENTS

ACKNOWLEDGMENTS

Many thanks are owed to the staff of the University Press of Kansas, including Nancy Scott Jackson and Rebecca Knight Giusti, and to Susan Eck-lund, an extraordinarily gifted (and patient) freelance copy editor. Thanks as well to the Muhlenberg College Center for Ethics and Leadership for supporting the physical preparation of the volume.

General Introduction

Groups, Selves, and the State

Christine Sistare

Aristotle claimed that the human is a *zoon politikon anthropos*, by which he meant that the individual human is *of and in* a social group. Since his time, philosophers, sociologists, and psychologists have endeavored to articulate the role played by social groups in the lives of their members. It has been suggested frequently that the relationship of individual to group is the central problem of social, moral, and political theory. But, as Aristotle also observed, individuals typically belong to more than one group or collectivity (*koinonia*). This feature of human social life is reflected in the sociopsychological language of "culture and subculture," of "primary group socialization and subgroup socialization," and of "plural socialization[s] ."

While the relationships, consonance, or dissonance of the larger society and smaller groups are of particular sociopsychological significance, political theorists and legal philosophers are more directly concerned to delineate the legitimate political and legal status of those subcollectivities within the jurisdiction of the larger state. Just such questions of proper relationship and allegiance have generated considerable literature, and more rhetoric, about the relationship of the federal and state governments of the United States. The conflict of "states' rights" and "federalism," among other issues, gave us the Civil War, on the bitter fruits of which we continue to feed. Similar conflicts of state sovereignty and federal oversight arise in far less dramatic situations, which are normally resolved by judicial decision or, in some instances, by the decorous retreat of one or both of the disputing parties. Such matters of state and federal authority are, at least in principle, resolvable by appeal to constitutional doctrine; or, if the Constitution is not understood as determining the issue, some reference to governmental efficiency or social utility can be made.[1]

But by what means and with reference to what concerns might we define legitimate relations between governmental institutions and the practices or interests of unofficial, politically indeterminate subgroups existing

1

within the larger society? A deceptively simple answer is that we should regard such groups as *mere aggregates*—collectivities no more than, and fully reducible to, their individual members. On this view, all interests, rights, and obligations of the members are to be determined as the products of democratic rule, constrained only by constitutional protections of *individuals*. The group, ex hypothesi, does not exist as anything other than an aggregation of individuals; thus, there can be no question of group rights, group obligations, or, in any illuminating sense, group interests. There is, then, no genuine legal or political problem, but only the illusion of one.

Yet this surely is too simple an answer—and a question-begging one, at that. Prior to any ontology of groups, prior to any moral or political assessment of the rights and obligations of groups, there is the indisputable fact of our ordinary recognition of the existence of groups other than mere collectivities. This recognition is manifest in our concepts of family, tribe, neighborhood, sect, institution, and other groups of significance for human and social living. Less appealing groups, as well, are acknowledged when we speak of youth gangs, crime syndicates, or political cabals. It will not suffice to dismiss these groups as merely nominal entities, linguistic conveniences referencing no real objects. No doubt an obsessively individualistic account of the human condition, such as that sometimes ascribed to Hobbes,[2] can be devised. But, setting aside the predetermined end of denying that "true" groups exist, how plausible are such accounts? If individuals cannot come together in groupings that genuinely affect their lives, creating wholes out of their individual contributions, how could we explain the presence of language-speaking, socially interactive adults in the world as we do, in fact, experience it? What feral infants, miraculously dropped into life, unaffected by interaction with family or tribe, entirely self-identified and independent, came together to form the first aggregate collectivities? And how is it that the fields of psychology, sociology, philosophy, even biology, have so persistently conceived of the individual as *social individual?*[3] Can our self-experience, our disciplines, and our language all be so thoroughly misleading as to present as an important feature of individual human existence something that in fact has *no real existence at all?* Granted that our mistakes often persist over time, nonetheless, it is reasonable to ask that the burden of proof fall to those committed to explaining away the reality of irreducible groups.

One need not succumb to an equally radical and question-begging social organicism to comprehend the role that groups which are more than mere

aggregates of individuals play in human life. G. H. Mead, who must be
ranked among the more thoroughgoing proponents of the social individual, acknowledged the interdynamic of that which is genuinely individual
and that which is socially constructed in the development of the person.[4]
Thus, the same thinker who insisted that "it is the social process itself that
is responsible for the appearance of the self; it is not there as a self apart
from this type of experience"[5] could also claim that "the self appears as a
new type of individual in the social whole. There is a *new* social whole because of the self *with its own assertion of itself.*"[6] Indeed, Mead argued that
while "a person is a person because [she or he] belongs to a community,"[7]
what "makes *society* possible is such common responses, such organized attitudes" of individuals.[8] The social individual is both construct and con-
structor, whole and part of whole.

The relation of group to individual, in Mead's view, is dialogic:

> We must not forget this other capacity, that of replying to the community and
> insisting on the gestures of the community changing. We can reform the order of
> things; we can insist on making the community standards better standards. We are
> not *simply* bound to the community. We are engaged in a conversation in which
> what we have to say is listened to by the community and its response is affected by
> what we have to say.[9]

Thus, both individual and group are the products and producers of a
process of interactive communication. And, even though "the whole (society) is prior to the part (the individual) and the part is explained in terms
of the whole,"[10] the individual has some degree or mode of independent
perspective whereby she adds her own voice, her own particular contribution, to the conversation of which part and whole are coordinates.

If we admit the interactive construction of individual and "society" at
large, can we deny the same relationship between individual and those
"small" group(s) of which she is a constituent member? Can the larger, perhaps national, community to which one belongs be more formative, more
immediately significant to the character of the individual, than are the
smaller communities of family, church, neighborhood, or other subsocietal
groups? This seems, at the least, counterintuitive. Certainly, one of the most
startling experiences of the aging process, especially for parents, is the discovery of the extent to which one is or has become "just like" one's own
parents. If it is true that the history of humankind repeats itself, it is even
more the case that family histories repeat themselves, and with a highly

personal intensity. For most parents, in fact, it is the transmission of values and the molding of character that are the ultimate tasks of parenting. Food and other necessities for life may come from any number of sources; parents, qua parents, are needed and understand themselves as needed to guide the development of the child into a more or less specific personality who can occupy a set of more or less specific social roles.[11] Even the phenomenon of youthful rebellion presupposes the efficacy of parental, familial, or tribal molding. We rebel, or seek to, only against that which does in fact constrain us. A rebel without a cause is really a rebel who does not recognize those against whom she rebels, for they *are* the cause of her rebellion.

Families, tribes, and similar kinship groups might be called *natural subgroups* within a larger civil society. That is, they appear to be groupings in which humans typically are found, despite other cultural or political distinctions. These natural groups by no means exhaust the collectivities that humans create, particularly in complex contemporary societies. Much attention is focused in discussions of groups—their rights, responsibilities, and possible agency—on *formally constituted groups*. The existence of recognized rules and roles in such groups is often cited as the ground for describing them as *agent groups* both accountable for their group acts and potential bearers of legal rights. It is the intentionally constructed and explicitly rule-governed character of such groups that is seen as qualifying them for legal status.

It is true that a formally constituted group, with its defined roles and rules, is more readily identified by *outsiders* as a group than is an *informal nonnatural collectivity* based on shared aims, tastes, or traits. Nonetheless, I would like to suggest that this emphasis on formal groups, notably political action groups and economic entities such as corporations, may distort our understanding of the grounds for recognizing the meaningful existence of closely knit informal groups. For these informal groups may be more properly regarded as *communities*, and not *mere* collectivities, than are the formal but internally less cohesive groups on which our attention is often focused. That is, whatever may be the good reasons for legal recognition and regulation of corporations, political action groups, and the like, they are not the same kind of reasons that would support a decision to afford legal status to informal groups. This should hardly surprise us, given that a similar disanalogy obtains between these formal collectivities and natural groups such as families. Indeed, it may well be the case that the grounds of legal recognition for informal nonnatural groups and for natural groups are more alike than those for informal nonnatural groups and equally nonnatural formal ones.

One possible source of this asymmetry between informal and formal nonnatural groups is that many of the former are based on and devoted to profit making or other socioeconomic interests. Corporations are *created for* the purpose of providing financial benefits to individuals, including management personnel and workers, as well as stockholders. So, too, many political action groups are created on the basis of economic interests that all the members have as individuals. The American Association of Retired Persons, for example, certainly can be understood as a collectivity based on the similarity of individual interests among the elderly, at least as much as on any purported genuinely *common good*. With regard to groups of these kinds, we are justified in arguing that there *is no common good*, as such. There are, rather, interests of individuals that happen to coincide and are most effectively realized through collective investment, lobbying, or policies. Such groups are not formed, or not primarily formed, out of the reciprocal identification of individuals; whatever interests or aims are held in common by the members of the group are individual interests and aims. The satisfaction of those ends can be, and is, enjoyed by each member *as an individual*, not *as a member or part of the whole*.

Without addressing the nobility of economic interests and profit-making motives, we can see that collectivities of the type just noted differ from groups such as religious, cultural, ethnic, or similar collectivities. Groups of the latter sort, which I am here defining as informal relative to corporations and political groups, *matter to* the individual in ways in which the more formal kind do not and, perhaps, cannot. As suggested earlier, a crucial feature of an informal subsocietal group is that individual members do, in fact, understand and identity themselves partly in terms of their belonging to the group. Interestingly, it appears to be this reciprocal identity, this sense of self-in-group, which makes it possible for great numbers of persons, even those geographically distant, to regard themselves as comembers of a single group. Thus, to be a Mason or a Catholic or a Jew is to stand in relationship with others who may not even be present to oneself. And these relationships may be very closely felt, such that two persons' being Masons is of greater significance to them than is their being, for example, coworkers or conationals.

In somewhat dated language, we might describe these relations as being "internal" rather than "external." Whatever the efforts of management to generate "team spirit" among employees, the latter primarily stand in exter-nal relation to one another. Their interests are alike but not genuinely uni-fied. Leave this job, take another job, and little changes *within the self*, except to the extent that the change involves either some shame or pride in self. Thus, I may be quite distressed to be fired from SuperSox Corporation, but my distress is not grounded in the loss of something central to my iden-tity. I have never understood myself, significantly, as a SuperSox person; I was simply a SuperSox employee. By contrast, to fall away from or, worse, to be excommunicated from a religious group of which one has been a "prac-ticing" member is to suffer great personal loss or to undergo significant iden-tity alteration. Surely, it is the belief that Baruch de Spinoza cared deeply about his identity as a Jew that generates such admiration of his accepting the loss of that community out of philosophical conviction. If we thought Spinoza cared little about his religious community, we would not consider his display of theoretical integrity to be worthy of special note.

Moreover, some common goods or interests can be satisfied—or their satisfaction be fully enjoyed—only *as a group member* or through identifica-tion with the group. To use a micro example, let us consider a sports team and its record of wins and losses. While it is undoubtedly preferable to be a group hero, playing for extended periods and visibly contributing to win-ning games, even the benchwarmer shares in the joy and pride *of the team, qua team*, when it does win. So, too, every member of the team experiences the disappointment or embarrassment of a resounding loss. It is the team that wins or loses, not the individuals, not even those most responsible for the outcome. And this, I believe, is the deeper reason for our use of the lan-guage of groups. "The team" is properly spoken of as an it, a one, a collec-tivity that achieves, fails, enjoys, and suffers *as a group*. We may wish to maintain that the concrete experience of satisfaction or dissatisfaction can only be individual,[12] but none of these individuals could have any such experience other than as a member of the team.

In similar fashion, a group may have a discernible character of its own, one not entirely reducible to any characteristics of the individual members. In some cases, unfortunately, the stability of this character is maintained in ways that do not respect individual members. And, in some cases, the character of the group may change over time because of changing attitudes and expectations of the members. What individuals bring to the group may be something that could alter the group character. That, of course, is pre-cisely why closed groups *are* closed, and why they may seem as hostile to some members as to nonmembers. The group character is not entirely independent of its membership over time, any more than would be its continued existence. A group the members of which were in complete disagreement with their predecessors is unlikely to exhibit the same group character as it formerly did. And a group to which no one cares to belong is a group that no longer exists.

Nonetheless, groups do have such discernible characters, and we reference them all the time in our ordinary discourse. It is often the externally manifest character of a group that attracts new members or binds present members. It is equally common that a perceived group character repels other individuals. Moreover, the perceived character of the group, its image in the larger society, may have these effects of attraction and repulsion whether or not the internal activities and traits of members warrant the response. Thus, I might be deeply ashamed to be known as a member of a certain group, even when I know that the shameful image is not accurate. I simply do not wish to be identified by others as one of those kind of people. Or I might join a group believing it to have a certain group character, only to find that I was mistaken or misled. In that instance, I will be unable to make the identification I desire. Such a discovery often has the quality of disenchantment: I am disappointed, even resentful, because I felt *justified* in believing the group to be a group of a certain kind. And that sense of justification is often well-grounded, in that the group appeared to me and others to have a recognizable character, just as individual persons do.

All of these features contribute to the claims that informal groups may make on legal and social institutions for "special" recognition or treatment. Self-identification through a group, the possible attainment of certain goods only as a member of the group, and external identification by others based on one's group membership(s) are concerns of great significance. But it would be a mistake to conclude that this significance or the grounds for legal status it supplies are easily reducible to individual concerns. For, as much as subgroup membership is of importance to individuals, the existence of subgroups is of importance for the larger social or national group. Only a state that sought the complete and exhaustive allegiance and self-identification of its citizens would profit from the elimination of all subgroups. And so, a totalitarian state ought not to entertain claims for legal recognition of subgroups—as Plato, Hobbes, and others have well understood.

A self-proclaimed liberal democracy, by contrast, ought to treat the claims of subgroups with special care and adequate sensitivity. It ought, to borrow a familiar phrasing from Ronald Dworkin, to take subgroups seriously. This attitude of seriousness, or respect, cannot mean that the larger society simply capitulates to every demand of every collection of persons who name themselves a group. Some requests cannot be honored, either in light of the character of the societal whole or because the degree of disjunction required between whole and subgroup would be too great. So, too, the societal whole may justly refuse to recognize some self-proclaimed subgroup as a legitimate collectivity, either because no genuine community is discernible or because of the practices and values of the group.

We might treat these as a taxonomy of considerations for the recognition and granting of "special" rights or privileges to subgroups. First, there is the character or self-conception of the larger system. Does the very nature of this society preclude its acceptance of the subgroup in question? Next, we would assess the expected effect on subgroup to society relations should the former's requests be met. The relations to be considered would include legal and practical ones, as well as more broadly cultural relations. Third, some evidence of genuine community and of significance in the lives of members would be required of the putative group. And, fourth, we would want to know whether the subgroup proclaimed values or demanded legal allowances at odds with the larger society's political morality. Some examples of the form and import of each of these categories will illustrate both the complexity and the poignancy of many instances of subgroup divergence from societal norms.

There are national societies that conceive of themselves as having particular historical or cultural character—one that may be understood as a national destiny to be fulfilled. Israel is clearly a nation of such self-identity; the United States, at least in its infancy, may be regarded as another example. *Could* Israel accept within its larger national group, a subgroup which proclaimed the Christian destiny of Israel? What could that possibly mean for the national identity? Could the United States, given its origins and history, accept a subgroup in which some persons were treated as the property of others to be bought and sold, injured or killed, at the will of the "master"? Would it make any meaningful difference to the fundamental inconsonance of these two groups that the "slaves" had somehow consented to the arrangement? The self-identity of the nation, I think, outweighs any merely political or legal resolution of this issue. The United States, at this point in its history, simply could not recognize the demands of a group of masters and slaves, however willing the slaves might be. In both cases, the national or societal character precludes acceptance of the particular subgroups in question. So, too, some nations might be unable to openly acknowledge any divergent subgroups. Such nations need not be "closed," in Popper's derogatory sense; they need not resort to abuse and suppression of subgroups. They might simply be so narrowly self-identified or so culturally precarious that no official recognition can be given to diverse elements.[13]

In other cases, the society may be able to accept the subgroup within itself but balk at troubling practical and cultural problems. How will day-to-day relations between the group and the society be carried on, if at all? Will the national postal system serve a group that declares itself, in all other ways, to be "off the grid"? How are police and emergency personnel to deal with injured people who refuse treatment or who are unable to communicate consent? If a subgroup demands freedom to use nationally illicit substances within its own confines, how will the national body prevent such substances from finding their way to the larger public? Moreover, and perhaps most problematically, how great a distance between national society and subgroup can or should be borne by any larger social whole? Even in a highly liberal democracy, one committed to tolerating differences of a degree never before acceptable in any nation, there must be *some* limits. Can it be desirable for one group to hold within itself a subgroup that constitutes, in effect, an entirely separate legal and cultural entity?

What kinds of evidence are needed for a larger societal whole to grant the status of genuine community to a subgroup? One espoused reason for the Supreme Court's refusal to acknowledge the Rastafarians as an American subgroup sufficiently genuine to warrant special legal permissions was that the American claimants appeared to have little shared history or connection beyond their hairstyles and interest in using proscribed drugs. Does this prejudice the argument against all "new" or recently developed groups as over against older or more traditional ones? Must a subgroup exist without official recognition or freedom to engage in group-specific practices for some allotted period before it merits such recognition? But, is there not a Catch-22 here? If the group survives or flourishes while *not enjoying* that official status, what is the force of any claim it may make as to the significance of the requested right or privilege? Or must the members of the group persevere in conduct that makes them liable to legal penalty so as to secure the future status of their group? This suggests, for example, that Christian Scientist parents must either continue exposing themselves to very serious legal penalty by employing the Christian Science approach to the care of their ill children or abandon that particular commitment and, thus, abandon their claim to its importance in their religious practice.

On the same lines, there appears to be an asymmetry, possibly unjust, between the readiness with which a national government may recognize those formal nonnatural groups discussed previously and the diffidence with which informal nonnatural groups are regarded. Formal entities have the real advantage of being self-consciously created and defined. Their more clearly delineated internal structures lend them an appearance of continuity and simplify the attribution of responsibility by the larger social system. The managers of the corporation will always be those to whom the national system addresses itself and will be those, unlike the mailroom clerk, who will bear the brunt of accountability to external authorities. But nascent religious groups or cultural communities seldom grow in such structured fashion, any more than do natural subgroups. And who, within a group claiming unified interest and having no "leaders," is to answer for the group's conduct in the larger world? Nonetheless, while the formal collectivity has visible structure, it is likely to have less internal unity than the informal one. If, then, the social whole is more ready to afford status to the formal group, it is so more because of convenience than because of conviction as to the community character of the group. Thus, the informal group that can claim more genuine ontic status and internal unity is undermined in its search for recognition by those very features that make it important in its members' lives.

Finally, there is the matter of the subgroup's values and political morality. Earlier, I considered the possibility of a group that wished to practice slavery. I argued that the United States could not accept such a group insofar as its practices conflicted with our national self-identity as a "free people" who had fought a civil war over the very issue of slavery (among other matters). Yet it is equally evident that this nation would have great difficulty in accommodating such practices. If a subgroup demands permission to treat its members in ways that directly conflict with our conceptions of individual rights, our national system will have great difficulty in treating those demands as legitimate. To the extent that members are subjected to treatment to which they and we object, our social response is easily determined. But if the outside culture tends to regard the will of the members as compromised, then it may have objections on behalf of those who would not make any objection themselves. Even if we assume that, in a system such as our own, fundamental individual rights must trump group rights or privileges, our determinations will not always be easily made. Whatever our choice, we must be resigned to misaffecting the interests of someone. And we may do damage to what all the persons directly involved do regard as their interests because we perceive internal injustice where they do not.

What all this comes to is this: however ordinary, familiar, and necessary to our normal lives, subgroups create deep theoretical and practical issues for any purportedly singular social and legal whole. We all exist as persons of many faces. When our subgroup faces confront our national or larger cultural faces, we may find ourselves at odds not only with one another but also within ourselves. The more divergent our group and subgroup identities are regarding authority, values, and commitment, the more deeply any conflict must be felt. Resolving, or reconciling, such conflicts is not only an individual concern; it is an equally vital matter for public culture and public institutions.

The chapters in this volume address the issues raised here and many more. The natures of groups and of subgroups are explored in Part I. How are we to conceive of groups and to distinguish them from mere collectivities? In what ways can groups and their members be responsible for the acts of some of their number? What does justice require of the larger system in holding some members of the subgroup personally accountable for the group's practices? How might subgroups, qua groups, be entitled to rights or privileges within the larger society? What, indeed, does the concept of group rights mean, and to what kinds of rights might groups lay claim?

In Part II, the authors consider the possibilities for appropriate treatment of subgroups in a democratic system. How can subgroups be recognized so as to avoid Mill's dreaded tyranny of the majority? What are the effective and reasonable limitations on recognition that the larger system can afford to subgroups? What is required of the majority society if it is to fairly distinguish between core and peripheral interests of the subgroup? Can the subgroup, itself, be expected to make such distinctions? In general, are there principles that function to reliably balance policy between indifference or disrespect, on the one hand, and capitulation or fragmentation, on the other?

Finally, in Part III, we engage some specific cases of conflict between subgroup and societal claims. Religious integrity, ethnicity, and gender are all elements in these chapters. Here the authors attempt to illuminate problems and develop theoretical approaches by exploring particular legal and political dilemmas. Thus, we confront in particularized contexts the issues of core versus peripheral interests, of individual member to subgroup rights, and of the possibility for social openness raised in the preceding parts.

The resulting collection is, I believe, unique in giving extended attention to the role of the subgroup in individual and social life within a philosophical context focusing on matters legal and political. We have, in these chapters, the coming together of social philosophy, moral philosophy, legal philosophy, and, perhaps, a bit of sociology and social psychology. An intriguing question is whether this volume, itself, reveals anything of a communal sense. Is there a distinctly liberal, rather than communitarian, libertarian, or conservative slant to the chapters, or are the pieces sociopolitically diverse? Is there any consensus about the ontic status of subgroups, their agency and accountability? Are secular groups more sympathetically regarded than religious groups or vice versa? Is there any emergent doctrine regarding the rights of subgroup members vis-à-vis the rights of the groups to which they belong?

I suspect that readers will respond diversely to these questions as they engage the work in this volume. It has certainly been the intention of the editors to offer some genuine variety of perspectives; whether and to what extent we have succeeded is the reader's determination to make. Each part of the volume is introduced by a substantive overview of the issues raised in that part and a discussion of the individual chapters. The parts might be read in any order; we present the ontological issues first as a grounding for the more concrete analyses to follow. So, too, the individual contributions to any part may be read independently of one another. Each chapter was selected on the basis of its being individually interesting, as well as for its contribution to the whole. This is the very nature of any thematic collection of works by several authors: to become an informative whole composed of discretely worthy parts. We, the editors and the authors, invite you to explore this community of reflection with us.

Notes

1. A cynical observer of our national history might be forgiven for suggesting that many purported instances of constitutional interpretation are disguised exercises in utility assessment or, indeed, the products of political maneuvering.

2. Karl Popper, perhaps more clearly than Hobbes, argues for a similarly reductivist conception of groups: i.e., that a complete account of any apparently societal action or event can be rendered entirely in terms of the lives of individual members.

3. Setting aside the peculiarities of Weber's notion of *Verstehen* as a kind of empathic communication among individuals, we can appeal, here, to his argument that individual conduct in some sense always is "social action." That is, the very meaning of any individual action, and often the fact that a person acts at all, depends on a social meaning. Being rude, playing a game (see Wittgenstein and Mead on the nature of "play"), dressing for a party—not one of these individual actions can be understood as having any meaning at all, except insofar as we already understand the social concepts of politeness, play, "dressing up," and partying.

4. Another apt conception may be found in Maurice Mandelbaum's idea of "societal facts," which both inform and respond to individual conduct, dispositions, and so on.

5. *Mind, Self, and Society* (Chicago: University of Chicago Press, 1934), 142.

6. Ibid., 192; emphasis added.

7. Ibid., 162.

8. Ibid., 161; emphasis added.

9. Ibid., 168; emphasis added.

10. Ibid., 7.

11. I do not mean to suggest that only birth parents can fulfill this type of socializing role. What is crucial is that *someone* do so. Indeed, where there is little or no such socialization from family or quasi-familial persons, the young will simply adopt the socialization of the larger environment in which they find themselves. That, of course, is the rationale of the claim that children need "role models" to develop properly.

12. While willing to give the nod to this sort of reductivism to illuminate the point that group membership may be the only means of achieving certain goods, I think it misses its mark in another way, as well. While it may be true that each individual in the group personally enjoys or takes pride in the team's success, this does not foreclose the possibility of another mode of feeling that the individual experiences not as him- or herself but as team member, *qua team member*. That the pleasure is experienced *by* an individual does not entail that it is pleasure taken or enjoyed *as* an individual.

13. I have in mind so-called primitive societies such as native tribes in the deep rain forests of South America and Africa, for whom the continuation of any cultural identity, some claim, requires their protection from novel or inconsonant cultural influences.

Part I

The Nature of Groups and Group Rights

Introduction

Alternatives for a Theory of Group Rights

Carl Wellman

Group rights are frequently asserted these days, often with great conviction. Examples that spring to mind are the right of colonial nations to self-determination, of Native American tribes to their traditional lands, of the Amish to educate their children according to their religious beliefs, of African-Americans to proportional representation in Congress, of French Canadians to preserve their culture, and of the Croatians to secede from Yugoslavia in 1991. Although none of these assertions is noncontroversial, a plausible case can be made for each of them. If we are to avoid dogmatism, we should at the very least do our best to understand them.

No doubt, some of us will try to understand them as rights of the individual members of these groups. However, one cannot imagine how any individual French Canadian could preserve an entire culture. What could it mean, then, to assert her right to do so? And although any individual Croatian could emigrate from Yugoslavia, only collectively could Croatians secede and form an independent nation-state. If there really is any right to secession, it is presumably a group right.

Let us, then, suppose that some moral philosopher accepts the existence of one or more group rights and wishes to develop a theory in terms of which to understand them. What theoretical decisions must she make? From what alternatives could she choose the elements with which to construct her theory? And what difficulties would she face in articulating an adequate theory of group rights? Because the examples I have mentioned here are usually thought to be in the first instance moral rights, it will simplify matters if we begin with moral group rights and only later consider legal group rights.

Conceptions of a Right

What is a right? This can be understood either as a request for some generic description of the nature of rights or as asking for a definition or analysis

17

of the meaning of the expression "a right." Either way, one obviously needs some conception of a right in order to identify the subject matter of one's theory of group rights, to indicate some of the essential features of group rights, and to suggest how group rights are related to the rights of the individual members of the relevant group. Fortunately, several plausible conceptions of a right are available in the literature.

Moral philosophers often distinguish between will theories of rights and interest theories. The former hold that a moral right consists in some special moral standing of the right-holder's will; the latter maintain that a moral right gives some interest of the right-holder special moral protection. Although this classification is not exhaustive, it is illuminating for anyone trying to understand group rights.

The most familiar will theory of rights is H. L. A. Hart's protected choice theory. He conceives of a moral right as a bilateral moral liberty protected by a perimeter of duties of noninterference. For example, the right to give ten dollars to the Salvation Army might consist in the liberty of either giving or not giving that amount, together with the duty of the bell ringer not to force one to give at gunpoint, the duty of one's companion not to prevent one from giving by physical restraint, and the duty of others not to interfere coercively in any manner with one's giving or not giving as one chooses. His conception of a right led Hart to suggest that the ascription of rights to babies or animals is idle. This is not to suggest that such ascriptions are meaningless; they may be asserting merely that we do have duties not to abuse babies or treat animals cruelly. But it is inappropriate to use the language of rights to assert this because we can say everything we want to say in the more fundamental language of duties, and in these contexts "a right" lacks the distinctive sense that gives it special importance in moral discourse. Now if one adopts Hart's conception of a moral right, presumably it would be idle to ascribe rights to any groups incapable of choice. Although one can understand pretty well what it is for Standard Oil to choose to raise the price of gasoline, it is difficult, if not impossible, to explain what it would be for any unorganized group, such as African-Americans, to make a choice. Are we to conclude, therefore, that it is idle to ascribe rights to racial or ethnic minorities?

I have argued that a right consists in a system of liberties, claims, powers, and immunities that, if respected, confer dominion on the right-holder in some potential confrontation with one or more second parties, and I define dominion in terms of freedom and control. Although this conception of a right does not presuppose that right-holders must have the capacity to choose, it does seem to imply that only agents could have rights because one can exercise freedom or control only by acting in some manner. Thus, my will theory of rights will also make it difficult to ascribe moral rights to any group incapable of acting as a unit.

One way to avoid these difficulties is to adopt an interest conception of rights. Neil MacCormick advocates an interest theory that is similar to my will theory in that it employs Wesley Hohfeld's fundamental legal conceptions and their moral analogues. MacCormick holds that a moral right consists in some interest of the right-holder protected by a set of liberties, claims, powers, immunities, and duties to promote or at least not to damage that interest. Joseph Raz proposes a similar but simpler theory in which a right consists in an interest-based reason sufficient to impose one or more duties upon others. If one adopts some such conception of rights, one can ascribe rights to groups without explaining how they are capable of choosing or acting. On the other hand, one must now explain how a group can have an interest as a group, some interest not reducible to the several interests of its individual members. It might (or might not) be easier to explain how African-Americans as a group have an interest in proportional representation in Congress than to understand what it would be for them in some unified way to choose to have or elect the appropriate number of representatives. In any event, any decision to adopt either a will or an interest conception of rights has important implications for any theory of group rights.

Joel Feinberg has developed an attractive hybrid theory of rights. He defines a right as a valid claim. Thus on his theory a moral right consists in a claim the recognition and protection of which is justified by the principles of an enlightened conscience. But what is a claim? One does not find claims among the furniture of the universe as either natural or nonnatural objects. To have a claim is to be in a position to make a claim, to demand something as one's due. This is a will theory of the nature of a right because it conceives of rights as claims and analyzes claims in terms of the action of claiming. Feinberg recognizes that his conception of a right seems to imply that babies and imbeciles, who are incapable of claiming anything as their due, cannot have any moral rights; but he thinks it obvious that babies do have rights, such as the rights not to be neglected or abused. How is this possible? It is because others, their parents or guardians, can act as their representatives and claim their rights in their name. What kinds of beings, then, can be represented by others claiming in their behalf? He argues that only beings who have or can have interests can be represented. On Feinberg's theory, a group incapable of acting as a group could possess moral rights if it could have group interests. These rights would, however, have to be claimed by representatives speaking in their behalf. It is an interesting question for one seeking to construct a theory of group rights whether this hybrid theory enables one to combine the advantages of a will conception of rights with those of an interest conception or burdens one with the disadvantages of both kinds of theory. Although Feinberg's conception does lend itself very well to a theory of group claim rights, I do not believe that it can be extended to explain other species of rights such as liberty rights and power rights. At least the former seem required for any complete theory of group rights.

There are, of course, other alternatives, conceptions of a right that do not require one to adopt either a will theory or an interest theory. One might, as many do, hold a claim theory of rights but reject Feinberg's definition of a claim in terms of the power of claiming. On this theory, a claim of the right-holder is simply the logical correlative of some other party's duty *to* the claimant. What makes any duty a duty owed to someone is that it is grounded on some property of the right-holder herself, not her relation to someone or something else. For example, what makes the duty not to kill Jane a duty to Jane might be her inherent value, not her value to her family or the loss of social utility that would result from her death. On this conception of a right, all that would be required to explain group rights would be to identify one or more properties of groups that ground one or more moral duties of others.

Although Ronald Dworkin's conception of a right seems inhospitable to group rights, a few moral philosophers have used it to explain them. The defining purpose and special importance of moral rights, especially those fundamental rights that are or ought to be recognized in constitutional law, lies in the way in which they protect individuals from mistreatment by society. Now if they were grounded on some interest of the right-holder or on social utility, it would be permissible for the government to infringe a right whenever it would be in the public interest or useful on balance to do so. Hence, one can take rights seriously only if one conceives of them as individual trumps over social goals. This is to say that any state action infringing an individual right must require some special justification over and beyond the appeal to some goal of the society. Dworkin's conception of a right seems to imply that only individual persons could be moral right-holders. But one can adopt an ontology in which groups are also individuals, and one can point out that some groups within a society need protection against mistreatment by the government in much the same way that individual citizens do. In this way, one might use Dworkin's conception of a right to construct a nonutilitarian theory of group rights.

There are two sets of passages in John Stuart Mill's *Utilitarianism* in which he describes the nature of a moral right. Although one set clearly asserts an interest theory of rights, the other need not be interpreted in this manner. He sometimes suggests that to assert that someone has a right is to say that society ought to defend, either by legal or by moral sanctions, one's claim to the possession of something. All that one would need to do to explain group rights on this conception of a right would be to describe some moral justification for the social protection of group claims to possess or enjoy certain things or conditions.

There is a certain progression, or regression, in this series of conceptions of a right. Most of those who have proposed theories of rights during the past few decades have tried to define what is distinctive and especially important about rights. Hence, they have rejected attempts to reduce rights to duties or to interpret them merely as means of maximizing value. The conceptions of Hart, Feinberg, and Dworkin are paradigmatic in this respect. But the last two conceptions that define a right in terms of duties to the right-holder or things that ought morally to be protected by society take rights to be less distinctive and to occupy a less special place in moral theory. This suggests that one who wishes to develop a theory of group rights may be faced with a trade-off. If one adopts a conception of rights that captures what is most distinctive and important about rights, it may be difficult to explain how groups can have rights; if one adopts a conception that makes it easier to understand group rights, these may turn out to be rights in a theoretically less significant sense than the rights of individual persons.

Species of Rights

However one may conceive of the generic nature of a right, presumably one will recognize distinct species of moral rights. Some of the distinctions between different kinds of rights are worthy of note by anyone constructing a theory of group rights. At best, some species of rights may be more appropriate for or valuable to groups than others; at worst, there may be some kinds of rights that groups by their very nature could not possess.

There are those, alas, who argue that the very concept of a right renders the notion of group rights incoherent. Enemies of natural rights, and by extension moral rights, argue that rights conceptually presuppose an unrealistic atomic individualism; friends of moral rights like Herbert Hart maintain similarly that the concept of a right is an essentially distributive concept. If either view is correct, it would seem that there could not possibly be any genuinely collective rights. There may be, however, an intermediate position open to those who distinguish between primary and derivative rights. A derivative right is one that is implied by some prior right; a primary right is one that is not grounded on any prior right. Now, it would be possible to hold that although only individual human beings, and perhaps nonhuman animals, can possess primary rights, these somehow imply one or more derivative rights of groups. Whether any such derivation is sound remains to be seen, but one should not rule out the intelligibility of the notion of a group right until one has explored this theoretical option.

Many moral philosophers have adopted D. D. Raphael's distinction between rights of action and rights of recipience. The former consist in the absence of any moral obligation to refrain from acting in some specific manner; the latter consist in the moral obligation of some second party to treat one in some specific way. Presumably a group could have a right of action only if that group is capable of acting in the appropriate way. It may, or may not, be relatively easy to attribute rights of action to corporate bodies but much more difficult to explain how unorganized groups could possess this species of rights. Because rights of recipience require only that some other party, the duty-bearer, act in some manner, group rights of recipience seem less problematic. One would, however, need to identify some plausible sort of ground for this kind of moral right.

Some, but not all, moral philosophers believe that there are two species of rights of recipience: positive rights and negative rights. Offhand, it is hard to see why it would be more difficult to explain how groups could possess positive than negative rights or vice versa. It might, however, be easier to defend the existence of negative moral rights like the rights not to be harmed or to nondiscrimination than to find adequate moral grounds to establish such positive rights as the right to be provided with the means to sustain a culture or to be given territory in order to enable a group to secede.

Some moral philosophers suggest that there are moral analogues of Hohfeld's fundamental legal conceptions. Thus Herbert Hart and I conclude that there are four species of moral rights corresponding to the four legal advantages he distinguished. Accordingly, we classify moral rights as liberty rights, power rights, claim rights, or immunity rights. The first two are species of active rights, rights one exercises by acting in some manner; the last two are passive rights, rights one can enjoy without engaging in any activity. Presumably only groups that are capable of action could possess the former, but it might be possible for a group lacking the ability to act to possess the latter. In any event, it is important for any theory of group rights to classify any alleged group right accurately in order to identify its content and its practical implications. It would also be helpful to have some idea of which kinds of rights are needed to serve the purposes of a theory of group rights and which kinds, if any, are merely incidental or even unnecessary for these purposes.

Kinds of Groups

No one alleges that every group or collection of individuals has or could have rights. It is hard to imagine what right could be ascribed collectively to the set of persons listed under "Smith" in the Saint Louis telephone directory and doubtful that the line of shoppers impatient to check out at a grocery store has any group right to faster service. What kinds of groups, then, should one consider when attempting to develop a theory of group rights?

Many moral or political philosophers articulate only a fragment of a theory of group rights because they are primarily concerned with only one kind of group. In business ethics, discussions of the social responsibility of firms have led to a consideration of the moral rights corporations might have. The doctrine that every nation has a right to self-determination has expanded to the view that every people has certain rights such as the right to their existence, to their economic development, and to national security. Many versions of political liberalism have championed the rights of ethnic or racial minorities to preserve their culture, to freedom from discrimination, and even to affirmative action programs. Some environmentalists have asserted that entire species of plants or animals have a right not to be made extinct. A good place to begin would be to survey this scattered literature on group rights and pick out those kinds of groups for whom the ascription of moral rights seems most plausible.

Although anyone attempting to understand group rights does not need an exhaustive classification of groups, it would be useful to have one that applies systematically to the most important kinds of groups for which rights are or might be alleged. Anyone who is attracted to an interest theory of rights might use Larry May's arguments that ethnic groups, sexually stereo-typed groups, and corporations have interests that ground moral rights. Those who find a will theory of rights more plausible could look to his explanations of how mobs, corporations, and informal associations are capa-ble of group action. May does not, as far as I know, deny that there are other kinds of groups capable of having interests or acting collectively.

I have proposed a classification intended to cover all the kinds of groups for which moral rights could plausibly be alleged. I suggest that the most fundamental distinction is between organized groups that are structured by a set of rules or norms that define specialized offices or roles within the group and unorganized groups that lack any such normative structure authorizing its officers to act for the group as a whole. Among the former I distinguish between corporations, such as Gulf Oil, that are constituted by a formal system of rules, and teams, such as a group of children playing sandlot baseball, constituted by a more informal understanding. Among the latter I distinguish between collections, such as the group of spectators that just happen to be watching the seals play on a sunny day at the zoo, and classes, defined merely by some common characteristic, such as being female. Although I argue that no group of any of these kinds could possess moral rights, anyone who wishes to challenge this conclusion might well find my classification illuminating.

I propose this classification for the limited purpose of explaining and defending my general theory of moral and legal rights. It would be wise to compare my speculations about groups with the more scientific group the-ory of sociologists. They typically distinguish between a social category, a class of individuals grouped conceptually because of some shared socially relevant characteristic such as age, sex, or occupation, and a social group consisting of individuals who interact in an interconnected set of roles. They then distinguish between primary groups whose members interact face-to-face, such as a family, and secondary groups whose members do not all interact personally and directly with one another, such as the Demo-cratic Party or AMINTAPHIL. They also classify social groups along the dimension of continuity. Corporations, whose members hold certain joint rights in property, tend to retain their identity over considerable periods of time even though their members change. Action groups consisting of individuals who assemble in some organized manner to perform some joint task may persist for a relatively long or short time. A crowd or gathering is by its very nature ephemeral. Whether some such classification of groups would be useful for anyone trying to construct a theory of group rights remains to be seen, but it is likely to provide some insight into the nature of various kinds of groups.

The Nature of Groups

There are three obvious alternatives regarding the generic ontology of groups. Some social philosophers hold that a group is nothing more than an aggregate or sum of its individual members; what we speak of as actions or interests of a group are more accurately described as merely acts or interests of one or more individual members of the group. Others maintain that a group is an entity other than, although not independent of, any or all of its members. It is an organic unity quite different from the multiplicity of its members. Although a human being uses her throat and tongue to speak, it is the teacher who gives a lecture, not her throat and tongue. Similarly, when the treasurer of a corporation writes a check and another employee delivers it to the supplier of raw materials, it is the corporation that has paid its debt, not the treasurer and employee theirs. Thus, a social group is something more than the sum of its members. An intermediate theory is that a group is neither a mere aggregate of individuals nor something more than its members; a social group *is* its individual members *in* their relationships. It is these relationships that enable its members to act as one or on behalf of the whole and to have joint interests distinct from the interests of any or all members as individuals.

No doubt groups do exist, and some version of one of these alternatives accurately describes their existence. Nevertheless, some moral philosophers have suggested that for the purposes of a theory of rights, one should think of social groups as constituted normatively rather than ontologically. Notice that a corporation like General Motors or Washington University is brought into existence by the granting of a charter, a legally valid act, and that which actions of its officers are recognized as acts of the corporate body is determined by its bylaws. Recall also that for sociologists what distinguishes a social group from a social category is not merely that its members interact with one another but that in doing so they enact social roles defined by social expectations or rules. Whether one needs an ontological theory or a normative theory of the nature of groups in order to understand group rights remains controversial. If one admits normative relationships into one's ontology, it would be possible to combine these two approaches. Whether this would be theoretically advantageous is quite another question.

Not every social or moral philosopher interested in group rights attempts to formulate a generic theory of the nature of social groups. Presumably all one needs is some account of those special characteristics of certain kinds of groups that enable one to explain the rights they have as groups. My incomplete sampling of the relevant literature calls to mind four examples of this sort of analysis.

Peter French has argued that a corporation is quite literally a moral person. It is, of course, accepted legal doctrine that in addition to natural persons, individual human beings, there are artificial persons, corporate bodies that have legal rights; but many jurists and philosophers of law regard this as a legal fiction. French maintains that the very same conception of moral agency that applies to human beings applies equally to corporations like Gulf Oil. Every corporation has its internal decision structure that licenses the redescription of actions of its members carried out pursuant to this structure as intentional acts of the corporate body. Thus, Donald Davidson's analysis of intentional action is as applicable to corporations as to individual human agents; both are moral agents in precisely the same sense. This would explain the capacity of a corporation to possess moral rights for anyone who holds a will theory of rights.

The right of a people to self-determination has for some time been widely accepted among moral philosophers, and more recently the Organization of African Unity has asserted a number of additional rights of peoples, including their rights to existence, to freely dispose of their wealth and natural resources, and to their cultural development. But what is a people? Vernon Van Dyke has suggested that all those who share a given culture and think of themselves as possessing an enduring collective identity are a people. Presumably a culture is identified by such characteristics as language, religion, and perhaps race, and by shared attitudes, customs, and traditions. Each and every culture has very great value, either in itself or for its contribution to the personal identity of its members, that grounds the group rights of each people to an independent existence and to preserve its culture. Some social philosophers regard ethnic minorities and aboriginal tribes as peoples in this sense.

It would seem, however, that some ethnic minorities lack sufficient unity to enable them to possess any genuine group or collective rights; they are what social scientists call *social categories*, aggregates of individuals classified together by observers because they share some socially significant characteristic. Michael McDonald argues that to be a right-holder a group must be self-collected. Its members must identify themselves with the group and share a normative understanding such that they think of themselves, at least much of the time, as acting according to their group functions and for the common good. This normative understanding enables them to engage in collective action and to pursue community interests. Hence, they can be claimants and possess group rights according to something like Joel Feinberg's conception of a right.

Larry May goes so far as to suggest that even a mob, such as the one that stormed the Bastille, can engage in collective action. The crowd is not literally a single social individual; rather, each member acts in solidarity with the others and in a manner that facilitates the actions of fellow members. The solidarity that renders the mob a unified group engaging in joint action arises from the awareness of each individual of the attitudes and actions of the others and the fact that they share some common interest or interests. Presumably, then, on either a will or an interest theory of rights, a mob could possess group rights. No doubt there are other analyses of the nature of some special kind of group that might enable one to understand how such a group could have rights, but these four examples are enough to hint at the range of alternatives available to one who is attempting to construct a theory of group rights.

Possible Right-Holders

We have already noticed that the way in which one conceives of a right has implications for the capacity of a group to possess rights. Although this is just what one would expect, it is only in the past two decades that moral philosophers have asked the general question, What kinds of beings could possess a right? and developed systematic theories about what is required in order to be a possible right-holder. Presumably before one asks whether groups *do* have any moral rights, one should ask whether groups *could* be moral right-holders.

I conceive of a right as a system of moral positions, such as claims, liberties, and powers, that, if respected, confer freedom and control over a defining core position upon the right-holder in a possible confrontation with one or more second parties. Because only an agent could exercise either freedom or contol, I infer that only a moral agent could possess a moral right. Most of those who adopt a will theory of rights will be driven to the same conclusion about possible right-holders. Although H. J. McCloskey does not adopt a will theory of rights, he also asserts that moral agency is required for the possession of moral rights. This is because exercising a right, acting on the basis of one's right, is essential to the concept of a right, and in exercising one's rights one must call upon one's moral capacities.

Obviously, if one accepts this theory about the capacity to possess rights, one must either deny that groups are possible right-holders or explain how groups can and do act collectively. Peter French, as we have seen, accepts this challenge head-on and argues that corporations are literally moral agents in their own right. David Copp, who takes a more indirect route to the conclusion that corporations are capable of action, distinguishes between primary and secondary action. An action is a secondary action if, and only if, it is attributable to the agent on the basis of the action of one or more other agents. For example, when my banker transfers funds from my bank account to that of Visa, it is I who have paid my Visa bill. Similarly, when one or more officers of a corporation perform some primary action within their authority, the corporation itself engages in a secondary action. Those who wish to attribute rights to groups other than corporate bodies must explain how they, too, are capable of acting collectively. Margaret Gilbert has developed a more general theory of groups as plural subjects capable of engaging in joint action. In order for a number of people to constitute a plural subject, it is necessary and sufficient for them to be jointly committed to doing something as a body. Although her most convincing examples of joint commitment consist of two or three individuals, Gilbert suggests that social conventions make it possible for even large groups to constitute plural subjects capable of acting as a body.

But is it really necessary to explain how groups can engage in collective action in order to ascribe rights to them? Neil MacCormick rejects every version of a will theory of rights because it implies that very young children, who have not yet developed their capacities for choice and moral agency, are incapable of possessing the right to be nurtured and cared for. He argues that to have a right is to have an interest, some component of one's well-being, valuable enough to impose duties upon others at least not to damage and often to protect and advance that interest. On this or any similar interest theory of rights, it is the capacity to possess interests that makes one a possible right-holder. Although Joel Feinberg does adopt a will theory of the nature of rights, he also believes that even infants can and do have moral rights. This is possible because they can be represented by others, normally their parents or guardians, who claim their rights in their name. Because only beings capable of having interests can be represented by others, all and only beings that can have interests are possible moral right-holders.

Now the task of anyone who wishes to ascribe rights to groups becomes, not explaining how a group as such can act, but how a group can have a collective interest that is not reducible to the interests of its individual members taken distributively. How, for example, could an ethnic minority have any interest in the preservation of its language over and above the several interests of its individual members in being able to use their traditional language in their many cultural, business, and political activities? Someone could argue that any interest in the preservation of a language must be a collective interest because no individual could preserve a language all by herself; only a community of language users can have a language. Similarly, political independence is often in the interest of some colonial people, but this is not something that could be obtained and enjoyed by one or only a few individuals living in a colony. If one can show that certain sorts of goods are by their very nature collective, it might well be possible to explain how groups can have collective interests that qualify them for the possession of moral rights.

A third theory about the capacity to possess rights is that only persons are possible right-holders. Mary Anne Warren defines personhood in terms of psychological traits such as consciousness, rationality, self-motivated activity, the capacity to communicate, and self-awareness. Although the law recognizes corporations as artificial persons, this is usually regarded as a legal fiction because corporate bodies seem entirely incapable of having any such psychological characteristics. The same objection can obviously be made to the ascription of personality to other sorts of groups. A moral philosopher who wishes to argue that in spite of first appearances, groups really are persons would need either to explain how groups can be conscious, rational, communicate, and so on or to propose some other criteria for personhood. A. I. Melden, who agrees that only persons can possess moral rights, rejects any definition of personhood in purely psychological terms. He argues that persons must be capable of joining their lives together in a network of moral relationships. Whether this would make it easier or more difficult to recognize groups as moral persons is not clear. Perhaps a good place to begin would be to ask, as Peter French may have done, what would be required to take literally the legal doctrine that corporations are legal persons. If one could explain this, it might be possible to extend this explanation to other groups as moral persons.

Even if one can explain how groups are persons, the question remains as to how this explains their capacity to possess rights. Why is it that many philosophers insist that all and only persons have moral rights? A traditional answer, and a fourth theory of possible right-holders, is that all and only persons are ends in themselves; it is their inherent value that grounds their rights and commands our respect. This suggests that groups might also be possible right-holders if they similarly possess inherent value. Whether this would be a fruitful approach for anyone developing a theory of group rights is problematic because the concept of inherent value is seldom clearly defined and moral philosophers disagree about what it is about persons that gives them this special sort of value.

Another theory of possible right-holders asserts that it is membership in the moral community that qualifies a being for the possession of moral rights. Annette Baier argues for this thesis on the grounds that rights are essentially social. To assert that someone has a right is to say that at least one other party has an obligation to the right-holder and that there is or should be a socially recognized means for the right-holder or her proxy to take appropriate action should that obligation be neglected. Moreover, one possesses a right by virtue of some social role. Martin Golding concludes that only members of a moral community can posses moral rights by a different line of reasoning. The expression "a right" is a forensic term used by a right-holder or someone speaking on her behalf to claim something from some second party. But how could one justify one's claim to this second party? This would be possible only if that second party recognizes that what one is claiming as a good for oneself is a good for himself also. Thus, every right presupposes some shared good, and, more generally, moral rights presuppose a social ideal that defines a moral community. Now are groups, as well as their individual members, capable of membership in the moral community? If they are, then on this theory of the capacity to possess rights, they are possible right-holders.

In a famous passage, John Stuart Mill suggests that to assert that one has a right is to say that society ought to defend one's claim to the possession of something. On this view, groups would be possible right-holders if society ought to protect them in their possession of something, perhaps their culture or their land or even their very existence. Accordingly, if one can make out a cogent moral justification for the collective protection of groups that is not reducible to a justification for protecting their members distributively, one could explain how groups are qualified for the possession of moral rights. On what grounds one could argue for the protection of groups as such remains to be seen.

In any event, there are at least six alternative theses about what is required for the possession of moral rights. Anyone constructing a theory of group rights could explain the capacity of groups, at least some kinds of groups, for the possession of rights by explaining how groups are moral agents, have interests, are persons, have inherent value, are members of the moral community, or ought to be protected by society. In choosing one of these theses, one should, of course, consider how well it coheres with one's conception of the nature of moral rights.

Grounds of Rights

It is one thing to explain how groups are possible right-holders; it is another to prove that groups actually do possess moral rights. To establish the existence of any alleged right, one must point to reasons sufficient to ground that right. Unfortunately, the least satisfactory area in the theory of rights concerns the grounds of rights. Still, one can describe the alternatives that seem most promising for anyone who wishes to justify claims about the moral rights of groups.

One who adopts an interest theory of rights typically infers that any right is grounded in some interest of the right-holder. For example, the reason a creditor has a right to be repaid is that repayment is in the interest of the creditor. One need not accept an interest theory of the nature of rights in order to hold that rights are grounded on interests. Although Joel Feinberg holds that to have a moral right is to be in a position to claim something as one's due, he occasionally suggests that it is some interest of the claimant that puts her in a position to make a morally valid claim. Now if moral rights are grounded on interests and if, as many argue, groups as such have certain collective interests, then presumably one should conclude that groups do in fact have moral rights.

This conclusion has been challenged by those who agree with H. L. A. Hart that the concept of a right is an essentially distributive concept; and even Neil MacCormick, who advocates an interest theory of rights, once suggested that rights secure individual goods individually enjoyed, not some collective good collectively enjoyed. For example, Jane's right to personal security protects her interest in not being injured or killed, and John's right to personal security protects his interest in not being injured or killed, but there is no right to security that protects the public as such from harmful attack. But does this line of reasoning really exclude group rights? Some-one could challenge the assumption that the only individual entities are individual persons. If groups of persons have a genuine unity and identity of some kind, then they should be taken to be individuals also. And if rights protect individuals in the enjoyment of some good, then rights might well protect groups in the enjoyment of some good. But can groups as such enjoy any good? Raz argues that there are some genuine goods that can be enjoyed only collectively. For example, public goods like national security or a healthy environment cannot be secured to only a few members of a soci-ety; either everyone enjoys them or no one enjoys them. Although Denise Reaume objects that a public good such as clean air can be enjoyed indi-vidually and might, therefore, be the object of an individual right, she argues that participatory goods, such as communicating in a shared lan-guage, can be enjoyed only collectively. In any event, if there are any essen-tially collective goods, these might serve to ground group rights that could not be reduced to rights of the individual group members.

Some moral philosophers attempt to ground group rights on the value of groups, at least certain kinds of groups, to their individual members. Communitarians, for example, argue that the individual self is not an aso-cial atom but is constituted in large measure by its social inheritance and continuing participation in a community. Strip away one's language, forms of thought, religion, and traditional practices, and there is no real self; who this or that particular person is depends on the political, economic, and cultural life he or she shares with other members of the community. It fol-lows that the preservation of the group or groups with which one identifies is of tremendous importance to one's well-being. Hence, group rights to certain aspects or features of the community might well be grounded on their value to the individual members of the group.

But is this theory of the grounds of group rights tenable? The problem is that it appeals to the purely instrumental value of certain groups, such as cul-tural communities or religious organizations. Any such appeal to instrumental value seems suspect. Consider the argument that chickens have a right to be well fed and protected from foxes in order that they be plump and juicy when they are slaughtered and cooked for our Sunday dinners. This sort of objection might be evaded were one to ground group rights not on individual values but on individual rights. If the individual person can develop her capacities to live a fully human life only by participation in the cultural, political, economic, and religious life of some group, then perhaps, as Carol Gould has argued, group rights are grounded on the individual's moral right to self-development as a human being. Again, given the pervasiveness in our society of racial discrimination, perhaps a group right of African-Americans to affirmative action programs can be grounded upon the individual rights to equal opportunity of African-Americans taken severally.

This last example suggests a fifth possible ground for group rights: social justice. John Rawls has recently tried to show that his liberal theory of social justice is not essentially atomistic, as some communitarian critics have alleged, by explaining how it can be extended to the law of peoples. To be sure, a people or a nation-state is only one sort of group, but many of the arguments for group rights do seem to be grounded on some principle of justice. Moreover, traditionally it has been assumed that there is some essential connection between rights and justice. Whether this assumption is justified is unclear, but this approach to the grounding of group rights is at least worthy of serious consideration.

Finally, one might try to ground group rights on utility. Although Ronald Dworkin and others have argued that rights could not be taken seriously were they grounded on social utility, David Lyons has defended something like Mill's utilitarian theory of human rights. Wayne Sumner has argued at greater length that the most plausible moral basis for rights is the utility of the rules that confer rights. If one is willing to take seriously the conceptions of rights proposed by Mill or Sumner, then one should take seriously a theory that asserts that group rights can be grounded on the utility, everything considered, of groups.

Legal Rights

Any complete theory of rights must deal with legal as well as moral rights. Is the range of options regarding legal group rights the same as those I have described for someone constructing a theory of moral group rights? Most, but not all, moral philosophers and jurists publishing in the theory of rights adopt a generic conception of the nature of a right, one that applies to all kinds of rights. Although they recognize that there are important differences between legal and moral rights, they insist that what is essential to their being rights is fundamentally the same. Given some generic conception of rights, the issues confronting anyone constructing a theory of group rights would be very similar whether one is considering moral or legal rights. For example, if one adopts a will theory of rights, then whether groups could possess legal rights depends upon whether they are capable of acting as groups, just as it does for whether they could possess moral rights. Again, if one accepts an interest theory of the nature of a right, then for moral and legal rights alike, whether groups are possible right-holders will depend upon whether there are any group interests irreducible to the interests of the several members of the group. If, on the other hand, one denies that any generic conception of rights is possible because moral and legal rights are essentially different, then one's conception of legal rights may provide a different range of theoretical options.

Almost everyone recognizes one important difference between moral and legal rights. Whereas the former are independent of any and all moral beliefs and social institutions, the latter are artificial in the sense that they are created by and thus dependent upon the legal system of some society. Some conclude that the limits upon possible moral right-holders do not apply to possible legal right-holders. Thus, Christopher Stone has argued that although natural objects may not be capable of possessing moral rights, the legislature or the courts could confer legal rights upon forests or rivers in order to protect them from environmental damage. One might reason analogously that because legal rights are created by administrative decree, legislative action, or judicial decision, a legal system could confer rights upon groups whenever a monarch, legislature, or court chooses to do so. Now I have no doubt that the officials in any legal system can do whatever they choose to do. However, the question remains whether their action, even granted that it is legally valid, creates some legal position that fits one's conception of a legal right, whatever that conception may be. It is a mistake to conclude from the fact that legal rights are artificial that there are no limits at all on the creation of legal rights, but it may be that those limits are different from the limits for moral rights.

Another relevant variable is one's conception of the nature of law. Legal positivists generally hold that the law is whatever rules are posited by the legally authorized actions of the officials of some legal system. Although natural law theorists generally admit that positive law is created by the actions of such officials, they insist that a posited rule is not legally valid, and thus not real law, if it is unjust or inconsistent with the natural law, a set of moral rules existing independently of the moral code of any society or any set of social institutions. If one accepts some natural law theory, one may be driven to recognize some moral limitations on the creation of legal group rights. Thus, if some legal group rights would be inconsistent with fundamental human rights, then any attempt to create them by legislative action might be bound to fail. For example, legislation purporting to confer upon an Indian tribe the group right to prevent the alienation of traditional tribal property might, by a natural law theorist, be considered legally invalid on the ground that it would violate the human right to property of the individual members of the tribe by preventing them from selling their holdings to more wealthy individuals who are not members of their group.

On the other hand, many legal positivists accept the sources thesis. This asserts that the content of the law in any legal system is entirely determined by whatever sources of law are recognized by the officials in that system to be authoritative. Now most of these will be texts of some sort such as a written constitution, proclaimed acts of the legislature, published administrative regulations, or the recorded opinions of the courts. This seems to imply that whatever these authoritative sources *say* is the law really is the law. This, in turn, suggests that if these sources say that groups have rights, then groups do have rights, from which it obviously follows that groups are possible right-holders whatever moral philosophers may allege to the contrary. Now it is probably true that in many legal systems there are authoritative texts that say, for example, that corporations have various specified rights. Hence, any legal positivist who accepts the sources thesis must admit that in some sense at least some groups—corporate bodies—can and do have legal rights. The question remains whether this sense of the expression "a right" as it is used in the law is the same as or consistent with the conception of rights required for the most adequate theory of law. If not, then in this theoretically preferable sense of "a right," the sense more relevant to philosophy of law, corporations may not have legal rights.

Whether or not one accepts the sources thesis, almost everyone will agree that the grounds of legal rights are different from, even if they include in part, the grounds of moral rights. This means that whether groups do have legal rights, and if so which rights they have, cannot be decided merely by discovering what moral rights, if any, groups in fact possess. Presumably the grounds of legal rights would include clauses in a written constitution, statutes enacted by the legislature, and in a common law system judicial decisions. Some of these, for example, the Canadian Charter of Rights and Freedoms, certainly seem to confer group rights upon aboriginal peoples or ethnic minorities. Whether such grounds do in fact confer legal group rights, rather than rights upon the individual members of the group, will depend in part upon the legally acceptable interpretation of the clause, statute, or decision that seems to do so. In any event, someone who wishes to construct a theory of legal group rights will need to adopt some view of the grounds of legal rights and then explain how these grounds do or do not apply to groups.

There is a certain logical priority to the questions that anyone attempting to construct a theory of group rights must face. The most fundamental question—Could groups have rights?—arises concerning both moral and legal rights, although the answers may be different for law and morals. If one's answer to this question is negative, then one must abandon one's project of constructing a theory of group rights. But if one believes that groups could have rights, the next question is, Do groups have rights? This question might also arise for both moral and legal rights, although whether groups do have legal rights may vary for different legal systems. Whether or not groups do in fact have legal rights, if they could have legal rights, then there is a third question, Should groups have legal rights? This question arises concerning the law, but not concerning morals, because the law is created and can be reformed by human action whereas morals are not artificial in this sense. Those who accept a political individualism and who fear that group rights will conflict with or unduly limit individual liberty often argue that there ought not to be any legal rights of groups. Communitarians who reject what they call atomic individualism and insist that the self is essentially social often advocate legal group rights to preserve and protect those communities they see as essential to the fullest development and most worthwhile lives of the individual members of certain social groups. The tension between these two viewpoints has recently led to a debate concerning whether political liberalism ought or ought not to advocate any legal group rights. The answer seems to depend in considerable measure upon one's conception of the ideal society. Thus Nathan Glaser has argued that although the ideal would be an integrated society in which only individual rights would be legally recognized, if the society contains minorities that cannot be effectively integrated into the mainstream and that are threatened with discrimination, then the law ought to confer some legal rights upon those groups.

The Final Alternatives

There are some legally valid documents, such as the Canadian Charter or international treaties, that seem to confer rights under domestic or international law upon groups. There are also moral wrongs, such as the persecution of religious sects, colonialism, genocide, and apartheid, that seem to cry out for the recognition and respect of group rights. In the end, each philosopher of law and moral philosopher must choose between different ways of dealing with legal documents and moral wrongs of these sorts.

The obvious alternative is to attempt to explain the appearance of group rights by constructing a theory of group rights in the strict sense, one that ascribes rights to groups as such. In this case, one will need to consider each of the sets of alternatives I have described far too briefly here. Because many of these alternatives pose challenges to the very possibility of group rights, this will not be an easy endeavor. It would, however, be premature to conclude that it must fail before seeing how well the best available theory of group rights solves the philosophical problems confronting it.

Some will choose the opposite alternative and attempt to interpret what seem to be group rights as rights of the individual members of the relevant groups. They may deny, for example, that African-Americans have any moral right to proportional representation in Congress but suggest that each black citizen has a moral right to representation in Congress that is equally effective as the representation of any individual white citizen. One may adopt this alternative because one believes that the very concept of a right is essentially distributive or because of the individualism central to one's political theory or social ideal.

These alternatives are illustrated by the International Covenant on Civil and Political Rights of 1966. Article 1 asserts, "All peoples have the right of self-determination." Although there is no explanation of what sort of group constitutes a people, this article clearly ascribes the right of self-determination to a people as a group. On the other hand, Article 27 reads: "In those states in which ethnic, religious or linguistic minorities exist, persons belonging to such minorities shall not be denied the right, in community with the other members of their group, to enjoy their own culture, to profess and practice their own religion, or to use their own language." In this passage the specified rights are ascribed not to the minorities as groups but to the individual members of these minorities. Many will read these two passages as illustrating a confusion in the thinking behind many human rights documents; others will insist that they show only that whether one should appeal to group rights in the strict sense or rights of the individual members of a group varies with the context, perhaps because what threatens important human interests and the most effective form of protection will vary with the situation.

There may be, however, an intermediate alternative. Some have proposed the concept of a group-based right. For example, if individuals have some fundamental moral right not to be harmed, and racial or sexual discrimination harms entire groups in a manner that cannot be reduced to the harms it inflicts upon individual blacks or women, then each African-American or female has a moral right that he or she, as a Black or woman, not be discriminated against merely for being a group member. Whether this really is a third alternative or only one of the former alternatives in disguise depends on precisely how the theory of group-based rights is articulated.

If none of these alternatives can be worked out clearly and in detail, one may have to fall back upon one last sort of theory. One might explain that there are legal and moral duties regarding groups that are not owed to those groups or to their members because of any right. The doctrine of the logical correlativity of rights and duties is no longer widely accepted; most moral and legal philosophers believe that there are some duties that are not grounded on rights. If so, then it may be that the legal, social, and moral causes championed by those who appeal to group rights can be served better by some theory of our duties regarding certain sorts of groups at least not to destroy or damage and perhaps even to sustain them.

My own strategy would be to develop a theory in which individual persons as members of groups have some moral rights and ought to have even more legal rights, but that also recognized a variety of moral duties regarding groups. But whether I am correct in my estimate of the alternatives remains to be seen. The final verdict cannot be delivered until moral philosophers and philosophers of law have spelled them all out clearly and fully. Only then will we be able to assess reliably their respective merits.

Our Contributions

The philosophical work of developing general theories or rights, and more specifically of explaining group rights, is well under way. The chapters in this volume are intended to advance this endeavor; those in this first part relate most closely to the alternatives I have described.

In my own chapter, I have not defended my choices between these theoretical options, much less attempted to integrate them into any coherent theory of rights. What I have done is to distinguish the different kinds of theoretical choices confronting anyone thinking about group rights, describe briefly the sorts of theories from which one might choose along each of these dimensions, and hint at some of the advantages or disadvantages of each alternative. I do not pretend to have contributed anything to the theory of group rights; my hope has been only to assist my philosophical colleagues to do so by reporting the relevant work that has already been done to formulate and defend more general and abstract theories of rights.

Carol Gould's primary contribution to the theory of group rights is her explanation of the nature of a social group. She rejects both the reduction of a group to a mere aggregate of its individual members and the thesis that a social group is an entity over and above its members. A social group is constituted by individuals-in-relations. What is most interesting in her theory is her suggestion that these are internal relations, social relations that make each individual who he or she is so that the members of a social group are themselves by their very nature social individuals.

Gould also proposes an original theory of the grounds of the moral rights of cultural minorities and oppressed groups. These group rights are derived from the moral rights of the individual members of these groups, and the relevant individual rights are in turn grounded on social justice.

Finally, she defends the thesis that cultural minorities and oppressed groups should have legal rights. However, she places certain limits upon these legal rights. The rights of the group must be compatible with the human rights of its individual members, must not violate the rights of any internal minority, and should support democratic decision making within the group.

Ann Cudd also focuses on the nature of social groups, especially nonvoluntary groups. The members of a voluntary social group share joint commitments or joint projects; the members of a nonvoluntary social group share social constraints consequent on their group membership. These constraints are imposed upon them by individuals who identify them through the socially salient characteristics they share with other members of their group and by social institutions that affect the penalties and rewards they reap for their actions. Although many of these social constraints result from intended collective actions, others are the unintended consequences of actions based on stereotypes that serve as default assumptions upon which people act.

Cudd then suggests that some such theory of nonvoluntary social groups is necessary to explain the social injustice of oppression. Whether she would go on to ground any moral group rights of oppressed groups upon social justice or argue for group legal rights in anything like the way that Carol Gould does remains unexplained, but advocates of group rights might well use her theory of the nature of nonvoluntary social groups for these purposes.

George Rainbolt discusses alternative conceptions of group rights. He assumes that some assertions that certain groups have rights are true and that the philosophically important question is what such statements mean. He then distinguishes two kinds of conceptual analyses of group rights. Individualists believe that all group rights can be analyzed as complex sets of individual rights; collectivists insist that at least some group rights cannot be reduced to any sets of merely individual rights.

Rainbolt also clarifies the nature of individualistic conceptions of group rights by eliminating several common misunderstandings. For example, individualism need not favor either left-wing or right-wing political viewpoints. It need not deny that individuals can have rights because of their group membership. And it is not committed to the view that a group right must be analyzed in terms of the rights of only the members of that group.

He then rebuts three very recent kinds of arguments for collectivism. The first argues that there are rights, like the right to assemble, to do things that only a group can do. The second and third presuppose that a right must be grounded on some interest of the right-holder sufficient to impose duties upon others and argue, on the one hand, that the value of participatory goods like enjoying a baseball game with one's family cannot be explained only by the individual interests of the participants and, on the other hand, that only the collective interest of a group is sufficient to impose the duties implied by some rights like the right to self-determination. Rainbolt's general strategy is to analyze assertions of these kinds of rights into conjunctions of statements about individual rights and then to define the content of these individual rights in terms of some action or interest of the individual conditional upon that of others. If one can deal with group rights with some such conceptual analysis, then one should be able to avoid the ontological problems Carol Gould and Ann Cudd face in explaining the nature of social groups.

Christopher Gray proposes a different classification of the types of social groups in terms of procedure, the sequence of behaviors required in order for an action to have force. Organizations, such as a social class or ethnic minority, maintain a group identity and carry out projects because members of the group have taken on functional roles. They are led and directed by persons in control, but the identity of the group and any inherent goals may remain out of sight. Moral persons, for example, families or nations like the Quebecois in Quebec, are social groups in which the exercise of power that directs others is understood as a function and its fulfilment a duty, as are the powers of the members to carry out tasks. The members are here recognized as entitled to act within their jurisdictions and seen as rights-holders, whereas in an organization individuals are seen only as performing contingent activities needed for the organization to function. Legal persons, such as the Bell Telephone Corporation or the Province of Quebec, are constituted by constitutions, charters, or bylaws that confer specified powers to act and liabilities for acting upon their members. Whereas moral personality is more or less reducible to the organs of power depending upon the participants' awareness of the group's identity, legal personality is indivisible and is an all-or-nothing matter.

Gray then argues that this classification has important implications for the question of whether social groups are possible right-holders. A group must be able to exercise its rights as modes of action. Because organizations, moral persons, and legal persons have systematically different capacities for action, this classification is useful in sorting out the kinds of rights that any social group could possess and to which it might be entitled. Thus, because only individuals can speak or write, only individuals could have any right to use their native language. (However, a linguistic group might benefit from this right even though it could not, as a group, exercise or possess any group right to use its language.) Although only a natural person could have any fundamental right to life, a social group might have an analogous fundamental right to exist. Because possession has many modalities and different types of groups have various capacities to hold and own possessions, social groups can and presumably should have some sorts of property rights. Finally, a group's political rights to determine public policy are more available as its capacity to perform these functions increases.

Thomas Simon argues that the debate about whether some social groups should have legal rights is philosophically problematic and politically counterproductive. It raises difficult ontological questions about the nature of social groups and conceptual issues concerning the meaningfulness of ascribing rights to groups. It pits individualists, who defend freedom of individual choice and legal rights as trumps over social utility or public goods, against collectivists, who believe that individual well-being depends essentially upon the social groups that enable them to become autonomous persons and give value to their lives.

Simon proposes a group-harm analysis as an alternative and more fruitful approach to the political issues at stake in the individualist versus collectivist debate. Both individualists and collectivists can find common ground in a proscription against group harm. And the conception of group harm is less problematic than that of group rights. A group is harmed when the harm directed against a member of the group because of that person's group status lowers the threshold of vulnerability for other group members. Any politically useful theory about groups must first address the lingering and current effects brought about by the forces of prejudice and discrimination. Hence, harms must become the central focus for political theory and action. This approach is especially relevant in the legal context because it speaks directly to the appropriate judicial remedies for the social injustices that any theory of group rights approaches only indirectly and ineffectively.

Although none of these chapters can claim to provide a comprehensive theory of group rights, as a group they have a right to be taken seriously. They illuminate the most perplexing alternatives open to anyone wondering whether, and if so how, to develop a theory of group rights. No doubt much of the philosophical work remains to be done, but some of it is begun in the later parts of this volume.

Chapter 1

Group Rights and Social Ontology

Carol C. Gould

The increasing globalization and universalization of culture worldwide has paradoxically been matched at the same time by increasing cultural particularism and separatism. These two conflicting trends are reflected in cosmopolitanism or the homogenization of cultures, on the one hand, and in claims to cultural autonomy or to ethnic and nationalist chauvinisms, on the other. At the same time that sixteen-year-olds all over the world are drinking their Cokes while listening to MTV and wearing their Levis (many sizes too large), their parents and siblings are often reviving ancient ethnic feuds, rediscovering their distinctive cultural identities, and attempting to exclude alien others from their midst. Against the background of an increasing awareness of the value of cultural difference, but also in the context of the alternative claims of equal and universal freedom and global interconnectedness, the question of group rights has recently reemerged with particular force and has been developed in newly sophisticated ways in social and political philosophy. What are group rights? Do we need to recognize them as a condition for preserving and enhancing cultural diversity? Are they fundamental rights, or do they instead derive from individual rights? And indeed, what do we mean when we speak of a "group" in this connection?

In my discussion, I will draw upon what I have called *social ontology*, as a theory of social reality, which I have developed in earlier work, and will use it as a framework for considering what constitutes a group and what normative claim there can be for group rights. In this chapter, the focus will be on the rights of cultural minorities in liberal democratic societies and the problems that arise when a democratic majority takes its dominant culture and language to be obligatory and adopts assimilationist or integrationist policies that deny rights of cultural self-expression and development to such minority ethnic groups. I will also briefly consider the somewhat different question of the rights of oppressed groups within a larger polity, where such groups are identified by discriminatory, exclusionary, or exploitative treat-ment. I will leave aside here the related questions of the rights of relatively smaller groups such as corporations, professions, and so forth, as well as of such larger collectivities as polities, whether at the local or the national level, where issues analogous to those of group rights might also arise.

Groups as Constituted Entities

In the discussion that has developed on group rights, there has been no lit-tle confusion about what the term *group* should be taken to refer to. It is commonly agreed that it is not simply an accidental aggregation of individ-uals, nor even one where the individuals share some common characteris-tic. This is far too abstract for a social group of the sort intended. It is also commonly agreed that it is not a reified entity, a collectivity that exists over and above its individual members, on the model of a Platonic class or a Durkheimian structure. Instead, a number of theorists have characterized a group as made up of individuals who stand in certain relations to each other, for example, as sharing a common purpose or having a common intention-ality, or acting together, or at least having a common interest. I developed a view along these lines in my book *Marx's Social Ontology: Individuality and Community in Marx's Theory of Social Reality* (1978),[1] in my 1979 paper to the Metaphysical Society entitled "Ontological Foundations of Democracy," and subsequently, in my book *Rethinking Democracy* (1988).[2] In the social ontology developed in these works and others,[3] I characterized a social group as an entity constituted by "individuals-in-relations," eschewing both aggregative and holistic readings. Further, I argued that while individuals as agents are ontologically prior to the groups that they constitute, they stand in internal relations to each other such that they become the individuals they are in and through such social relations and may therefore be described as social individuals. By internal relations we mean relations among entities that are at least in part constitutive of the identity of these entities; a change in these relations would therefore effect a change in the character of the entity itself. In external relations, by contrast, the identity of individuals is independent of these relations. Thus, where such internal relations are social relations among persons, for example, in those between teacher and students or between parents and children, the characters of the individuals are trans-formed by the interactions between them. The ontological priority of the individuals is retained, however, in virtue of their agency, as a capacity to change these relations and to choose new ones (either by themselves or together with others).

The sociality of individuals consists not only in their interactions, which may take reciprocal or nonreciprocal forms, but also in what I have called *common* or *joint activity*. I argue that participation in such activity is one of the main conditions for individual self-development. In this framework, groups are defined by such joint activity or common purposes, whether explicitly recognized or not. On my view, groups are constituted entities, that is, they come into being by virtue of actual relations among their constituent individual members, but are not reducible to the individuals distributively, taken apart from these relations. We may observe that constituted entities are not the less real for being constituted; but they do not exist independently as Platonic universals. Rather, they exist only in and through the individuals related to each other in the group and cease to exist when these relations no longer hold.

Norms and Ontology

The normative question of whether there are group rights is distinct from, though related to, the ontological question of what constitutes a group. My view here differs in this respect from that of Allen Buchanan, who, in his book *Secession*, argues that although there are group rights, the question of ontology is irrelevant. He claims that liberalism is committed to individual moral rights but is not limited to an individualist ontology that would preclude an emphasis on the sociality of individuals. He holds that liberalism's individualism is moral and not ontological.[4] Whatever one thinks of this particular claim about liberalism, I do not accept Buchanan's sharp fact-value or ontological-moral distinction with regard to social facts and would instead suggest that the social ontology of both individuals and groups makes a difference to the normative arguments about group rights.[5] To take the extreme cases: it would obviously make quite a difference if one argued that only individuals exist and that their relations to others are simply external relations that had no effect on who they fundamentally were; or, by contrast, that the identity of individuals derives entirely from their group membership and that they had no independent existence apart from this. It would be odd to attribute moral values or rights to groups in the first case, where only individuals are held to exist; or to deny such group rights in the second, that is, where individual identity is seen as deriving from group membership. Indeed, I would suggest that the social ontology itself is already in a way normative—for example, that the very characterization of individuals as agents or persons with cultural identities supports an argument for certain rights as valid claims of such individuals. Conversely, the values and rights recognized are partly dependent on how one characterizes the existence of individuals, social relations, and groups. This does not render such an ontological account "metaphysical" in the sense pertaining to "being as such," since it remains a regional ontology concerned exclusively with concrete human beings in their social inter-relations and practices.

How to Derive Group Rights from Individual Rights

We begin from the principle of justice as equal positive freedom, which (as I have argued elsewhere) is the normative conception that goes along with such a social ontology of individuals-in-relations and constituted social groups. This principle entails a (prima facie) equal right of individuals to the conditions of their self-development or to the exercise of their freedom over time. Since participation in common activity is one of the main conditions for such self-development, it follows that individuals as agents have prima facie equally valid claims or rights to such opportunities for participation in joint activity. Among the modes of such activity involving a shared understanding of common interests and a mutual recognition as participants in it are work, political life, culture, and also various forms of voluntary association and face-to-face interactions. If we focus on culture here, it is because it is a pervasive source of social identity, providing a context for thought and action that involves language, values, modes of behavior, education, socialization, practices, traditions, and shared history. Cultural life, in these terms, essentially involves common or joint activity with others, as members of the cultural group. Common activity is taken here in the generic sense to include not only joint participation in explicit and organized or institutionally defined practices, such as the celebration of holidays or historic events, but also the more tacit forms of activities expressing shared beliefs or values, such as modes of social behavior, styles of dress or speech, and so forth. It is evident from this pervasiveness of culture, then, that an individual's participation in some mode of cultural life as a form of common activity is a condition for self-development. It therefore follows that if individuals have equal rights to the conditions of their self-development, they have equal rights to have the opportunity to participate in a culture. We may say that there is an equal right of access to the conditions of cultural self-development.

This remains a relatively transparent right, tacitly assumed, as long as there is no special problem concerning access to or participation in one's culture. Thus for dominant cultures what may be at issue is equal educational opportunity or cultural literacy or the availability of cultural resources in a fair distribution. However, for minority cultures what is at stake is precisely the question of their continued existence or the denial of the conditions of access to or participation in the life of that culture. This may result from lack of means for learning the language or the history and traditions of a minority culture; or it may mean deliberate discriminatory repression of the minority culture. In such a case, the provision of the equal rights to the conditions of cultural development may justify a claim for group rights.

A number of very sharp issues concerning the rights of cultural minorities have thus become the focus of the current discussion on group rights. The normative framework proposed here may therefore be characterized as a theory of cultural justice,[6] where this concerns the rights of groups to the expression and development of their own cultures within the framework of a different dominant culture, and, more generally, the rights of individuals to cultural self-development.

The other focus of this recent discussion is on the rights of oppressed groups that are not characterizable as—or not simply characterizable as—cultural minorities, for example, women or African-Americans in the United States context. There is, of course, some overlap, since some oppressed groups are at the same time clearly identifiable as cultural minorities (e.g., Native Americans, and to some degree African-Americans). Moreover, oppressed groups may develop shared modes of understanding and action that may be characterized as cultural. So, for example, some have attempted to talk in this way of "women's culture" or again of "a culture of poverty," but clearly some reification is entailed in attributing such a common culture to all members of these groups. (The same may well be true of more standardly identified cultural groups.) In talking about groups and their rights, then, one has to be sensitive to the degree of diversity even within the framework of a common culture and certainly in those contexts in which the term *culture* is used by metaphoric extension.

But what exactly is a group right as against the rights that individual members of a culture have to their own cultural expression and development?

And how would such group rights be derived from the cultural rights of individuals? Part of the confusion in talking about group rights derives from an ontological error, specifically, to consciously or unconsciously reify the conception of a group as something independent of or abstractable from its constitution by individuals, in the specific relations that characterize them as members of that group. Such a group as an abstract entity cannot have rights. Even if one were to identify a culture with such institutional or social facts as language or a system of values, or structures of belief, these entities would themselves be constituted by the actions, beliefs, and linguistic practices of individuals-in-relations. On the other hand, individual members of a culture, whether majority or minority, cannot develop their cultural activity except with respect to the existence of a culture to which they belong, namely, to a relatively persisting and emergent form of cultural life, which they in turn appropriate in the course of their interaction with others.

Group rights therefore pertain to groups as constituted entities and thus are rights derived from the rights of the constituent individuals who are members of the group and who have these group rights insofar as they are members of the group and not apart from these relations to each other. The group rights that a cultural minority can bear are therefore rights to the cultural conditions for the self-development of its members. Since it is not the group that has the equal right to cultural self-development but the individual members of the culture, these group rights are derivative from and instrumental to the equal rights to self-development of the members. They are not rights of the group sui generis. Yet group rights are not reducible to or identifiable with the distributive rights of each individual to the conditions for his or her own cultural development, but rather are rights of the constituency of the culture in the literal sense of those who constitute the group collectively. As a necessary condition for the exercise of individual rights, the group can make a valid claim against the majority culture to provide the individuals with these conditions. Thus, a minority culture that may be expressed in a language other than a dominant language of the majority would have a group right to provide the means for the perpetuation of that linguistic community through its educational system and other means. This does not entail, however, that the cultural minority could insist that all of its members were required to be educated only in that language, but rather that the choice to be educated in this way would be available to its members.

This addresses a special problem concerning group rights of minority cultures, namely, the preservation of the human rights of members of the culture and their freedom of choice to remain members or to leave the group, or indeed to combine their cultural identity in the group with other cultural identities or affiliations. I will have more to say on this later.

Another condition for cultural participation of members of a minority culture could be the freedom to observe certain cultural traditions or practices, whether religious or secular, for example, the celebration of certain festivals or commemorations or the observation of dietary rituals. Here, again, the right of the group would consist in its access to the means to provide for these practices and not to be interfered with in them by the dominant culture or the powers of the state. Yet here, too, an important constraint will be noted later, namely, that the practices of a minority culture cannot be such as to violate the human rights of its members. In other words, the special group rights must be compatible with the universalistic human rights to which the dominant culture is presumably committed. Where this is not the case and the dominant culture is itself repressive and in violation of the human rights of its members, the minority culture is not thereby absolved from this constraint.

The approach I present is related in certain respects to the views of such theorists of group rights as Will Kymlicka, Charles Taylor, Michael Hartney, Michael McDonald, Allen Buchanan, and Vernon Van Dyke. A full account of the similarities and differences between the view I develop here and these others would require a more extended discussion than I can give in this chapter. Suffice it to note a similarity with Kymlicka, Buchanan, and to some degree Taylor, in the general strategy of regarding culture as a condition for the agency of individuals or their development.[7] In addition, like Taylor and McDonald (and Van Dyke earlier), I would argue that there is a need to go beyond traditional liberal individualism in recognizing the claims of cultural groups or communities.[8] However, I am wary, as is Hartney,[9] of a tendency among such theorists toward a collectivist interpretation of groups or an assignment of independent value (e.g., survival) to the group as such.

A difference between my view and nearly all of these others concerns their characterization of what constitutes a culture or a cultural group. In general, they operate with a strong or overarching conception of culture not only as "encompassing" (in Margalit and Raz's term)[10] but as national and territorially based, or, in Kymlicka's phrase, as a "societal culture."[11] The idea here seems to be something like that of a national minority with group claims against the majority nation-state in which it finds itself. In this way, culture is thought of in terms of such group rights as property right, political sovereignty or self-determination, and secession. While the question of the group rights of national minorities or societal cultures is clearly an important one, there is a wide range of culturally defined groups that lies outside of this strong definition of cultural identity. As will be seen, it is this range that is my focus here, in the context of contemporary multicultural societies and the phenomenon of multiple cultural identifications.[12]

There is one other important and systematic difference between these other views and the one developed here. Although the philosophical discussion by these theorists is often sophisticated and the concrete examples very rich, it seems to me that there is as yet an insufficient attention to the social ontology of cultural groups and therefore to the relevance of such an ontological analysis for the normative question of rights. I think it could be shown that each of these theorists does in fact operate, at least implicitly, with an ontology of individuals and groups. Nearly all of them advance a criticism of the one-sided alternatives of ontological individualism and holism or collectivism. Several of them go on to explicitly reject the relevance of any ontological analysis, either because of the unacceptability of these dichotomous alternatives for the case of cultural rights (e.g., Kymlicka)[13] or because of the belief that moral or normative values like justice or rights are independent of the "factual" characterization of entities such as individuals or groups (e.g., Buchanan, Hartney).[14] I have already criticized this latter approach in my earlier discussion of Buchanan. As to the former view, which correctly perceives the inadequacy of the presumed ontological alternatives in this case, one can respond that there is in fact an acceptable mediated ontology that is relevant to the issue of cultural rights which moreover avoids the criticisms that can be leveled at the one-sided views. This position, while it draws on the strengths of both individualist and communitarian emphases, integrates them in an ontology of social individuals. Such a social ontology, in turn, supports a notion of group rights that neither reifies the group as a rights-bearer nor reduces these rights to the distributive rights of individuals.

Oppressed Groups and Group Rights

Before proceeding, I might note that there is a parallel construction for the derivation of group rights from rights of individuals in the case of oppressed groups. As I noted earlier, an oppressed group is characterized as a group within a given society that is excluded from the equal rights and benefits of other members of that society or is subjected to discriminatory or exploitative treatment severely affecting the freedom and/or well-being of its members. An oppressed group is excluded in some systematic and effective way from whatever norms of equality may prevail in the society at large. The special rights of an oppressed group would bear on the rectification and compensation for unequal treatment in the past and would aim at providing what has been characterized as a "level playing field" for present members with respect to the rest of society. So in this case, the group rights—whether in the form of affirmative action, compensatory treatment, the removal of special barriers to participation in political and economic life, desegregation, and so forth—are justified by reference to the same principle of prima facie equal rights to the conditions of self-development, hence from the rights of individual members of the oppressed groups.

Here the basis for membership in a group is not a matter of social identification or common purpose or shared understanding, though these elements of solidarity among the oppressed may develop as a common consciousness of their relevantly similar situation. Rather, it is a matter of objective circumstances of being put in a particular situation of oppression not by choice; and of what has been called an ascriptive identity, that is, what members of the group are taken to be by others and in particular by the dominant group. While such oppressed groups may also be regarded as constituted entities in the sense that the groups do not exist apart from the individuals in relations of oppression, nonetheless such groups are not defined by shared purposes of their choosing or the sort of intentionality often characteristic of cultural groups.

Constraints on Group Rights for Cultural Minorities

An interesting and not uncommon problem arises with respect to group rights for some cultural minorities: When the practices of a cultural minority, which are to be supported by group rights, themselves violate the human rights of individual members of the culture, does the autonomy of the cultural group permit the violation of human rights? I would argue that any of the rights of a minority cultural group would have to be compatible with the human rights, for otherwise the justification of the group rights on the basis that they provide conditions for the equal freedom of self-development of the individuals who are members of that group would be undermined. Since the human rights are the fundamental conditions for the exercise of agency and hence are given priority in the application of the principle of equal positive freedom, they cannot be abrogated by group rights applied or interpreted in such a way as to violate them.

This has particularly important bearing for the difficult question of the pervasive oppression of women within many cultural minorities (and majorities as well!). Thus, for example, a traditional practice of female genital mutilation is still condoned within certain cultural groups. The claim has been made that the autonomy of a culture demands noninterference or nonintervention even with such practices. Without addressing the difficult issue of intervention here, we may say that cultural group rights would not justify such practices, since such practices entail a violation of human rights. Further, insofar as women's equality is formally protected by the human rights, it can be appealed to as a ground for eliminating other cultural practices that oppress women.

Other constraints on cultural group rights that need consideration, though I cannot deal with them here, include the issue of the democratization of decision making within a cultural minority where autocratic or other antidemocratic practices may prevail. A related issue is that of who is authentically representative of the cultural minority and can speak for it. Another important constraint on the scope of group rights concerns what we may call "minorities within the minority." Especially in territorial situations where a minority culture holds sway over a geographic region, there will inevitably be minorities living within this minority cultural framework. Clearly, the rights of these subminorities to their own cultural expression need to be respected, and these minorities within the minority should not suffer the same suppression or discrimination that the minority culture had itself suffered. This norm of the protection of minorities within what were previously oppressed cultures or nationalities has been widely and wildly violated in recent history and at present. I would also hazard the suggestion that the issue of such subminorities has not received enough attention from political philosophers.[15]

A practical question emerges from this issue of minorities within a minority. How large must a cultural group be before it is legitimated in its demands for cultural autonomy and recognition of group rights? Will we be led on a slippery slope here to the absurd condition that any group of two or three may call themselves a cultural group and may demand special rights for the preservation and the practice of their "culture"? Clearly, some measure of good judgment is required here, especially in a historical period in which long-suppressed minorities of ethnic, religious, or linguistic sorts have emerged to make claims not only for recognition and cultural self-determination but also for secession and national identity.

From Separatism to Multiculturalism

Perhaps the most salient development in the recent period has been a move away from monocultural identity associated with the traditional nation-state to multicultural identities in which there is an interaction and an admixture of two or more cultures. This is to be distinguished from mere assimilationism, in which an older or parent culture yields to a dominant culture that essentially replaces it or corrupts it. Especially in large cities and in the context of major waves of immigration, populations have become culturally heterogeneous. Likewise, with the development of the world market and the globalization not only of the economy but also of communications and the media, an increasing cosmopolitanism has emerged. There are two aspects to this: the first is a rapidly changing world culture, especially as a youth culture transcending national, ethnic, and geographic barriers; the second is the interaction among existing cultures and the pluralization of cultural identities.

This phenomenon has been identified as *multiculturalism*, but this is a term that has been used in importantly ambiguous ways, meaning different things to different people. We may distinguish between two uses of the term: in one use, multiculturalism designates an aggregate or collection of different and relatively separate cultures together with an awareness within an older dominant culture of these differences and of the contributions of the cultures of oppressed groups—paradigmatically, the recognition of the contributions of African-American, Latino, and other minority cultures in the United States—or an awareness of non-Western cultures beyond the dominant Eurocentric canon. The term *multiculturalism* has also been used to designate a new interactive model of culture, where cultural identity itself is open to plural definition and where there may be cultural creation through the appropriation of diverse cultural influences. (A noteworthy example of this is American jazz, and there have been newer forms of this as well, especially in art and music.) Yet this does not necessarily entail a homogenization of cultural strains, and it is also a continuation of the historically common phenomenon of cultural diffusion. But we may say that this has become a more intensely dynamic phenomenon than it was in the past, due in part at least to the powerful contemporary technologies of global communication.

On the normative side, from the standpoint of a single individual, these developments contribute to the possibilities of cultural choice and change. Customary views of cultural, ethnic, or political identity have most often seen this identity as simply given, as a matter of birth into a culture, or ethnic group, or community; or else have considered this identity to be ascriptive, that is, determined by what salient or authoritative others take one to be. I would argue that cultural identity and group membership need to be defined in such a way that they are open to choice and to the possibility of multiple cultural identifications. This would add an important element of self-definition and the appropriation of diverse cultures to the more passive traditional characterization of cultures as matters of birth or ascription.

These normative considerations, as well as the fact of increasing multiculturalism, raise a host of practical and interesting questions concerning cultural group rights. Since determining whether groups have rights and what rights they have also depends on the answer to the question of what makes an individual a member of a group, multiculturalism significantly complicates the identification of a given cultural group, as well as the question of which group rights any given individual can lay claim to. This would be especially difficult if we wish to move to a multicultural policy within the public sphere in which there would be public support for cultural groups as a matter of group rights.

We may clarify the relations between cultural differences and the public sphere by considering some models of the state in regard to culture, as well as ethnicity and nationality. In particular, we may distinguish five alternatives:

1. The purely political or universally abstract model of the state, which is defined entirely independently of any condition of or relation to ethnicity, nationality, or culture. In such a neutral state, cultural differences may exist, but they are irrelevant to the definition of the state as a polity and are assigned to the private sphere.

2. The multicultural state, in which a diversity of cultures exists and is recognized in various ways by the state. These cultural differences are not only tolerated but supported by the state, though they are not requirements for citizenship, which is defined apart from them. Such cultural affiliations

do not bear any essential relation to ethnicity or nationality in the strong sense of characteristics given by kinship or country of origin.

3. The monocultural integrationist state, in which there is a dominant statewide (and in that sense national) culture, in which all citizens are required to participate, but which is open to anyone regardless of their particular ethnic, national, or cultural affiliations. In this case, the different cultural, ethnic, or national identities are tolerated as pertaining to matters of private preference, but integration within the state requires the adoption of its official or national culture.

4. The binational or multinational state, which combines two or more well-defined nationalities within a single political entity. Here there is formal recognition of ethnic or national affiliation, and specific rights are given to each of the constitutive nationalities with respect to certain areas of state law and policy. This case also involves the formal recognition of two or more official languages. In this model, the nationalities could be of relatively equal size, or one might constitute a majority and the other (or others) a national minority (or minorities).

5. The nationalist state, which, in its strongest version, makes a particular ethnicity or nationality a condition for citizenship and thus for full political rights. Such a state is exclusively national in that it makes no provision for the equal treatment of minority ethnic, national, or cultural groups and regards them at best as resident aliens or denies them rights to reside there altogether.

When considered from the standpoint of cultural minorities within the state, the fifth model is clearly normatively unacceptable, and so in most formulations is the fourth. The crude, exclusive nationalism of the fifth by definition leaves no scope for equal rights for members of cultural or ethnic minorities within it. The best that one could have on this model would be democracy for the right kind of people, but even this is highly unlikely given the authoritarian bent of most nationalistic regimes. The fourth model is more complicated, since it provides for representation and cultural self-determination for a set of different cultural groups. Nevertheless, there will certainly be minority cultures within a binational or multinational state that are not included among these nationalities, ethnicities, or recognized minority cultures. Therefore, despite the attempt to represent cultural variety in the context of political equality, some will inevitably be excluded and thus will be discriminated against, in terms of the expression of their culture, even if they possess equal rights as individuals.

The third model, of monocultural integrationism, despite its toleration of minority nationalities and cultures outside the political domain, still has a coercive dimension, in its imposition of the official national culture as a requirement for citizenship. This national culture also tends to be the culture of the majority, so that even with fully democratic procedures of majority rule, minority cultures could have their interests subordinated by the votes of a permanent majority. Interestingly enough, the first model of the neutral state is open to a similar problem in practice, with respect to the dominance of permanent cultural majorities. Although in this case there is no explicit imposition of acceptance of the dominant culture, democratic majorities may still deny equal treatment to cultural minorities, by discriminatory allocation of resources or the adoption of policies that privilege members of the cultural majority in public life.

In terms of the protection of rights of cultural minorities, the second model, namely, that of multicultural democracy or cultural pluralism, which is presently in its nascent form, is normatively the most acceptable. While it shares with the first the priority of a framework of equal individual and political rights, it promises to offer greater protection for minority cultures by explicitly building in support for a diversity of cultural expression and development. It also differs from the other models in providing for the facilitation and encouragement of interrelations among different cultures, thus making possible a richer cultural environment for citizens. But the question of how public support for cultural groups could be allocated without being unfair to some individuals remains a difficult problem. More generally, the implementation of the normative requirement of prima facie equal rights of access to the conditions of cultural self-development in a multicultural society would present practical problems of enormous complexity and difficulty. One hopes that the study of group rights and their relation to individual rights will contribute to a rational framework for such policy deliberations.

Notes

1. Carol Gould, *Marx's Social Ontology: Individual and Community in Marx's Theory of Social Reality* (Cambridge, Mass.: MIT Press, 1978), esp. 31–39.

2. Carol Gould, *Rethinking Democracy* (Cambridge: Cambridge University Press, 1988), esp. chap. 2.

3. Cf. especially Carol Gould, "Beyond Causality in the Social Sciences: Reciprocity as a Model for Non-exploitative Social Relations," in *Epistemology, Methodology and*

the Social Sciences, Boston Studies for the Philosophy of Science, ed. R. S. Cohen and M. W. Wartofsky (Dordrecht: Reidel, 1983), 53–88; and Gould, "Ontological Foundations of Democracy" (paper presented to the Metaphysical Society of America, 1979; published in revised form in *Rethinking Democracy*).

4. Allen Buchanan, *Secession* (Boulder, Colo.: Westview Press, 1991), 8, 79–80.

5. We might observe that Buchanan himself appeals to numerous arguments that are social ontological in this sense. See, for example, ibid., 39, 77.

6. See my "Cultural Justice and the Limits of Difference" (paper presented at the annual meeting of the American Society for Value Inquiry, American Philosophical Association, Eastern Division, 1994); and my "Hard Questions in Democratic Theory: When Justice and Democracy Conflict," working paper no. 5, University Center for Human Values, Princeton University, Princeton, N.J., March 1994.

7. Cf. Will Kymlicka, *Multicultural Citizenship: A Liberal Theory of Minority Rights* (Oxford: Clarendon Press, 1995), 76, 82, 93; Buchanan, *Secession*, Clarendon Press, 53–54; Charles Taylor, *Multiculturalism* (Princeton, N.J.: Princeton University Press, 1994), 61.

8. Cf. Taylor, *Multiculturalism*, 56–61; Michael McDonald, "Should Communities Have Rights? Reflections on Liberal Individualism," *Canadian Journal of Law and Jurisprudence* 4 (July 1991): 217–37, esp. 237; and Vernon Van Dyke, "Collective Entities and Moral Rights: Problems in Liberal-Democratic Thought," *Journal of Politics* 44 (1982): 21–40.

9. Michael Hartney, "Some Confusions Concerning Collective Rights," in *The Rights of Minority Cultures*, ed. W. Kymlicka (Oxford: Oxford University Press, 1995), 202–27.

10. Avishai Margalit and Joseph Raz, "National Self-Determination," *Journal of Philosophy* 87 (September 1990): 448.

11. Kymlicka, *Multicultural Citizenship*, 18, 75–80.

12. Although some of these theorists do consider aspects of this wider range of cultural groups, e.g., Kymlicka in his discussion of "polyethnic" and immigrant groups (*Multicultural Citizenship*, 30–31, 78, 96–98, 176ff.), this does not fundamentally affect their theoretical framework, which is drawn from the narrower national conception of culture.

13. Ibid., 34–35, 46–47.

14. Buchanan, *Secession*, 79–80; Hartney, "Some Confusions Concerning Collective Rights," 208.

15. An exception is the essay by Leslie Green, "Internal Minorities and Their Rights," in *The Rights of Minority Cultures*, ed. W. Kymlicka (Oxford: Oxford University Press, 1995), 256–72.

Chapter 2

Nonvoluntary Social Groups

Ann E. Cudd

We enter schools, join clubs, play, work, make friends, buy and sell, travel, read, vote, converse, marry, and procreate. These are some of the social activities that we (more or less) choose to participate in, and by doing so we self-determine the course of our individual lives. But our lives are also shaped by social facts about us that we cannot choose. We are born into families that we do not choose, with abilities and disabilities, skin color, sex, and sexuality that we do not choose but that have profound consequences for the choices we will be able to make. We are shunned or welcomed by others for our parents' social status and wealth; we find ourselves with a native language and dialect, and in a culture whose attitudes toward wealth, power, technology, and individual freedom will deeply affect the way we think about the world. Our societies are already there for us, with complex sets of traditions, expectations, stereotypes, norms, practices, and explicit rules that enable and constrain our beliefs, desires, and activities. Changing them is like turning an aircraft carrier—it can be done, but not in a hurry, not with a sailboarder's precision, and not by one person acting alone.

These are among the common circumstances of human social life familiar to us all: that we are individuals who belong to social groups, some of which we choose to belong to and some of which we belong to whether or not we would choose to belong if we could. There is wide disagreement over whether the concept "social group" is empty or whether it is useful explanatorily or normatively. Among those who take social groups to be real, there is disagreement about a fundamental point about what social groups are, and how they are formed and maintained. There are two broad categories of approaches here. One, the intentionalist approach, claims that social groups are formed and maintained by individuals who intentionally enter into them and maintain them through rules and norms, explicit or implicit. The paradigm kinds of social groups for the intentionalists are the social club, the modern state, or the conversational pair. With this approach we can associate names such as Jean-Paul Sartre, Max Weber, and Margaret Gilbert. The other approach, the structuralist approach, claims that social groups are structural features of the social environment, formed by rules, norms, and practices, explicit and implicit, and include individuals who may never consider or even see that they are a part of them, even though membership in the group has some effect on their lives. The kinds of groups that structuralists focus on include social classes, races, genders, and cultures. Among the important structuralists are Karl Marx, Émile Durkheim, and Michel Foucault.

Intentionalists and structuralists see their positions as diametrically opposed because they share the mistaken notion that intentionalist psychology is incompatible with the existence of irreducible social forces. I hold a compatibilist position, that while action is intentionally guided, many of the constraints within which we act are socially determined and beyond the control of the currently acting individual; to put a slogan on it, intention exists within structure. On this view, acting individuals, whose actions are intentionally guided, though perhaps not toward the ends they achieve, exercise social control of the social constraints. These individuals are themselves working within socially determined constraints, and so on. The intentionalist is correct to see that action begins with the beliefs, desires, and capacities (both psychological and material) of the individual acting agent, but wrong to suppose that that rules out social forces beyond the control of that agent, forces that affect her beliefs, desires, and capacities. The structuralist is correct to see that from the point of view of the acting individual, there are groups to which she can choose to belong and unchosen groups to which she either belongs or does not, but which she cannot choose to enter or leave. But the structuralist mistakenly attributes these to immutable forces of history located beyond the influence and responsibility of individual human beings. The intentionalists generally attempt to take the ontological high ground to deny the existence of social groups of the structuralist sort, while the structuralists defend the political high ground, claiming that the intentionalists focus on the weak force of interpersonal relations while forces of history move with structural social groups. Both camps claim that they have found the uniquely "basic" social group. Although I believe that each of these negative claims is misguided, in this chapter I shall address only the negative claim of the intentionalists. These two approaches highlight two causally continuous but distinct kinds of social groups. One sort of social group consists of persons who have voluntarily entered into the group, the other of primarily nonvoluntarily socially determined members. Ignoring or denying one and focusing entirely on the other leads us to make bad normative prescriptions or insignificant social theory. A comprehensive social theory must recognize social groups postulated by both camps. I shall adopt the terms *voluntary* and *nonvoluntary*, which aptly capture the distinction between them.

A Theory of Nonvoluntary Social Groups

Social theorists (especially nonliberal ones) commonly talk about collections of persons who suffer various forms of oppression. A short list of such collections in the context of contemporary U.S. culture would include women, African-Americans, Native Americans, Asian Americans, the poor, the working class, Jews, gays and lesbians, and the disabled. Likewise, there are their correlatives, the dominant collections: men, white Americans, Christians, the middle class, straight people, and able-bodied persons. There can be no doubt that we can cut the world up this way, since we do so all the time; the question I want to pursue is whether it is an explanatorily useful way to do so, and whether these categories are forced on us by the social facts of our world. I take it that if the answers to these questions are affirmative, then we will have reason to call such collections social groups.

Social groups, whether voluntary or nonvoluntary, are collections of persons who share something that is socially significant. As Gilbert argues, members of (voluntary) social groups share joint commitments or joint projects.[1] The members of a nonvoluntary social group share social constraints consequent on their membership. They need not intend to share the social constraints, but they are (without drastic intervention) inescapable; other agents and the social structures agents put in place constrain the group members because of their membership in these social groups.

There are many social constraints on individual actions. By social constraints I mean facts that must be considered in deciding how to act or how to plan one's life, or facts that shape beliefs and attitudes about other persons. They are the factors that must be modeled in rational choice explanations of actions, as the choices, common beliefs, strategies, and payoffs that agents consider in making decisions or as the default assumptions that agents use when they act on intentions that are not fully or rationally considered. These constraints include legal rights, obligations, and burdens;

stereotypical expectations; wealth; income, social status, conventions, norms, and practices. Many of these constraints are the result of intended collective action, such as laws that prohibit social funding of abortions, judicial practices that normally assign child custody to mothers, tax structures that favor the middle class. But many of them are the unintended consequences of other intentional actions: stereotypes of women as overly emotional likely came about from the fact that women have been relegated to spheres of life in which emotional expression is important and appropriate. Some social constraints might be partly intended and partly unintended: racial segregation in the cities comes about not because all the people want to live in segregated cities but because a few want to live with only their own race, some others want to be in the racial majority, others want not to be the only ones of their race on their blocks, still others want to sell before their property values are completely depleted, and so forth. Some social constraints might also have partly natural causes: deaf persons are rarely born in a culture where they can share the native language. Social constraints are not unchangeable facts; they are purely exogenous variables in a social theory only in the short run. But as John Maynard Keynes pointed out, we all live in the short run; social constraints are among the facts we have to face in planning our lives.

Social constraints affect actions through the penalties and rewards that one can expect from them.[2] Individuals are motivated to act in their interest and the interest of others about whom they care. If it is a social fact that in a certain area of town women are likely to be harassed or assaulted, then individual women will be motivated to avoid the area. That does not mean that all women will avoid going there (indeed, some feisty women might even take it as a challenge to go there), but just that for any woman there will be a cost to going there that she ought (rationally) to consider in making a decision about where to go and by what route. Social constraints help to explain individual actions by explaining the incentives that individuals have by virtue of the visible, socially salient characteristics they share with others.[3]

Some social constraints form assumptions that affect individuals' beliefs and attitudes. According to cognitive scientists, we make implicit assumptions, called *default assumptions*,[4] all the time in our thinking about what holds true in normal circumstances, and we apply these assumptions until and unless some feature of our situation forces us to reassess things. Without the ability to make such assumptions without thinking about them first, we would be hopelessly mired in the frame problem, unable to find the relevance of any situation for our own needs and desires in time to act effectively. Of course, sometimes these assumptions are false, but given our finite cognitive capacities, the complexity of facts we would need to think everything through, and the need to act relatively quickly in many situations, default assumptions are an evolutionary necessity.

Among the kinds of default assumptions we make are stereotypes about individuals based on visible features that they share with others. Women are relatively small and weak, Asians are good mathematicians, Blacks are from the South or the inner city, effeminate men are gay, women and minority professors got their jobs to fill affirmative action quotas. Stereotypes become social facts by being the default assumptions that we normally make when we first meet someone or when we hear someone described to us or see someone on the street. Stereotypes guide us to form beliefs about an individual before we have the kind of evidence for those beliefs that we would require if that individual did not share some other attribute with the collection to which that stereotype attaches. We have an Asian student in our class and ask her to do the class report on game theory rather than the one on hermeneutics. Default assumptions not only make false beliefs easier to form when they do not hold but also make it more difficult to form the correct belief that is quite plain to see. We see a woman and assume that she could not lift the box in front of her, even if, were it a man of approximately the same build and size, we would think that he could. And we make the assumption even when we see that she is wearing the uniform of a UPS driver.[5]

Finally, stereotypical default assumptions cause us to have attitudes toward the groups that we attach stereotypes to. Assuming that women are weak and small, many men form a superior and protective attitude toward women in contexts where there are physical challenges. Assuming that Asians are good at mathematics, many Whites form a resentful attitude toward Asians in math and science classes. Other collections of persons have no stereotypes attached to them: Is there any belief or image you form upon hearing that some otherwise anonymous individual has attached earlobes? How or why we form particular default assumptions and not others is an interesting and important matter, but it is not necessary to explore it here to make the argument that there are nonvoluntary social groups.

Social constraints are often assigned to individuals based on the default assumptions that others make about them. This means that individuals themselves have no control over those rewards and penalties unless they can make it clear in the relevant situations that the default assumption is false. Of course, if one is getting a reward that one does not merit, it is tempting to try to look like an average normal member of the collection to which the stereotype attaches and to make it look like the stereotype is true in a great percentage of cases of members of that collection. Where one wants to show that a stereotype does not apply, it can be difficult. Counterexamples are often honestly construed as misperceptions rather than as true counterexamples, in social life as well as in science.

A nonvoluntary social group is a set of individuals who face (or would face in the same circumstances) the same social constraints. Membership in a nonvoluntary social group is socially and not individually determined. The patterns of distribution of social rewards and penalties according to stereotypes generate social groups. Nonvoluntary social groups, then, are formed not by the intentions of the individuals in them to join together and share in a particular project but by the actions, beliefs, and attitudes of others, both in the group and out, that constrain their choices in patterned and socially significant ways. Members of nonvoluntary social groups experience constrained or enhanced choices by comparison with others who are similarly situated in every respect except membership in that group. So, for example, on this view a Black man and a similarly placed White man in America face different constraints on their choices due to their membership in one pair of different nonvoluntary social groups. This is consistent with experience. The Black person in a color-conscious society can expect to be treated and judged differently because of his Blackness even when he outwardly behaves the same as the White man who appears to be of the same social class. In stores the middle-class Black is likely to be followed by employees; in White neighborhoods he is likely to be harassed by police. Women clutch their purses when they see him on the elevator, and people expect that he likes sports and plays them well. Likewise, although he may not notice his privileges, the White man is treated differently from the Black—he is not followed, he is given the benefit of the doubt by police, and so forth. These social constraints affect the actions one considers and the choices one makes in clear and predictable ways: the Black man does not expect to be left alone, so he acts as one would when being watched; he expects police harassment in certain situations, so he either avoids those situations or adopts an attitude of innocence, deference, or defiance to cope, and so on.

Nonvoluntary social groups come in and go out of existence when attitudes and actions change. Sometimes such social groups lose their nonvoluntary character, but some members choose to form voluntary social groups.
For example, Irish Americans used to be a significant social group—being
labeled as an Irish American would have many consequences for one's possible actions. But now there are not very many such consequences, unless
one chooses to name oneself Irish and participates in voluntary activities
with other Irish Americans, making it difficult to argue that it is a nonvoluntary social group.

One of the important differences between voluntary and nonvoluntary
social groups is that one need not recognize that one is a member of a particular nonvoluntary social group to be a member. All that is required for
membership is that one objectively faces the constraints that other similarly situated members face, whether or not one recognizes them as patterned constraints that one shares. I take this to be a good feature of my
account because it is common for people in oppressed groups not to recognize their oppression, not because they do not recognize that they face
constraints but because they tend to see them as their own individual problems.[6] My account of nonvoluntary social groups can accommodate groups
whose members are conscious of themselves as forming a social group or
groups whose members are not yet aware of their grouphood, as well as nonvoluntary social groups with members who mistakenly deny that they are
members.

Although one need not be conscious of oneself as a member of a nonvoluntary social group, social awareness of a particular social group has significant consequences for the members. Membership in some nonvoluntary
social groups may give one a sense of identity, group solidarity, or self-worth.
These psychological benefits come only when one becomes aware of oneself
as a member of this social group. (Likewise, there can be psychological costs
to becoming aware of oneself as a member of a social group.) Awareness of
one's social group membership does not make the group into a voluntary
group, though, because that also requires that there be some shared project
and the common knowledge of that sharing. Still, groups that have become
self-conscious are on a continuum closer to voluntary social groups because
self-awareness is the first step toward self-assertion.

How does one come to be grouped into a nonvoluntary social group?
There are different signs for group membership depending on the social
group, but in each case membership is assigned by others through default

assumptions that go into effect when they recognize or think they recognize some typical trait or behavior that is very salient in the culture for grouping. So, for instance, skin color, hair length, dress, voice pitch, word choice, size, and walking or sitting style are all well-known signals of race, gender, class, and sexual orientation. Some of these are more or less matters of choice for the individual doing the choosing, and nearly all of them are, given enough, sometimes drastic, intervention, changeable. In that sense one could say that there is a voluntary aspect even to nonvoluntary social groups. But this sense of choice is not the same that is in play with voluntary social groups. These choices are not negotiable or malleable by the individual—who chooses neither to be in this nonvoluntary social group nor that there is no room for a pooling of wills or joint choice. In the marketplace of social group norms, the individual is a norm-taker, not a norm-setter.

In order to explain some features of social life, it is essential to recognize nonvoluntary social groups. For instance, how do we explain the door-opening ritual, as it is called by feminists, in a case where a small man with packages rushes to open the door for a large, able-bodied woman? It does not make sense unless we include in the explanans reference to default assumptions about social groups, namely, the stereotype of women as weak and small. It is precisely where the social constraints that compose nonvoluntary social groups are involved that we need to refer to irreducibly social facts to explain human behavior.[7] Thus we cannot do without the concept of social groups.

Some Objections

One kind of objection to my account of nonvoluntary social groups argues that because there are interacting sets of social constraints that each individual faces, there is no way to individuate a set of them that picks out a unique social group. This objection takes two different forms: one to the existence of the social group itself, and one to our ability to discern accurately the consequences of belonging to the social group. I take it that the first is the more crucial objection for me to block, since if it is correct, there are no social groups at all. But I find that these two forms often come together and originate from different theoretical and political directions.

An instance of the first form of this objection to social groups comes from recent work in feminism that claims that there is no way to separate out the "woman part" from a woman, that is, to separate her womanness from her other social attributes, such as race, class, and sexual orientation. Thus, any account of social groups that tries to set aside one of these categories to name a group will be unable to come up with clear identity conditions for group membership. Elizabeth Spelman, who holds this view, writes: "One's gender identity is not related to one's racial identity as the parts of pop-bead necklaces are related, separable and insertable in other 'strands' with different racial and class 'parts.' "[8] One way to interpret this objection is to say that what we cannot do is locate in the individual the identities that match up with social groups. But my account is not trying to do that; mine is an externalist account that is trying to locate in the world the social constraints that compose social grouphood. Spelman's objection may be reinterpreted against my account as follows. My account supposes that in the world there are constraints that apply to all women, others to all men, others to all Blacks, and so forth. It is what I prefer to term a *vector force model* to suggest the analogy with mechanics. As with mechanics, it is an empirical matter whether objects on earth or in space, moving in a straight line or a curve, in the presence of friction or on a frictionless surface would all behave the same way in the presence of two different sources of inertial force. But they do; the vector force model works. I contend that it works, modulo the imprecision of social facts, in the social world as well. To determine the social constraints that an individual faces, one needs to add up the entirety of social constraints of her social group memberships. As with contending forces in mechanics, some group memberships will change the direction or intensity of some social constraints. Spelman might contend, however, that the individual vector forces change in the presence of different other forces. For instance, she might argue that being a man would contribute positively to one's overall life choices if one is White, but negatively if one is Black. In fact, I think this is the main example that antiessentialists like Spelman use.[9] On one point I would agree: it is an empirical question whether the vector force approach works. However, I disagree with the analysis of this example. Over a wide range of measures of social outcomes, being a man and Black leads to greater achievement than being a woman and Black. Black men outearn Black women, have a wider range of professions open to them, and are physically dominant in the sense that vastly more men of all races kill, beat, and rape women than vice versa; more Black women are relegated to the servant jobs of society; and most Black political, religious, military, and social leaders are men. Objections of the form "White women think of themselves as superior to Black men" are red herrings to the question of whether the vector force model works. To compare the constraints that form the social groups of men and women, one must compare within race, class, and other significant social groupings.[10] While it may be difficult to measure with any precision the effect of constraints, or worse, to compare different sources of value like psychological well-being versus life expectancy, these difficulties do not tell against the existence of the patterns of differences in social constraints, and so the existence of nonvoluntary social groups.

The second form of this objection is raised against our ability to accurately locate such nonvoluntary social groups amid the tangle of social facts that characterize individual lives. One obvious way to locate nonvoluntary social groups, well articulated by Lester Thurow, is to begin with statistics by looking at various collections of persons to see whether they have different outcomes (e.g., levels of income, life expectancies, frequency of imprisonment) from other identifiable collections.[11] It is then necessary to determine whether there is reason to believe that some systematic social constraint is in operation that denies equal opportunity to these persons as a group, or whether the different outcomes are due entirely to voluntary behavior. However, Anthony Flew contends in *Thinking About Social Thinking* that it is a fallacy to argue

> that because members of one social set are not represented in some occupation or organization in the same proportion as in the population as a whole, therefore members of that social set must be being, whether intentionally or unintentionally, discriminated against. . . . [This argument] can go through only on the assumption that abilities, inclinations and the senses of actual choices fall into the exactly the same distribution pattern in the social set in question as in the population as a whole.[12]

Flew is correct to worry about the indiscriminate use of statistics to infer discrimination, but statistics can give us a lead on what collections to investigate. We then need a causal analysis of how those statistics come to be determined, whether it is because of discrimination by others or voluntary behavior by the disadvantaged group members. More important, "discrimination" in the sense of conscious action by individuals against others is not the only problem. The "inclinations and the senses of actual choices" are endogenous variables in the equation that relates a social group's treatment to the outcomes of its individuals; that is, how one is treated helps to determine what one believes one can reasonably choose, and so one's desires as well.

I think that Flew is more concerned about the implication that statistical patterns of discrimination against a social set would show that there are any nonvoluntary social groups at all, that is, the first form of this objection. Flew uses the term *social set* explicitly to avoid having to postulate that there are any social groups, which he takes to be organized groups, rather more like Gilbert's voluntary groups than the nonvoluntary social groups that I am arguing for. He writes: "We employ the expression 'social set,' rather than 'social class' or 'social group,' in order to disown any undesired implications that the social sets in question must be either social classes or else other social or racial groups which may either be seen by others, or see themselves, or be organized, as such."[13] If it is Flew's concern to suggest that there are no social groups that suffer discrimination, however, showing that statistics about outcomes cannot alone reveal such discrimination does not do it, nor does it show that there are no nonvoluntary social groups.

Conclusion

By way of conclusion, I want to suggest some of the uses to which this theory of social groups might be put. First, any account of oppression that distinguishes it from other harms that can come to individuals and locates it as a social injustice requires an account of social groups. But if only voluntary collections can be social groups, then socially structured harms perpetrated on members of what I have been calling nonvoluntary social groups could not be seen as systematic oppression.

Second, this theory of nonvoluntary social groups dissolves the alleged dichotomy of individual and social responsibility. There are social theorists and philosophers who claim that persons should be held responsible only for their intentional actions, and so if some group of individuals is harmed by the unintended consequences of many individuals' actions, there is no responsibility on anyone to correct the harm or to compensate the victims. For instance, Flew objects to redistributing wealth or exercising affirmative action to the victims of institutionalized racism or sexism because they are victims of unintentionally inflicted harms. Indeed, he objects to the very concept of structural or institutional racism because "racism, in the only proper sense of that properly abusive word, is an essentially intentional [act]."[14] On the other hand, there are other social theorists and philosophers who suggest that individuals are to be excused for their actions when they are members of oppressed classes, and that to blame them for self-destructive actions is to "blame the victim." The choice between holding only individuals responsible for their intended actions and holding only society responsible for the actions of individuals acting under constraint is a false choice. Oppression of nonvoluntary social groups is an urgent matter of social injustice that requires rectification. The just society should come to see this as a collective responsibility. But not all individuals in society are equally well placed to alleviate oppression. The oppressed themselves are to be held responsible not to act self-destructively or unjustly, but the nonoppressed must be held responsible to loosen the social constraints caused by their actions, even though the harms may have been unintended. For we are always held responsible for the unintended but foreseeable consequences of our actions, and admitting that there are nonvoluntary social groups is a first step in foreseeing the oppressive consequences of our actions.

Notes

1. Margaret Gilbert, *On Social Facts* (Princeton, N.J.: Princeton University Press, 1989), 198.

2. I intend the word *constraint* normatively neutrally, more in the sense of *frame* or *guide*. Whether a constraint is overall a negative or a positive for the agent in the situation in question depends on factors that I do not intend to discuss in this chapter. Still, I think it is arguable that rewards can reframe a situation in a way that is negative for an individual actor. An example of Larry May's in *Sexual Harassment and Male Solidarity* illustrates: suppose a professor offers a marginal graduate student a fellowship on condition that the graduate student sleep with the professor. The offer is a new opportunity that the graduate student could not have expected, and thus one might object that it constitutes an additional choice, not a constraint on choice. However, as May argues, the offer changes the situation for the student in a way that she might well not have chosen: she must now live in an academic environment in which she knows that her professor considers her as a sexual object and not simply as a student, and in which her sexuality makes a difference to her academic success. Thus, the reward offered has changed the situation arguably for the worse for this student. Likewise, examples can be concocted in which a social penalty reframes a situation positively for an individual; consider the constraint on men not to cry.

3. For a compatible view of the role of rational choice theory in structural explanations of behavior, see Debra Satz and John Ferejohn, "Rational Choice and Social Theory," *Journal of Philosophy* 41 (1994): 71–87.

4. Douglas Hofstadter, "Changes in Default Words and Images, Engendered by Rising Consciousness," in his *Metamagical Themas* (New York: Basic Books, 1985), 136.

5. Laurence Thomas, a Black Jewish professor of philosophy at Syracuse University, tells the story of being in an elevator in Jerusalem with a White American woman whom he did not know. When he got into the elevator with her, she looked at him nervously and clutched her purse. Laurence Thomas, "In My Next Life, I'll Be White," *Ebony*, December 1990, 84.

6. Betty Friedan, in *The Feminine Mystique* (New York: Dell, 1974), wrote about "the problem that has no name," by which she was referring to a series of similar psychological, sexual, and material problems that many middle-class white women in the 1950s faced, but that no one had ever seen as systematic oppression.

7. John Connolly uses John Stuart Mill's analysis of women's willing participation in their own oppression in *The Subjection of Women* to argue for the need to postulate what he calls "reference groups," which are social groups in much the same sense as my nonvoluntary groups. John Connolly, "A Dialectical Approach to Action Theory," *Inquiry* 19 (1976): 427–42. Gilbert (*On Social Facts*) also rejects methodological individualism because voluntary social groups bring into being the irreducible concept of the plural subject. I think that she is right, and that the refutation of methodological individualism is overdetermined.

8. Elizabeth V. Spelman, *Inessential Woman* (Boston: Beacon Press, 1988), 15.

9. Spelman (*Inessential Woman*, chap. 5) draws here on the work of Angela Davis (*Women, Race, and Class* [New York: Random House, 1981]). I believe that it is a misinterpretation of Davis to read her as endorsing this objection, however.

10. For an excellent critique of Spelman's antiessentialist claims using recent empirical evidence of the similarity of women's oppression across races and cultures, see Susan Moller Okin, "Gender Equality and Cultural Differences," *Political Theory* 22 (1994): 5–24.

11. Lester Thurow, "A Theory of Groups and Economic Redistribution," *Philosophy and Public Affairs* 9 (1979): 25–41.

12. Anthony Flew, *Thinking About Social Thinking* (Oxford: Basil Blackwell, 1985), 10.

13. Ibid.

14. Ibid., 15.

Chapter 3

What Are Group Rights?

George Rainbolt

Consider such claims as "The Quebecois have a right to speak French" and "Georgia State University has a right to $325 from Ed." These claims assert that certain groups have rights. At least some claims of these kinds seem to be true. If a resident of Georgia registers for a class at Georgia State University (GSU), then (subject to certain conditions) GSU has a right to $325. In these claims, groups are the subject of a right. The group has the right. In other cases, people make claims in which groups are the object of a right. "Addurrahim has a right that the quartet play (because he paid for a private performance)." In these cases, the group has the duty correlative to the right. There are claims in which groups are both the subject and the object. "The Hopi have a right that the United States meet its treaty obligations."[1] (Rights have three parts—subject, object, and content. Take the statement "Amanda has a right against Joyce that Joyce not burn down Amanda's house." Amanda is the subject, and Joyce is the object. The content of the right is "that Joyce not burn down Amanda's house.")

What are group rights? In other words, what is the proper analysis of claims in which groups are said to be the subject and/or object of rights? Some, let us call them *individualists,* think that all group rights can be analyzed as complex sets of individual rights—rights in which only individuals are the subjects and the objects. Others, let us call them *collectivists,* think that some claims of group rights cannot be analyzed as complex sets of individual rights. In this chapter I will clarify the nature of individualism and consider a new family of arguments against it.

Individualists (and collectivists) are defending a conceptual analysis. By *conceptual analysis* I mean the task of determining what a concept is.[2] When one wonders what knowledge is, when one seeks to determine what it is to have a belief, one is doing conceptual analysis. Questions such as What is law? and What is knowledge? are typically requests for conceptual analysis. A successful conceptual analysis does not show that the concept

71

being analyzed does not exist. Suppose it were shown that knowledge is justified true belief. This would not show that we do not know anything. A correct conceptual analysis shows that X (the concept being analyzed) is identical to Y (the analysis). So if Y exists, then X must exist as well. Some, but not all, analyses are eliminative. An eliminative analysis makes two claims: that X is Y and that, since Y does not exist, neither does X. Dragons are large, flying, fire-breathing lizards, and there are no such lizards, so there are no dragons. An individualist, as defined previously, might defend an eliminative and/or a noneliminative analysis of group rights. An eliminative individualist thinks that there are no group rights and therefore that all claims of group rights are false. A noneliminative individualist thinks that there are group rights, that some claims of group rights are true, and that all group rights can be analyzed as sets of individual rights. I find eliminative individualism implausible, but, to save space, I will not defend that view here. Hereafter *individualism* refers to noneliminative individualism unless otherwise noted.

The distinction between eliminative and noneliminative individualism shows that one must distinguish conceptual analysis from questions about the truth conditions of claims. When, if ever, are claims of group rights true? is a question distinct from the question What are group rights?[3] (I suspect that some in this debate have overlooked the distinction between conceptual analysis and truth conditions because they use the term *reduction* without clearly defining it.) Both (noneliminative) individualists and collectivists can consistently assert that some claims of group rights are true. One reason we are interested in conceptual analysis is to help us determine the truth conditions of claims. A good conceptual analysis must preserve the truth conditions of clear uses of the concept being analyzed and give us plausible truth conditions in the unclear cases.

Some in this debate object to conceptual analysis in general. While discussing group responsibility, Virginia Held has made an objection that might be thought to apply to group rights: "To require a reduction of such statements [i.e., statements of group responsibility or group rights] to statements about individuals would often be tantamount to abandoning such statements altogether." She thinks that "such translations would . . . be clumsy, long and vague, where the original statement . . . was clear, brief and intelligible."[4] (Held conflates reduction, translation, and conceptual analysis. It would be tedious to lay out the necessary distinctions. Held's basic point would be unaffected.) If this objection is valid, it shows that one should never do conceptual analysis if the resulting analysis is complex. All else being equal, a simple conceptual analysis is preferable to a complex one. There are, however, cases in which a concept is a complex one. No simple analysis of knowledge will be adequate. Even if it were the case that knowledge were justified, true belief, one would need to know: What is justification? What is truth? What is a belief? The answers to these questions will be complex. This is no objection to the analysis. Most people operate in the world successfully without knowing what knowledge is. Moreover, there is no guarantee that a collectivist analysis of rights will be simpler than an individualist analysis. No one is suggesting that any proposed analysis of group rights will be used by most people most of the time. Most of the time we can determine the truth or falsity of a statement of group rights without such analysis. It is only in hard cases that individuals will actually use the analysis. Analyses are principally of philosophical interest.

On the individualist view, group rights are similar to my legal right to free speech. This right can be analyzed as a complex set of individual rights. Here are some members of that set:

1. A right against Newt Gingrich that he not interfere (in certain legally specified ways) with my saying that Bill Clinton is a man of poor ethical character
2. A right against Newt Gingrich that he not interfere (in certain legally specified ways) with my not saying that Bill Clinton is a man of poor ethical character

One can generate some other members of the set by putting in someone else's name in place of Newt Gingrich's as the object of the right and/or by changing the content to refer to my right to say something else. In addition to the claims just above, the legal right to free speech contains a large set of Hohfeldian liberties, powers, and immunities as well. Space prevents me from presenting and using the full Hohfeldian apparatus. (I have provided a more complete analysis of rights to free speech elsewhere.)[5] The individualist thinks that, just as my legal right to free speech can be analyzed as a complex set of individual rights, all group rights can be analyzed as complex sets of individual rights.

Individualism is politically neutral. It does not entail one particular individualist analysis of group rights. Different noneliminative individualists might defend different kinds of group rights. It is therefore possible for individualists to disagree among themselves about which statements of group rights are true. A more right-wing individualist might, for example, assert that some claims of corporate rights are true but all claims that ethnic groups have rights are false. A more left-wing individualist might defend the opposite view. Individualism is, therefore, not necessarily a right-wing or a left-wing view. (For the same reasons, collectivism is also politically neutral.)

The individualist need not deny that individuals can have rights because they are members of groups. Let us suppose that the American Philosophical Association (APA) contracts with a certain book supplier and, according to this contract, the book supplier agrees to give APA members 10 percent off its regular prices (perhaps in exchange for the use of the APA mailing list). In that case, I, because I am a member of the APA, have a right to buy books from this supplier at 10 percent off the regular price.

The individualist is not committed to the view that the subjects, objects, or contents of the individual rights that make up a group right must be the same as the subject, object, or content of the group right itself. Consider GSU's right to $325 from Ed. The individualist is not committed to the view that some individual in the employ of GSU has a right to $325 from Ed. GSU's right to $325 might be identical to a large set of rights of a large set of individuals, none of whom have a right to $325 from Ed. Rights in this set might include the right of certain employees in the registrar's office to send Ed's file to the transcript office, the right of certain employees in the transcript office to refuse to give out Ed's transcript, the right of certain employees of GSU to send Ed's file to an outside collection agency, the right of a judge to enter a order to garnish Ed's wages, and so on. Like my analysis of the right to free speech, this analysis is incomplete. There are two reasons I cannot provide a full analysis here. First, as noted earlier, a full analysis would require a presentation of Hohfeldian terminology and an explication of how that terminology can be used to analyze rights. Second, the precise shape of GSU's legal right to $325 from Ed is determined by the legal system. A fully precise analysis would, therefore, require legal knowledge that I do not possess.

The individualist is not committed to the view that group G's rights must be analyzed only in terms of the rights of members of G. Part of the analysis may refer to the rights of individuals not in the group. Larry May has claimed that corporate rights cannot be analyzed as the rights of stockholders and managers.[6] The individualist might argue that corporate rights can be analyzed as the rights of stockholders, managers, *and other individuals—*

such as employees *and* certain legal officials (e.g., judges). So the following two views are compatible: individualism is true, and there is no plausible analysis of corporate rights as the rights of stockholders and managers. May also claims that one cannot analyze corporate rights as individual rights because no one stockholder owns or controls all of any corporate asset. This overlooks the point that the content of the individual rights into which a group right is analyzed can differ from the content of the group right. The individualist is not, therefore, committed to an analysis of classic corporate property rights as classic individual property rights of stockholders and managers. As May points out, classic property rights are complex bundles of rights, and different individuals have different sorts of property rights. Stockholders are often said to own corporations, but their property rights in the corporation are clearly lacking some of the elements that one finds in classic property rights, such as my property right to my car. In particular, in the typical case, no one stockholder controls any corporate asset in the way I control my car. But this does not imply that the rights of corporations cannot be analyzed as complex sets of (limited) rights of managers, employees, stockholders, suppliers, judges, and so forth. The individualist might argue that corporate rights may be analyzed as a set of individual rights in which one individual has part of the classic property right bundle and another individual has another part. (This could be made more explicit with Hohfeldian analysis.) Finally, May also argues that corporate rights cannot be analyzed as individual rights because the law limits corporate liability but does not limit personal liability. He thinks that this shows that corporate rights cannot be analyzed as individual rights. This does not follow. All that May has pointed out is that some of the individual rights in a plausible analysis of corporate rights will be rights of limited liability.

With the nature of individualism clarified, we can proceed to consider one family of arguments for collectivism. I believe that Carl Wellman and Michael Hartney have refuted most of the arguments for collectivism.[7] But there is a new family of arguments for collectivism that Wellman and Hartney have not refuted. This family of arguments begins by noting that there are some things that only groups can do. I will consider three members of the family and argue that all are flawed.

There are some things that, as a matter of logic, only groups can do. Only a group can play a quartet, secede, have a philosophical discussion, or get married. A collectivist might be tempted by the following simple argument:

1. Only a group can marry.
2. X can have a right to do A only if X can do A.
3. Therefore, only a group can have a right to marry.[8]

One could replace *marry* with *play a quartet, secede,* and so on. Something seems amiss with this argument. It implies that neither you nor I have the right to marry. It seems that individuals do have the right to marry, and yet, in some sense, only a group can marry. Mark, an individual living in 1850, did not have a right to attend GSU. GSU did not exist in 1850, and so no one had a right to attend. The existence of GSU is a necessary condition for Mark having a right to attend GSU. I have a right to marry. More precisely, I have a right to marry someone—but only if that person agrees to marry me. That Jana agrees to marry me is a necessary condition for me having a right to marry Jana. "Only groups can marry" in the sense that an individual has a right to marry only if another agrees to marry her. The fact that Jana's agreeing to marry me is a necessary condition for my having a right to marry Jana does not show that only the group Jana-and-I has a right to marry any more than the fact that the existence of GSU is a necessary condition for anyone having a right to attend GSU shows that only the group GSU-and-Mark has a right to attend GSU. This argument also applies to the right to have a discussion, play a quartet, or secede.

Denise Réaume and Jeremy Waldron have presented the second member of the family of arguments that we are considering. They have argued that there is a certain subclass of the actions which only groups can perform that cannot be analyzed as sets of individual rights.[9] They begin by noting that certain goods are participatory. The crucial feature of participatory goods is that, not only does one value them, but that one values the fact that one is valuing them with others. I enjoy watching baseball games with my family—my mother and my sister. I enjoy watching a baseball game by myself as well—but not as much. The difference is that I enjoy the fact that, as a family, we are enjoying something together. My mother and my sister have similar feelings. This is, as Réaume and Waldron point out, an important feature of many activities. Attending movies with my wife is more fun than going alone. The thrill of the World Series is augmented by the fact that I know that baseball fans all over the country are enjoying the games. My family's enjoyment of a baseball game is not plausibly analyzed as my enjoyment of watching a game by myself and my mother's enjoyment of watching a game by herself and my sister's enjoyment of watching a game by herself. Many group rights seem to be rights to participatory goods. Consider the Hopi's right to engage in their religious rituals. I suspect that many of the Hopi not only want to practice their rituals but also wish to do so with other Hopis. An individual Hopi would feel a genuine loss if he were the only person performing the ritual actions. The participatory rights argument, however, does not seem to apply to some group rights, for instance, corporate rights. Perhaps some value being in a corporation with others, but most seem to be motivated primarily by individual monetary considerations.

The next step in Réaume and Waldron's argument is the assumption that an entity, E, has a right to do A if and only if E's interest in doing A is a sufficient reason for others to have a duty. They borrow this analysis of rights from Joseph Raz.[10] Réaume and Waldron think that no adequate account of the desirability of participatory goods can be pinned down to an individual. Therefore, no individual's interest in participatory goods can be a sufficient reason for others to have a duty. According to Réaume and Waldron, the duty to realize these goods is grounded not in an individual's interest but in the group's interest. On this view, an individual's interest in a participatory good cannot ground a right because we cannot say that it is for the individual's sake that the duty is imposed. As Waldron puts it: "Since no adequate account of its [a participatory good's] desirability can be pinned down to either X or Y or Z, there can be no *point* in saying that it ought to be pursued as X's or Y's or Z's right."[11]

This argument is not sound. First, the individualist is not committed to the view that group rights must be analyzed as disjunctions of individual rights ("X's or Y's or Z's right"). In most cases, group rights will be analyzed as conjunctions of individual rights. Second, it is true that my enjoyment of a baseball game is increased if my family members are enjoying it with me. It is also increased if I have a bratwurst. Individuals can value many things—including bratwursts and the fact that other individuals value something. The individualist has no more problem providing an analysis of rights to participatory goods than she does of providing analysis of rights to bratwursts. I have a right to watch a baseball game while eating a bratwurst. This right is not plausibly analyzed as my right to watch a baseball game and my right to eat a bratwurst. My family has a right to watch baseball games together. This right is not plausibly analyzed as my right to watch a game by myself and my mother's right to watch a game by herself and my sister's right to watch a game by herself. It is, however, plausibly analyzed as my right to watch a game *with my family* and my mother's right to watch a game *with her family* and my sister's right to watch a game *with her family*. (If one wished, one could provide a Hohfeldian analysis of these rights in the same way that I analyzed the right to free speech and GSU's right to $325 from Ed.)

Joseph Raz provides the third member of the family of arguments that we are considering.[12] He offers an example of a right, the right to self-determination, which, he argues, cannot be analyzed as a set of individual rights. Raz begins by noting that Yassir Arafat has an interest in Palestinian self-determination. Palestinian self-determination is one of his important long-term projects. As noted previously, Raz thinks that E has a right to do A if and only if E's interest in doing A is a sufficient reason for others to have a duty. Does Arafat have a right to Palestinian self-determination? According to Raz, Arafat's interest alone is not sufficient to justify the far-reaching duties of others that a right to Palestinian self-determination implies. If there is a right to Palestinian self-determination, then a large collection of individuals all over the world have a duty to help the Palestinians gain self-determination. Some would have negative duties not to interfere with Palestinian efforts to gain self-determination. Others would have positive duties to vacate land and give it to the Palestinians. Arafat's interest, by itself, is not sufficient reason for such a large set of others to have such extensive duties. His interest is not, by itself, sufficiently morally important to justify all these duties. So, according to Raz, Arafat does not have this right. Arafat is, however, not alone in having an interest in Palestinian self-determination. Many other Palestinians have a similar interest. If there is a right to Palestinian self-determination, it is only these interests, *collectively*, that are sufficient to justify the far-reaching duties that the right implies. According to Raz, the right to Palestinian self-determination cannot be analyzed into the rights of individuals because no single individual's interest, by itself, would justify the correlative duties, and an individual has a right only if that individual's interest is *sufficient* to justify correlative duties. Raz thinks that there are many rights that have the same structure as the Palestinians' right to self-determination. He thinks that there are rights to many public goods (e.g., clean air, a cultured society) and that they cannot be analyzed as sets of individuals' rights.

This is an extremely interesting argument. I think it shows that if Raz's theory of rights is true, then individualism is false. Raz's theory, however, is independently implausible.[13] He holds that E has a right to do A if and only if E's interest in doing A is a sufficient reason for others to have a duty. In other words, E's rights must be justified by E's interests and no one else's. There are cases, however, in which rights are granted not to protect the interests of the right-holder but rather to protect the interests of others. The rights of public officials are frequently justified in this way. A judge has a right to impose sentence. It is not plausible to hold that the judge has a right to impose sentence if and only if the judge's interest in imposing sentence is a sufficient reason for others to have a duty. This right is not justified by the judge's interest. It is justified by the interests of other individuals in having criminals punished. There are cases in which the person who has a right has explicitly said that it is not in his interest to have the right. Congress decided that the chairman of the Federal Deposit Insurance Corporation (FDIC) was to have a large set of rights concerning the disposal of the property owned by failed savings and loans. The chairman of the FDIC, William Siedman, opposed being granted these rights. He felt that he already had too many responsibilities and that someone else ought to be appointed to dispose of the property. Congress gave Siedman these rights in spite of his objections.[14] The "sufficient reason" for these rights is not to protect Siedman's interests but to protect the interests of other individuals (e.g., taxpayers). Raz's theory of rights therefore implies that Siedman did not have a right to dispose of the property. This is implausible.

I believe that the preceding arguments, when added to the work of Wellman and Hartney, show that every known argument for collectivism is unsound. Of course, we still need an independent argument to show that individualism is true, but space limitations prevent me from considering such an argument here. Let me briefly mention the most common argument for individualism, which begins by comparing paradigm right-holders (e.g., typical adult humans) with paradigm non-right-holders (e.g., rocks) and asking: What are the necessary conditions for having the ability to have rights? Wellman argues that the ability to make choices is a necessary condition for having rights.[15] Joel Feinberg argues that having a conative life, having the mental states needed for purposive behavior, is a necessary condition for having rights.[16] Tom Regan argues that sentience, the capacity to have sensations or feelings, is a necessary condition for having rights.[17] Because sentience is a nomologically necessary condition for having a conative life or making choices, Wellman and Feinberg are committed to the view that sentience is a necessary condition for having rights. Groups are not sentient. Groups are composed of sentient individuals, but they do not themselves feel anything. (This does not imply that claims that groups feel, suffer, and so on, are false. Because conceptual analysis is distinct from questions of truth conditions, it only implies that claims about group interests, like claims about group rights, are analyzable as sets of individual interests. Although he does not frame it as an analysis, I believe that May has offered a plausible analysis of group interests as individual interests.)[18] If sentience is a necessary condition for rights and groups are not sentient, then either ascriptions of rights to groups can be analyzed into sets of the rights of sentient individuals or there are no group rights and all claims of group rights are false. Since some claims of group rights are true, the rights of groups must be analyzable as sets of individuals' rights.

There are a number of ways that one could attack this argument. One could take on the view that sentience is a necessary condition of being able to have rights. The rights of the dead, the irreversibly comatose, and future generations are hard cases for this view. In theory, one could argue that groups are sentient, but I know of no such argument in the literature. One might argue that, while groups are not sentient, they have features that are sufficiently like sentience to warrant the claim that groups may have rights that are not analyzable into sets of rights of individuals.[19]

What are group rights? I have not answered the question, but have merely clarified the nature of individualism and argued that three versions of an argument for collectivism are flawed. I obviously believe that clarification of individualism makes it more plausible. I am not, on the other hand, fully convinced that individualism is true. While I believe that all extant arguments for collectivism have been refuted, no one has developed an argument for individualism that I find fully satisfactory.

Notes

My thanks to Angelo Corlett, William Edmundson, and Steve Rieber for their comments on an earlier draft of this chapter.

1. Here and throughout the chapter I will use legal rights as my examples. The arguments apply to moral rights as well.

2. For more discussion and examples of the kind of conceptual analysis I am doing here, see the work of H. L. A. Hart, "Definition and Theory in Jurisprudence," in his *Essays in Jurisprudence and Philosophy* (New York: Oxford University Press, 1983), and *The Concept of Law* (New York: Oxford University Press, 1961).

3. Noncognitivists should feel free to substitute *valid, appropriate,* and so on, for *true* here. The arguments below, mutatis mutandis will be unaffected.

4. Virginia Held, "Can a Random Collection of Individuals Be Morally Responsible?" in *Collective Responsibility*, ed. Larry May and Stacey Hoffman (Savage, Md.: Rowman and Littlefield, 1991), 90, 92–93. The second passage is quoted by Held from Ernest Gellner, "Holism vs. Individualism," in *Readings in the Philosophy of the Social Sciences*, ed. May Brodbeck (New York: Macmillan, 1968), 258.

5. George Rainbolt, "Rights as Normative Constraints on Others," *Philosophy and Phenomenological Research* 53 (1993): 93–112. For Hohfeld's own views, see W. N. Hohfeld, *Fundamental Legal Conceptions* (New Haven, Conn.: Yale University Press, 1919). While I cannot defend the point here, I believe that many collectivists have overlooked the power of Hohfeldian analysis.

6. Larry May, *The Morality of Groups* (Notre Dame, Ind.: University of Notre Dame Press, 1987), 125–34.

7. Carl Wellman, *Real Rights* (New York: Oxford University Press, 1995); Michael Hartney, "Some Confusions Concerning Collective Rights," *Canadian Journal of Law and Jurisprudence* 4 (1991): 293–314.

8. I am not sure that anyone has explicitly made this argument. Allen Buchanan has suggested something like it, but he was not focusing on conceptual analysis. See "Liberalism and Group Rights," in *In Harm's Way*, ed. Jules Coleman (New York: Cambridge University Press, 1994), 1–15.

9. Denise Réaume, "The Group Right to Linguistic Security: Whose Right, What Duties?" in *Group Rights*, ed. Judith Baker (Toronto: University of Toronto Press, 1994); Réaume, "Individuals, Groups, and Rights to Public Goods," *University of Toronto Law Journal* 38 (1988): 1–27; Jeremy Waldron, "Can Communal Goods Be Human Rights?" in his *Liberal Rights* (New York: Cambridge University Press, 1993), 339–69.

10. Joseph Raz, *The Morality of Freedom* (New York: Oxford University Press, 1986), chaps. 7, 8. I have simplified Raz's analysis to avoid complications irrelevant to the issue at hand.

11. Waldron, "Can Communal Goods Be Human Rights?" 359.

12. Raz, *The Morality of Freedom*, 193–216.

13. I have defended an alternative view in the article cited in note 5.

14. Here I recount an interview broadcast in July 1989 on the *MacNeil/Lehrer News Hour*. I am unable to discover the exact date.

15. Wellman, *Real Rights*.

16. Joel Feinberg, "The Rights of Animals and Unborn Generations," in his *Rights, Justice and the Bounds of Liberty* (Princeton, N.J.: Princeton University Press, 1980), 159–84.

17. Tom Regan, "The Case for Animal Rights," in *Applying Ethics*, ed. Jeffrey Olen and Vincent Barry (Belmont, Calif.: Wadsworth, 1992), 356–63.

18. May, *The Morality of Groups*, chap. 5.

19. For examples of this move, see Larry May and Peter French, *Collective and Corporate Responsibility* (New York: Columbia University Press, 1984).

Chapter 4

Institutions: A Technique
for Analyzing Group Entitlements

Christopher Gray

In order to identify how groups ought to be treated at law, one useful approach is to identify first what groups are. This opens possibilities that some jurisdictions may have already closed. *Yoder v. Wisconsin*'s confirmation of group educational rights for the Amish is nearly the sole acknowledgment of group rights under the U.S. Bill of Rights, whereas group protections for minority aboriginals and multiculturals proliferate in the Canadian Charter of Rights, and membership in a group is integral to significant standing for many purposes from Bosnia to Israel to Zaire. The constitutional practices peculiar to one jurisdiction, however, do not determine in advance how investigators in the philosophy of law will be able to characterize groups and their entitlements.

Groups of human beings can be sorted in many ways. In law, the axis most frequently used is whether a group is or has *legal personality* or, short of that, has *moral personality*. Groups that have neither are *organizations*. Legal consequences follow this usage, so it is a route worth investigating, even though at some point legal personality becomes a fiction.

While the analytic criterion of *procedure* (the sequence of behaviors required in order for an action to have force) is used to distinguish stages of group reality, the language of *personality* (one kind of reality that can be ascribed to a group) is retained as being true to practice, and to keep important features from neglect. Of course there is no question of constructing Victorian group substances out of merely an analogy.[1] The only persons involved are humans; insects and angels are moot for this purpose. This should not tempt, however, toward the unimaginative claim that only individuals are real. The relational reality that groups *are* is not any the less real, for not being the substantive reality that their individual members *are*.

Stages

Organized groups, or *organizations*, are effective in maintaining an identity, not to mention modifying it, and in carrying out projects because members of the group have taken on functional roles. They are effective because members act as organs of the group. This does not mean they are comparable to bodily organs in the manner of classical organicism; it means only that they are active in a division of labor. Such distinction of functions facilitates group accomplishments by reducing confusion and inertia.

What is not needed is that members give their labor a direction toward manifesting and maintaining the group's identity. Organizations may be led and directed by persons in control, and their exercise of power may be enough to lead the members to accomplish their tasks. This might be the sole locale in which creative initiative is deployed. The identity of the group and any goals inherent in that may remain out of sight. Achievement of the initiator's ends is all that guides his or her power. For their analysis by members or outsiders, attention need be given only to the actions of members and to their effectiveness, either the individual initiatives of leaders or the directed outcomes of others. This focus on what is accidental to their reality as organizations keeps organizations short of moral personality.

The term *moral personality* is used in the contexts both of law and of social philosophy. Used in the legal context, it is synonymous with one sense of personality, namely, that applied to some groups; the other sense is applied to human beings. In a social context, it is ascribed to any sort of group, or else to only those groups that meet some prerequisites for legal personality beyond organizational capacity.

In some groups, the exercise of power that directs others is understood as a function, and its fulfillment a duty. The same may be true for the powers of the members to carry out tasks. The duty and function are often discovered in terms of who the group is, even its name; or in terms of what it is, the kind of group it is, the recognition of its type, what it does. This process of discovery is analogous to grasping what the group's purpose, goal, or task is (or what they are) and judging the group's actions in view of that. This has been referred to as the group's "consciousness" of its "end."

The way such groups grasp their functions is by making the acts in which power is exercised persist, as facts. Some acts of organizations are thought, rightly or not, to be worth keeping and confirming. This regularizes organizations, rather than creates them. The acts are not prolonged in some mystical manner but are imitated or repeated. Procedure is developed whereby action of a type can be performed again. At a fuller stage of organizational development, a member's failure to conform to the procedure makes an action voidable, or even void. Procedure limits power in manner and form, while bringing into confirmed reality powers that hardly existed as a matter of fact within the group. One way this form becomes more pronounced and members become more conscious of it through procedure is by reforms made to the organization's division of labor. This, too, becomes no longer a matter of fact but a matter of jurisdiction, and of a right to that jurisdiction. Power does not simply fall apart but is separated; and its separated divisions may be made to balance each other and thus to limit each other.

Recognizing that other persons are entitled to act within their jurisdictions presents members to each other as rights-holders. This is unlike the organization, where individuals need be seen as phenomenal individuals in no more than contingent activities needed for the organization to function. As rights-holders, now, they are seen as substantive persons. In addition to this, by grasping who or what their group is, the members and leaders also become aware that other groups can have a similar stature as moral persons. It is this focus on persons in their substance that makes legal entitlements conceptually possible, both for individuals and for their groupings. This substantiates the term *moral personality* for this sort of grouping.

In the infrequent political perversions where no further state legal order exists, moral personalities' legal entitlements await no mandate from elsewhere. In what is now frequently called "civil society" again, these groups create a statutory law toward other persons, moral or natural, and a disciplinary law for members. It seems an ideological imposition upon the normativity, responsibility, and liability of moral persons to require sovereignty—a monopoly on the use of public force—in order for moral persons to have law and a legal standing.

The features just ascribed to moral persons are limitations upon power; the limits are proportionate to participants' awareness of the group's identity, that is, what it is about (its "idea," as mentioned in the notes). Its features can be greater or lesser; and "moral personality" is, in turn, an ascription that can be filled more or less. The counterpart to this is that the moral personality is decomposable to a greater or lesser extent, and is more or less reducible back to the organs of power.

This is not the way *legal personality* operates, for it either is the case or is not the case. It is indivisible. (This is not inferentially connected with sovereignty being either indivisible, as in imperative theory, or not.) This is the very reason for constituting legal personality: to further the group's stability more than moral personality does. Still subject to contingencies that affect its identity, moral personality may decompose. For group projects thought to be worth protecting, the legal fiction of incontingency may be placed upon moral personality or, indeed, upon organizations. Like every legal fiction, it is not unreal for being fictitious. It is so real that it tends to outrun the specificities with which it was achieved, as described later. If moral personality is called the "face" that organization shows, legal personality is the "mask" upon that face.

If moral personality prolongs individuals' acts in procedure, legal personality at most reacts to that and does not initiate. It does not create any more power for accomplishment than is generated by persons in economic, social, and political organizations. But, as power tends to organize group members, it tends to organize even itself; this is what legal personality effects.

The consciousness of purpose that members experience, often with conflicting convictions, is limited by competing jurisdictions.[2] But it is an act of rationality, more than this simple consciousness, for power to limit itself, as follows. Recognizing now the incompleteness of law in the ways it is instanced among moral personalities, despite the benefits of separated jurisdictions, group members "*auto*limit" power. (This has nothing to do with systems' limitation by the binarity of "legal/nonlegal.") Regardless of the apparent inconsistency of this event for *Grundnorm* theories, or for theories of sole parliamentary sovereignty, it is constant experience that legislatures separate their powers, that federalisms divide their powers, and that constitutions both limit their power for as long as they limit it and provide routes for amendment so as to change those limits.

Each such act is deemed "rational" because it is the abstract equality of rights, or at least of immunities, among participants in this balanced public life that is now in view. This is an equality of distributive justice to persons qua citizens, and to their groupings. It extends beyond the narrower justice that corrects transactions among the moral personalities in civil society.

Further, the autolimitation of power is rational insofar as it involves self-awareness by the group as a group, as well as by its members. This awareness is not simply their awareness of interests or of types, as is the awareness within organizations or within moral personalities. This makes the legal personality to be subjective, and not only objective, in its identity.

That this subjectivization is contemporaneous with the rise of the state is not surprising. Although sovereignty as the monopoly on public force is not necessary, a sufficiently centralized authority is needed if groups as legal personalities are to act upon the legal order and not simply within it. This makes it possible that, while legal personality is continuous in development with moral personality and organization, it can occur even without them. It can be constituted purely by law. Examples are the authority in a nation-state constituted by its members' own political will expressed in a constituting convention, where no integrated civil society preceded; or the corporation commencing with its charter or letters patent, with no commercial or charitable grouping preceding it or even following it.

These are extravagant instances, however. The ordinary case is that none of these stages occur separately. Just as sensation and concept occur absent one another only perversely, so purposefulness normally accompanies organization and accompanies moral personality even when something other than a corporate legal person is constituted (e.g., by syndical statute or by university charter).

Like any other distinction among stages of development, lest a process be made into a progression, another monitum is needed: stages are only the usual way for many developments to occur; one or more may be skipped in a given development, another may return to an earlier stage, the sequence may be altered, and so forth. But consequences will follow from any such digression from the standard process.[3]

Benefits and Burdens

The second task is to describe any effects as to the distribution of benefits and burdens that this distinction among stages of groups' development will have. This will involve locating those groups currently of greatest public concern in terms of stage and of benefits or burdens. To accomplish these tasks involves bringing into play further axes of analysis: the degrees of voluntareity in group membership, details of historicity in the group's identification, and modes of distributivity among benefits and burdens. Thereafter, a schema may be set up for expressing this result.

It is the core feature of *procedure* that differentiates moral personality from organizations on one side and from legal personality on the other. In turn, procedure concretizes the capacity for receiving and exercising benefits and burdens, and so is the threshold rationale for distributing them among groups. Groups without a procedure that members exercise (recall, as their agreement with the limitation upon power) are unable to identify representatives to speak and act for them. In organizations any representation must be self-declared by the singular persons who perform it. In legal personalities, on the other hand, the holding out of individuals who may make the group liable for acts becomes visible from their charters and bylaws. Moral personalities remain as the more indeterminate area, wherein scrutiny of the facts is the only way to discern a procedure and its outcomes.

The benefits and burdens for which groups may be candidates can be spread along the usual spectrum of rights relating to singular persons. To the extent that procedure permits a group to be and act in a manner analogous to singular persons, this group will be fit for receiving the benefit or burden.

At the far end of the spectrum will be the capacity of the *natural person* at law. This is the capacity to do anything of which it is capable and that is not explicitly prohibited. "Everything is permitted unless proscribed." The contrast here, drawn by Dicey, is to the capacity of a group at law, which is a capacity not to do anything, except what is explicitly permitted. "Everything is proscribed unless permitted." Natural capacity is attributed to legal personalities, or to some of them, by law. The utter naturalism on one side of this equation and the utter positivity on its other make it no more than a starting point, although an extremely useful one.

Some capacities may pertain to groups, short of natural capacity, by reason of *derivation* from the capacities of the individual persons who make up the groups. Singular persons have a right to association with others, which is often protected by constitutions in modern democracies. This right does not import anything about the rights that belong to these persons' grouping. The distinction, however, is sometimes so difficult to draw that only the detailed arguments in a particular litigation are enough to distinguish the group's derivative entitlements from those that might pertain to it qua group.

Capacities that are neither natural nor derivative are those for the exercise of fundamental freedoms, of legal rights, and of civil rights. Fundamental freedoms of *life* and possession belong to natural persons because it is impossible for them to exist otherwise. There is only an analogous rationale as to groups, since for them to "live" is almost metaphoric. Even if they can nonmetaphorically be said to exist, as relational existences, attributing life does not follow. *Possession* has so many modalities that the group's continuing to exist while having severely modified capacities to hold and to own is readily feasible; no claim can be made that, because the group is of such a sort, its holdings must be unlimited for it to survive. Or, if that argument can be made out, it does not follow that the group's survival requires anyone to support a particular form of holding property.

Fundamental freedoms of *belief and its expression* are only analogously among the capacities of groups. The queries about an individual person's conversion, skepticism, and sincerity are out of place about a group. While expression is certainly an activity of which a group is capable, the belief to which it gives expression need belong to no member of the group. The sense in which it is an expression is that the pronouncement expresses conditions for membership or entitles reliance in contractual justice or expectations in distributive justice. It then becomes other parties who are the focus of this right, and who can enforce against the group's resources.

Movement and association, finally, are more available to the group, the less it is a moral personality. To the extent that it is confirmed as an organization by and to a particular jurisdiction, its territoriality and those other groups with which it can associate are the more confined.

Besides fundamental freedoms, the group's *legal rights* to sue and to be sued or prosecuted, and in turn to be protected in its exercise of these, are relative to its group character. The more responsibility its procedurally assigned officers can take and the fuller its possession of attachable resources, the greater is its capacity for litigating with legal rights.

Similarly, the *civil rights* to own and to contract and its *political rights* to determine public policy are more available as the capacity to perform these actions increases. The group cannot perform them unless it has some degree of procedurally assigned spokesmanship and liability. Again, this is more the capacity of legal persons than for moral persons or organizations.

Thus far, discussion has proceeded upon the assumption that for the group to have rights, it must be able to exercise rights as modes of *action*. When the optic on rights is changed to whether the group can *benefit* from such rights without having to act upon or in accord with them, then a different set of results appears, for the group may simply have a benefit for its being a group even when it cannot act as a group out of this benefit.

This is the consideration that requires the distinction between *collective* and *distributive* benefits. To take the example of language use and the rights to education in that language, rights can only be exercised by the individuals who speak and sit in classrooms. But the benefit of the right accrues as well to their group collectively, so far as it is not diminished in its numbers and in the power of its defining characteristics. Similarly, only procedurally selected officers may have the exercise of voice in an assembly of constituent groups, such as a legislative house where constituent units are represented. Here, too, the collective interests of the groups are not identified with the distributed interests of their representatives, any more than with those of their populations.

The distinguishing factor between collective and distributive benefits is whether actions pursuant to the benefit can only be exercised as a whole. In the earlier example, it may be the case that every individual person in the group can continue exercising his or her language, while the linguistic group itself is reduced to the status of a marginal, folkoric, and clientized association. It is "quaint" to gape at its denizens on a holiday tour. As distinct from individual members' survival in a mere organization, for group survival to occur, if that is judged worthwhile, the exercise of prerogatives that benefit the group collectively is indispensible.

As well as distributivity, historicity affects the group's position before benefits and burdens under the law. Having an awareness of being formed by conditions of historical oppression (or benefit, it might be added) is how entitled groups are often characterized today. In fact, under influences from Marxism and Mannheim to feminism and Foucault, most find it hard to agree that there is any role at all for groups' formation by their members' autonomous awareness; every feature of groups may appear to be an ascription that others use to form the group, in their "social constitution of reality." What needs notice is that such social conditions may have been present, without their being what formed the group. Moreover, it should be observed that historical formation may occur without anyone's being aware of it. Where the latter is true, awareness of the historical formation may be gained long after and much more rapidly than the development of the group. A few short weeks under journalistic search, discovery, and consciousness-raising for social causes may suffice. This possibility can make the movement from organization to moral to legal personality highly volatile and unpredictable.

One final factor cutting across group realities is the *voluntariness* of belonging to the group, or to the group in its present condition. Joining groups one does not have to have joined is one extreme; having attributes that relegate one to a group unavoidably is the other. Nearly all cases fall between, as more or less one or the other. Membership in groups demarcated by race, gender, disease, nationality is no longer considered as obviously involuntary or unavoidable. And citizenship, religious membership, and sexual preference are no longer considered as purely matters of choice. The degree of voluntareity or of stasis for members within a group cannot be considered as a natural evolution of groups any more than the group's stages can be visualized simply as a movement "from status to contract" or vice versa.

But whatever the effect of such reevaluations upon the individual members, for the grouping itself an increased voluntareity, especially in adherence to burdensome dimensions of the group, implies that the group's procedural limitations upon power are more effective. This is because a group cannot afford frequent resistance, abuse, or alteration when members can readily walk away.

While distributivity cuts across the stages of group reality by requiring a distinction between exercise and receipt, historicity does so by juggling loose the placement of particular groups upon that template, and voluntareity does so by adjusting the procedural focus. The one remaining factor for consideration is that here, as in all evaluative matters, there is a role for *importance* and for the principle that *lex non curat de minimis*. A group may meet all the criteria for deserving the full range of benefits and burdens and yet be so unimportant in the public view that devolving rights upon it or withdrawing them from it seems unnecessary. This is especially likely to be the case when size, influence upon public life, or social visibility as a test case and standard does not appear to warrant significant use of public resources.

Types

The groups about which most controversy swirls can be placed in an order ranked from organization to legal person as follows.

Organizations	Examples
Social, economic classes	The unemployed
Races, genders, sexual orientations	Women
Nationalities, ethnicities	
Sequestered	Haitians in Canada
Integrated	Greeks in Canada
Linguistic groups	Anglophones in Quebec

Moral persons	Examples
Nations	Quebecois in Quebec
	Haitians in Haiti
Families	The Grays
Interest groups*	AMINTAPHIL
Schools, school boards	Concordia University
Unions, syndical groups	Concordia University Faculty
	Association
Legal persons	
Professional corporations	Canadian Philosophical
	Association
Religions, churches	Solar Temple, Methodism
Corporations (commercial, nonprofit)	Amway, Canadian Red Cross
Public corporations	Canadian Postal Service
Political units, states	Canda, Quebec, Montreal

*Unincorporated, either public or private, for health, educational, social, economic, cultural, recreational, occupational, commercial interests.

Consequences

Placing designated groups upon a grid for their group reality can contribute to dealing with several focal problems of group entitlement.[4]

Democratic Structure and Democratic Participation of Groups

Participation in organized action is without any gesture toward self-determination. Even with procedure, which brings the idea of the institution into shared pursuit and introduces group personality, democratic participation in neither of its senses is in view—neither majority rule by voting nor principles of equal respect and concern. Supporters insist upon democratic structuring in preinstitutional reality, in order to ensure democratic prerogatives in the final institution, the political state, because of analogies they draw between one of those senses of democracy at the level of the democratic state and that same sense within the group.

But there is a better analogy to be made. This is between the undemocratic group and the individual person, however bigoted. The person's participation in the democratic state is ensured so long as the bigotry remains within private activity, even publicly expressed. This is protected as long as the bigotry does not enter the public procedures in such a way as to undermine their process. It is a different matter if, through those democratic (majoritarian) procedures, democratic (egalitarian) principles are in danger of being lost. Then the latter, principiative notion of democracy must override the results from the initial, majoritarian exercise. For democracy to fail its majoritarian goals through honoring its egalitarian principles is less damaging than for it to fall short of those principles.

This license for majoritarian democracy within the intragroup range prevents imposition of democratic ideology where it does not belong. Some worthwhile human values are achieved more valuably by nondemocratic means, in the groups who pursue them. Equal entitlement and opportunity have rationale only in the fully matured legal personality of the state. As well, exclusion of nondemocratic groups makes poor precedent; for democratic majorities are far more likely to exclude from democratic public participation those groups that, while edifying by reason of their internal democracy, are devoted to promotion of public or private practices that are perceived at large to be immoral.

Self-Determination by Groups of Themselves and Their Members

The group achieves its identity by means of those characteristics it assimilates and pursues; this is equivalent to the values of the groups from which it selects its prospective members, and the values into which it educates its existing members. Solely the liberal constraints of the harm principle, thinned almost to excluding no more than abuse, are appropriate for determining state interference with this self-identification by its constituent groups and in turn with their representation in the legal state.

Of course, a democratic state's own policies for selecting and educating its members cannot follow the same course. For it, unlike the nondemocratic groups it may recognize, has a legal personality identified by law, that is, the rational and abstract equality of all before the public distribution of benefits and burdens. Just as their undemocratic constituent groups may be free riders on the practices of their democratic national state, so the nondemocratic states may participate as legal entities in democratic international affairs. While nondemocratic states do not have the prerequisites for legal personality, they can be constituted as legal persons by the fact of international recognition. Here again, in cases of nondemocratic national states just as in cases of nondemocratic subnational groups and in private corporations, legal personality may be pure legal fiction yet nonetheless real for that fact.

No group can join that international community of democratic or artifactual legal persons unless it has legal personhood. To separate from a national state, a group must have had legal personhood precedent to federation, or else by virtue of its internal nature, and be blocked in its exercise. These conditions set in institutional terms approximate current criteria at international law for self-determination, whether by internal "domestic nations" or their ethnocultural emulations. This is not equivalent to a national group's having the control of government in a political unit forming the legal person. Nor is it equivalent to the national group's having the majoritarian assent of its members. Nor is it sufficient in itself for secession. For example, a legal person entering a federation alters its identity by agreeing with other legal persons to form a new federated legal person. Here there can be no self-determined separation from the federated legal person any more than an individual legal person can unilaterally renounce debts, family, or identity.

Group Identity and Group Benefits for Imitative Groups (family)

Groups at a certain level of function and structure have a justified claim to receive the same benefits and burdens as others at that level. This is not to claim that they have the same identity as other groups at that level. This claim is most current in groups pretending to the status of family; these include purely voluntary communes, unformalized heterosexual liaisons, and same-sex unions. The identity of family is recognized with its distinctive legal status. If warranted (*ad demonstrandum*), the like level of group identity on the part of pretenders is appropriately met with an appropriate legal status, perhaps with no fewer benefits and burdens, advantages and disadvantages. Such rights and duties may be equal to those belonging to families, and may even be similar in kind. Nonetheless, these are not the rights and duties of families, and the legal identity associated with them is not that of families.

These examples of current legal concern with groups—their democratic participation, self-determination, and appropriation of status—have been addressed in terms of the structures for analysis developed earlier in this chapter. These are the characterization of organization, of moral personality, and of legal personality. Axes of development invoking the "social construction" of reality such as voluntareity, distributivity, historicity, and importance were grafted onto these. This graft is a fine-tuning to the formation of institutions by their members. That local tuning does not remove from the phases of institutional development their suprajurisdictional import for social and legal analysis.

Notes

1. An assortment is available in Francis W. Coker's *Organismic Theories of the State: Nineteenth-Century Interpretation of the State as an Organism or as Person* (New York: AMS Press, 1967). The interplay of moral personality as substantive and as relational ascription is seen most prominently in the ecclesial institution. For the religious philosopher, this is not otiose but is a typical instance of the exemplarity used in the *triplex via*: as justice, e.g., is found truly only in divinity, as revealed in scriptural narrative and tradition, but is known empirically now only by analogy drawn from human justice, so too for group reality. In particular, church as a group is moral personality identified mystically (none the less really for that) with divine personhood. The slide back and forth between relational personality and substantive person is both encouraged and cautioned, from the medievals' treatises *de ecclesia*, to the two Vatican Councils' documents (*Consilium de emendanda ecclesia* [1537]; *Lumen gentium* [1964]), and most explicitly in the encyclicals *Mystici corporis* of Pius XII (1943) and *Ecclesiam suam* of Paul VI (1964). Pierre Teilhard de Chardin was one recent scholar who brilliantly got the point, if wrongly. The analysis of its value for legal philosophy remains to be undertaken.

2. Consciousness of purpose need not imply unanimity, and hardly ever does. What to call the group's purpose and, hence, how to identify its position upon any point of its own interest or that of the broader society is to be announced by the group in line with its own procedures for determining this or, where lacking (as in an organization), by the legal authority's best estimate of it.

3. This is a recapitulation of some facets of the institutional theory of law of Maurice Hauriou (1856–1929), dean of law at Toulouse and commentator on decisions by the French administrative high court. The many features of institutions are caught in these definitions from the final stage of its thirty-year development. Of these, the most important (the idea) is downplayed here, and its empirical facet (procedure) is played up.

"The major lines of this new theory are the following: an institution is an idea of a task or project which is realized and lasts in a legal manner within a social milieu; for the realization of this idea, a power is organized which gives it organs; on the other hand, among the members of the social group which is interested in the realization of this idea there are produced manifestations of communion which are directed by the organs of power and are regulated by procedures." Hauriou, "La théorie de l'institution et de la fondation; Essai de vitalisme social," *Cahiers de la nouvelle journée* 4 (*La cité moderne et les transformations du droit*); reprinted in *Aux sources du droit; le pouvoir, l'ordre et la liberté* (*Cahiers de la nouvelle journée* 23) (Paris: Bloud et Gay, 1933), 96.

"In gathering these characteristics of the *instituted social organization*, which is at the same time the *incorporated institution*, we are led to the following definition: a social organization becomes durable, i.e., it keeps its specific form despite the continual renewal of the human matter which it contains, when it is *instituted*, i.e., when on one hand the directive idea, which is in it from the moment of its foundation, has been able to subordinate the power of government, thanks to the balances of organs and power, and when on the other hand this system of ideas and power balances has been consecrated in its form by the consent of the institution's members as well as that of the social milieu. In summary, *the form of the institution, which is its enduring element, consists in a system of balances of powers and consents which is built around an idea.*" Hauriou, *Précis de droit constitutionnel*, 2d ed. (Paris: Librairie du Recueil Sirey, 1928), 73.

4. For a construct of this legal status, see C. B. Gray, "Family as Closely-Held Company," in the AMINTAPHIL volume *Perspectives on the Family*, ed. R. Moffat and M. Bayles (Lewiston, N.Y.: Edwin Mellen, 1990), 171–84, although deemed unrealistic in its preface.

Chapter 5

Groups: Rights, Wrongs, and Culture

Thomas W. Simon

The connection between groups and democracy seems tenuous, especially since the received political wisdom today makes a strong connection between democracy and individuals, not groups. No one proclaims democracy as "rule by, for, and of groups." After all, *demos,* the stem of the word *democracy,* means "people," that is, a collection of individuals. This commonplace view of democracy depends upon treating a highly political concept, democracy, as not politically contestable. If people have disagreed over the meaning of *demos* or *people* throughout history, then democracy's tie to individualism weakens. Perhaps the sense of *people* associated with *democracy* means a collection of artificially determined groups. This may not be so farfetched as it might seem. The word *democracy* has close etymological connections to *demes.* Cleisthenes, often designated as a founder of Athenian democracy, created artificial political units called *demes.*[1] He tried to break up Athens's traditional tribal boundaries, which had served as the units of governance, and aimed to undermine the political power of some tribal groups over others. He plotted to use demes to weaken tribal units by replacing them with administratively drawn lines that lacked historical and sociological rationales. Demes represent an ancient form of electoral districts. So, democracy may have begun by administrative fiat. Cleisthenes imposed a replacement of "natural" group divisions with artificial ones. On this account, democracy begins to look like an administratively imposed leveling force. Given the current force of group identity politics, should some rights revert to pre-Cleisthenes tribal groups? The idea of group rights has enjoyed a sudden resurgence. The voices of opposition to group rights have proved equally adamant.[2] I shall focus on one claim made by proponents of group rights: groups, that is, minorities, have rights to their culture.[3] Each interrelated term of the claim requires analysis. Here I shall further narrow the focus to the issue of what group rights protect. Also, I shall direct a great deal of my critique at Will Kymlicka's writings.

96

Kymlicka, who ranks as one of the leading liberal proponents of group rights, has argued that special rights should protect cultural membership. In contrast, I put forward an alternative formulation, not in terms of group rights but in terms of group harms. I shall argue that strongly formulated discrimination provisions should protect individuals from harms inflicted upon them because of their perceived or actual group affiliation. Before analyzing the, surprisingly unanalyzed, term *culture* in this debate, I shall clarify, at least in a perfunctory fashion, the ideas of groups and of rights.

Group Rights

Many commentators see human rights as the centerpiece of law and politics. Lawrence Beer puts the case eloquently: "Human rights provide the omnidirectional transcultural axis around which the gyroscope of constitutional government, law and politics should spin."[4] The number of rights proposed has proliferated in recent years.[5] Discussions of rights in international law incorporate three generations of rights: first-generation political/civil rights, second-generation social/economic rights, and third-generation collective/solidarity rights.[6] Only the third generation, including the right to cultural identity, appears to require a concept of groups. Even the idea of rights has become an object of attack.[7] According to these critics, the individualistic quality of rights creates an immediate and perhaps insuperable barrier to any group claims.[8] Further, the critics contend that an examination of rights cases in legal history reveals that rights represent, at best, mild concessions given to disadvantaged groups by dominant ones. A jaded view of United States history might highlight the reluctance with which (first-generation) voting rights were accorded to African-Americans and women only after the entrenchment of (second-generation) economic and social disadvantaged status of these groups. Finally, other critics, while embracing the idea of human rights, reject the dominant conception of rights. For them, the Western powers have unjustifiably dictated the terms and conditions for rights. The West stands accused of having hijacked the global human rights debate. Westerners consider rights only as they apply to the individual, and Western individualism conveniently ignores many non-Western societies where human rights operate within a communal and group context. Roughly sketched, this view holds the following: personal identity evolves through group identity;[9] individual rights in terms of "freedom of" (civil and political rights) or "freedom from" (economic and social rights) mean nothing if divorced from community; rights derive from interactions and relations with others. Overall, as evidenced by these critical stands, the debate over group rights has centered on the comparative status accorded to individuals and groups.[10] The individualist-collectivist debate has dominated the group rights controversy.

Debates in international law and politics reflect competing visions for protecting human rights. Individualist, universal conceptions of human rights vie for support against collectivist, group-specific conceptions. The theoretical debates have political and historical roots. The United Nations Charter symbolized a post mortem pronouncement on the League of Nations' allegedly aborted attempt to protect minorities. Many commentators thought that the League had failed because of its misguided efforts on behalf of minorities. Today, many other critics complain that the United Nations has not done enough for minorities, and a reinvigorated movement to advance minority and group rights has emerged. According to a Working Group of the Human Rights Commission, "The fundamental question of whether to follow an individual or collective rights approach remains unresolved."[11] The positions appear at loggerheads: the individualists prize individual freedom, and collectivists promote social goods.

The idea of freedom of individuals to choose undergirds the individualist position. Individuals choose their ends. It does not make sense to talk about a collectivity choosing its ends. Group rights make sense to individualists only if groups consist of nothing more than individuals.[12] Otherwise, for individualists, it does not make sense to talk about group rights. Granting rights to individuals gives a trump card to individuals over the welfare of the collectivity. The collectivity should not choose the individual's ends. Group rights, according to individualists, necessarily give individual interests second-class status. In contrast, collectivists argue that collectivities have rights independent of the rights of their members.[13] Collectivists can employ the group rights of federal units and corporations without resorting to identity politics, but positive group identity has become central to some collectivist programs. Group identity politics celebrates group membership. These collectivists recognize and prize group attachments.

In Canada, Aboriginal tribal councils have the right to determine what hunting will occur to help preserve their culture, and the Province of Quebec has the right to preserve its distinctive culture and language. These examples, taken from Kymlicka's work, raise important questions about the debate between individualists and collectivists. Aboriginal tribal councils and the Province of Quebec have a curious status, neither individual nor collective. What is the difference between conferring legal rights on administrative bodies, states, and corporations and accepting rights for groups? Some theorists deny that words such as *state* and *corporation* refer to collective entities. Corporations are legal persons. In other words, they are fictitious persons.[14] For legal purposes, corporations are pretend persons, fictive individuals. Other analysts see groups as different in kind from the examples of legal fictions. They then dismiss the notion of a legal fiction, at least for purposes of philosophical analysis.[15] The first stage of this collectivist strategy has merit. It takes more than filing rules of incorporation with the state to form a group. Groups form through complicated means. Yet, the strategy of treating a collectivity as a legal fiction, while it may not prove philosophically satisfying, pragmatically accomplishes a great deal. The collectivity, armed with rights and obligations, now has legal protection. Within American constitutional law, corporations, while unable to vote or hold office, enjoy numerous rights.[16] If we confer rights on federal units and corporations, why not on groups? Unfortunately, collectivists would remain dissatisfied, since they would find groups-as-legal-fictions demeaning to those groups. After all, groups are more than just fictions. A focus on harms provides a strategy for maneuvering past the seemingly endless individualist-collectivist minefield.

Beyond the Individualist-Collectivist Debate

Despite their different orientations, individualists and collectivists have a common ground. Both positions accept a proscription against group harm. (I shall briefly describe group harm later.) Individualism comes in many varieties, with some strands more concerned with an individual's well-being than others. All individualists, however, would accept the seemingly innocuous claim that harm directed at individuals because of their group status would curtail and stifle the freedom of choice of those individuals. If individuals suffer because of their actual or perceived group membership, their ranges of choices thereby become limited. Further, group harms have the potential to spread from one activity type to another. Group discrimination in education curtails employment opportunities and so forth. Similarly, collectivists would also deplore group harms. Collectivists regard group identity as something to be cherished, honored, and defended. Group harms undermine attempts to establish a positive group identity. On this view, harms directed against my group constitute attacks on *who-I-am*. So, individualists and collectivists would accept a proscription against group harm.

A group-harm analysis avoids many of the controversies over rights.[17] All sides to the debates over rights would have to accept the minimalist account offered by a group-harm analysis. For those who see rights as basic to the rule of law, a commitment against group harm would stand as fundamental. Rights theorists see rights as protecting interests. An interest against being harmed would rank highly among the interests worth protecting. If rights protect anything, they should protect individuals (as members of groups) against harm. The ascription of a right imposes a duty on others not to harm or, more strongly, to prevent or rectify harms. The rights theorists might still want to preserve an appeal to rights to establish, for example, the weightiness of claims to avoid the harms.[18] However, even this could be done in terms of the severity of the harm without invoking rights discourse. I am not urging anyone to abandon rights-talk entirely. I am suggesting that harms-talk can mediate disputes among rights theorists and their critics. A harms perspective brackets (perhaps only temporarily) rights-talk. Initially, it appeals to (a presumably more mutually agreeable) harms. Harms pose as common enemy number one.

Those who reject rights discourse would also accept a group harm analysis. An initial commitment against group harms does not require use of rights language. Again, an adequate group-harm analysis would require providing a ranking of the severity of harms (a topic that cries out for further analysis elsewhere). Further, a group-harm analysis directly addresses the suspicion that animates the critiques of rights discourse. Critics of rights discourse, including some Critical Legal Studies proponents, find that rights discourse impedes rather than enhances the welfare of disadvantaged groups. A harm analysis centers directly on the status of disadvantaged groups. Finally, group rights advocates would welcome a group-harm analysis, but they would claim that it does not go far enough in protecting vulnerable groups. Yet they would pay a price for going further. A harm analysis does not have to reify groups or cultures; there does not have to be something over and above a legal fiction. This problem receives detailed attention in the next section, which presents arguments against using culture as a key (necessary or sufficient) notion in assessing, promoting, and adjudicating group claims. Most discussions of group rights, such as Kymlicka's, concentrate on the concepts of groups and rights. Theorists pay little attention to what those rights protect, thereby presenting an incomplete and misleading analysis. They assume a right to cultural identity without fully defining *culture*.

Defining and Valorizing Culture

Kymlicka also attempts to cut across the individualist-collectivist divide and finds that whether an individual or a collectivity bears a right is not critical to group-differentiated issues. Kymlicka undermines the individualist versus collectivist debate by illustrating how it fails to address the complexities of group-differentiated claims. He demonstrates the complexity thesis with numerous and sometimes inconsistent distinctions. He distinguishes between group rights and special rights,[19] and accuses collectivists of confusing the two. Collectivists, thereby, fail to acknowledge that special rights need not be incompatible with liberal principles. Group rights protect the group against individual dissent; special rights protect the group against external pressures.[20] For Kymlicka, group rights raise certain theoretical but few practical problems (at least in Canada). Special rights confront fewer problems. Cutting across the individualist versus collectivist debate, special rights can apply to individuals (thereby allaying the individualist's worries), a community (e.g., a tribal council), a province (Quebec), or a territory. Kymlicka's scheme, then, allows for two types of bearers of rights, namely, individuals and governmental or quasi-governmental units. Kymlicka claims that liberals should find either type of bearer of special rights acceptable. Liberals do not call the right of an individual to practice a religion a group right simply because it involves membership in a group. Further, they do not hesitate to ascribe legal rights to governmental units or other legal fictions, such as corporations. The granting of legal rights to institutional structures, including governments, bolsters the case for minority rights. Many groups, such as Canadian Aboriginal and French-speaking Quebecois, make their claims as recognized legal fictions. Other groups, such as the Roma (Gypsies), might claim legal-fiction status. These legal rights would become moral rights if the rights protect important interests.

Does Kymlicka's scheme enable him to safely traverse the minefields of problems and bypass (theoretically and practically) difficulties, such as the problem of internal minorities?[21] I shall assume an affirmative answer and focus on one aspect of Kymlicka's program for casting aside the differences between individualist and collectivist that remains problematic. At every turn, Kymlicka's case depends upon and appeals to the idea of culture. If he has a quarrel with the unrepentant individualists, it lies in their failure to appreciate the critical importance of culture. Collectivists, for Kymlicka, also have a problem with culture. They fail to realize how cultural issues can be addressed within liberalism. Whatever problem Kymlicka addresses, the idea of culture prevents the success of other theories. Culture remains a constant factor that enables Kymlicka to provide solutions. Yet, despite a few attempts to provide a clarification, he treats culture as a given. Culture represents the clay given to the sculptor Kymlicka to shape and fit within the rocks and crevices of liberalism. Further, Kymlicka molds the culture-clay to fit onto an already hardened human rights statue.

Kymlicka pays the price of unjustifiably valorizing a largely undefined phenomenon, namely, culture, in order to erect a bridge across the individualist-collectivist divide. Definitions of culture often contain localized valuations, and Kymlicka's approach to culture has a distinct Canadian flavor. He defines culture, which he takes as synonymous with nation or people, as "an intergenerational community, more or less institutionally complete, occupying a given territory or homeland, sharing a distinct language and history."[22] The Aboriginal and Quebecois qualify easily under this definition, but the Roma people, or Gypsies (not found in Canada), have a questionable status given their lack of institutional completeness and territory.[23] It just so happens that Kymlicka's definition captures those groups currently making the loudest claims to cultural identity in Canada. Individuating cultures according to their degree of institutional completeness affords protection to those groups that have the least need for it. The more institutionally complete a group, the more devices it has at its disposal to counter harms to its members based on their group affiliation. Quebec has a well-established political party, which, when in power, has all the tools of a provincial government at its disposal. The Roma have discombobulated political organizations. On any index (infant mortality, longevity, etc.), the Roma, in principle, have a greater need of protection than the Quebecois.

Several international instruments, especially the 1978 UNESCO Declaration on Race and Racial Prejudice, refer to a right to maintain cultural identity. The force of culture appears powerful indeed. For Raz and Margalit, "culture determines the boundaries of the imaginable" and "the limits of the feasible."[24] Given the alleged power of culture, it would seem easy to define it. However, that does not prove to be the case. Defenders of cultural rights rely on vague and equivocal senses of culture. Something seems worth preserving, yet that something remains elusive. Kymlicka takes up an aspect of the communitarian cause within liberalism. He constructs a case for minority rights around the claim that individuals need access to societal cultures to make meaningful choices about their lives: "We decide how to lead our lives by situating ourselves in cultural narratives, by adopting roles that have struck us as worthwhile ones, as ones worth living."[25] What does Kymlicka means by his claim?[26] If by *culture* Kymlicka means nothing more than context, then the culture thesis holds but says little. "Asocial choices" make little sense. The qualifier *cultural* adds hardly anything to the idea of context. If, however, the idea of cultural context becomes overly valued, it might result in an exclusive focus on symbols and rituals surrounding a group's actions. Cultural myopia might then exclude attention to other, often more critical, factors, such as economic ones.[27] Further, a "cultureless" context may have a greater value than a culture context. The context within which a person is situated may include a critique of what the dominant fellow group members think of as their culture. The critique may require a person to step outside a culture to assess the culture. The critical perspective is situated, but it is unclear what it means to say that it must be situated in a culture (another culture, other than the one critiqued?) to be meaningful.

Let us say that we want to account for someone's career choice. Certainly, we would want to know something about the context and background of the person's choice. Yet it remains unclear, if not unintelligible, to advocate the preservation of context. If, alternatively, "having a culture" means something specific, such as "having a language," we know what it means to "preserve a language." Nevertheless, it remains unclear how a career or any other life choice becomes meaningful depending on access to a particular language structure. A student's choice of schools does not depend for its meaningfulness on the student's ability to deliberate about the choice in Dutch, English, or Japanese. Admittedly, the degree of access to language does condition, limit, and perhaps enable choice. Language accessibility, however, does not determine the meaningfulness of choice. Language may influence the choice, but it does not determine the choice's meaningfulness.

Kymlicka, in a footnote, admits to the difficulty of defining a "minority cultural community." He glosses over the challenge by drawing on an attitude, made familiar in constitutional debates over obscenity. Basically, Kymlicka assures his readers that we know certain things when we see them, despite our difficulties in defining them. However, Kymlicka applies the we-know-it-when-we-see-it principle more to the notion of minorities than to culture. Even if precise definitions fail, Kymlicka knows a minority; culture still remains elusive. The title of Kymlicka's recent book *The Rights of Minority Cultures* suggests that rights attach to cultures, albeit certain kinds of cultures, namely, minority cultures. For Kymlicka, individual choice operates within a background of culture. To make choices fully rational, an individual needs to bring the background into the foreground. To adopt a critical perspective toward culture, an individual must also have culture in the foreground. If individuals want to be in a position where they can take account of their cultural values and also subject them to rational critique, they need to know what to look for and how to find them. Given the centrality of culture, Kymlicka must provide a clear definition of it.

In an earlier work, *Liberalism, Community and Culture*, Kymlicka paid more attention to defining culture. He differentiated his concern with culture from the "character of a historical community." He therefore was not using the word in the sense of the norms, values, and their attendant institutions in one's community.[28] Instead, Kymlicka claimed to be referring to the culture's structure as a context of choice. He readily acknowledged that a culture's character changes; however, even in the midst of such change, its structure remained constant. Cultural extinction provided the lone exception to the rule. French Canadians radically transformed their culture's character in the 1960s, from a religiously based set of values to a more secular, political one. Despite the character changes, the structure of French-Canadian culture, on Kymlicka's view, remained intact. Yet the distinction between a culture's character and its structure does not hold. For one thing, it proves difficult to describe character apart from structure.[29] Kymlicka hints that something remains stable throughout cultural change. He finds the changes in French-Canadian culture of the 1960s more aptly described as changes in the dominant character of the culture. For Kymlicka, something still persists in Quebec through all the changes. The "something left over" is "structure," yet the idea of structure adds nothing to our understanding of the Canadian example. The phrase "French-Canadian culture" might include references to different culture characters at different historical periods. The appropriateness and adequacy of this formulation do need to invoke a constant structure across the change. Nonstructural elements, including myths woven together by political leaders, produce some forms of cultural continuity over wide time periods. Historical studies provide few structural continuities tying Serb culture in 1389 to Serb culture today. Did the Iranian Revolution preserve Iranian culture? It brought religious, political, and economic structural changes, but something distinctively Iranian persisted throughout the changes. Perhaps, in Iran, structure changed but certain aspects of character remained intact. The ease with which we can switch between arguments for the stability of character and for the stability of structure indicates problems with the distinction between the two.

The idea of structure enables Kymlicka to hold on to the notion of culture, to reify it. Allen Buchanan strengthens and extends Kymlicka's arguments. In Buchanan's hands, the reification of culture becomes even more pronounced. According to Buchanan, culture rescues "the individual from the paralysis of infinite possibilities" needed to make meaningful choices in one's life, and it "connects what otherwise would be fragmented goals in a coherent, mutually supporting way."[30] This is a heavy burden to place on something not defined or indefinable. The persistent problems that plague appeals to culture should provide sufficient grounds to look elsewhere. The idea of group harms opens a fruitful "window of opportunity." If a theorist insists on a rights framework, ideas such as special rights could still play a role. Special rights, however, would not operate primarily to enshrine a culture. They would protect those individuals who are particularly vulnerable to harm because of their group affiliation. These concessions to minority rights do not lead right back to a culture perspective. Kymlicka also professes a deep-seated concern for group harms, but he mischaracterizes group harms.

Mischaracterizing Group Harms

Different groups experience different types of harms. We need to describe the harms adequately. I do not have the space to develop fully the description here except to offer a sketch. Again, Kymlicka's analysis will prove useful as a foil. Kymlicka differentiates harms inflicted upon Blacks and Indians. Blacks seek assimilation, but Indians seek distinctiveness: "But whereas racism against blacks comes from the denial by whites that blacks are full members of the community, racism against Indians comes primarily from the denial by whites that Indians are distinct peoples with their own cultures and communities."[31]

Kymlicka mischaracterizes the differences. Harms suffered by Indians often occur because of white recognition of the distinct identity of Indians. For Kymlicka, the primary harm at stake is damage to self-respect. To the contrary, the "sense that one's plan of life is worth carrying out" may be the least harm.[32] In fact, it may not even qualify as a harm. Many defenders of cultural identity pay too little attention to the social and economic harms inflicted upon different groups. Attacks on a group's traditions, language, and history might have the opposite effect, enhancing self-respect among group members. In contrast, dire economic circumstances and deplorable health conditions might do more to undermine self-respect than not recognizing a group's distinct identity. If the loss of self-respect constitutes a harm, then it is a secondary harm relative to the harms inflicted through material conditions. The critical harms do not lie in the damage to respect for a culture. Rather, their more pronounced manifestations lie in the horrid conditions group members experience.

Perhaps we can put Kymlicka's concern in more social and less individualistic terms than the term *self-respect* connotes. "Cultural preservationists" fear cultural assimilation. However, assimilation (a complex process indeed) alone does not constitute a harm for any one group over any other. Assimilation per se does not constitute a "badge of inferiority."[33] The harms, if any, in assimilation policies lie in their attendant practices and consequences. Assimilation, as practiced on indigenous peoples in the United States, included educating Indian children. In many instances, education programs included work ranging from modified slavery to forced labor, school jails, overcrowded accommodations, and inadequate food and health care, to say nothing of the psychological and social damage done by separating children from their families and community.[34]

Kymlicka recognizes the disadvantaged status of some groups. However, he focuses on a curious form of inequality, namely, the inequality of having to pay for secure cultural membership.[35] Non-Aboriginal members of the dominant culture in Canada supposedly do not have to expend resources to assure their culture's existence. "And since this inequality would remain even if individual members of aboriginal communities no longer suffered from any deprivation of material resources," collective rights are needed.[36] Yet, if all members of an Aboriginal community enjoyed material well-being, then they could support the growth and vitality of their culture's structure (providing they knew what Kymlicka meant by *structure*). Cultural membership is not the primary good in need of protection. Rather, individuals need protections against harms inflicted upon them because of their perceived group affiliation, and the idea of culture does not adequately capture the realm within which these harms occur.

Discussions of culture often ignore questions concerning economic well-being and other indices of social welfare. The context within which individuals make choices may include squalid living conditions, abject poverty, dilapidated housing, and lack of sanitary facilities. The situation of a culture and its associated items—language, tradition, and symbols—often pales in comparison to other more oppressive background conditions. Kymlicka often uses *culture* in the sense of what T. S. Eliot calls "reduced culture," that is, "as everything that is picturesque, harmless and separable from politics, such as language and literature, local arts and customs."[37] Colorful dances can hide the lives of the dancers from tourists' view. Further, emphases on culture may stifle attempts to give modern interpretations to group claims. Let us return to Kymlicka's example of Aboriginal hunting and fishing rights. According to a "frozen rights" theory invoked in Canadian courts, an Aboriginal right to hunt and fish holds so long as it is in keeping with the traditional practices of the culture.[38] This interpretation allows for spears and reef nets but not fleets of seine boats. Accepting the ideology of cultural traditions may prove economically harmful to the group.

This does not mean that cultural concerns ought to be thrown aside. Within a group-harm framework, culture becomes something that the claimants largely define for themselves and use to ward off harm. This means that culture is primarily socially constructed, not that it is subjectively defined. Culture could include maintaining or reviving a language or a dialect; forming institutions, such as schools, independent from the dominant institutions of the state; and establishing rituals and employing symbols unique to the group members. Merely tolerating the revival of a language could avert harms. The harms in question might call for stronger measures, such as state support for teaching a language. The circumstances would dictate the particulars of the remedy. Reviving a language, invoking residency requirements for voting, establishing schools, and engaging in traditional activities—all of these may serve as means to ward off harms. Success in these "softer" realms could place the group in a better position to improve its economic, health, and other conditions.

Thus, the harm approach permits sidestepping the vexed question of what constitutes a culture. It operates with the far more tractable concept of harm. The harm approach has one further virtue. The problem of defining *groups* becomes more tractable within a harm perspective. A group becomes identified (at least, for purposes of devising remedies) by those inflicting the harm. The Nazis, not the Jews, defined *Jew*. As with the following two sections on the role of the judiciary and an analysis of group harm, these ideas can only be telescoped here, but it is important at least to note them to give a picture of the strength of the harm approach.

Judicial Remedies

The heated controversy over group rights raises a question about political institutions. What institutional mechanisms should implement group rights? Assuming a separation of powers, should the executive, legislative, or judicial branches have the primary responsibility for group rights? The institutionalization of group rights within executive or legislative structures often favors some groups or one group over others. In Malaysia, the rules of composition of the executive council, the Conference of Rulers, guarantee Malays executive offices.[39] In the former Czechoslovakia, the minority Slovaks had guaranteed equal representation in the legislative Chamber of Nations.[40] The Malays have and the Slovaks had unwarranted power over other groups (Indians and Hungarians, respectively). What arguments support the judiciary as the primary means of determining the viability of group claims? While the judiciary in the United States has come under attack as countermajoritarian, one aspect of this criticism speaks in favor of, not in opposition to, the judiciary. Adjudicatory mechanisms can operate as a buffer to protect the minority groups against the tyranny of the majority. Other institutional devices, such as proportional representation for minority groups (whereby certain groups have guaranteed legislative representation), might serve the same purpose but only at the risk of empowering some groups at the expense of others.[41]

Debates over group rights seldom address remedy issues. Instead, they focus on legislation, constitutional amendments, and similar mechanisms. While, at least at this stage, I do not want to downplay the efficacy of these other fixes, it is important to acknowledge the role of the judiciary. Courts could play a crucial role in dealing with group harm beyond providing a more expansive interpretation of discrimination and constructing remedies to rectify these harms.[42] They could also issue declaratory judgments that require positive governmental action.[43] These declaratory judgments would have to be tempered by political accountability. A general claim to language rights might require governmental funding of schools for group members, or the remedy for housing discrimination against the group might mandate governmentally sponsored housing.

Even more substantially, courts could issue structural injunctions that mandate the expansion of institutions to rectify group harms.[44] For example, a court could require a school board to add facilities to enforce group language educational rights.[45] Or the situation could call for the creation and development of institutional structures, such as entire schools, and not just additional programs within a school. Perhaps a group, like the Roma, is so decimated and its members so vulnerable to harm that the group has few, if any, institutional structures to build upon. The remedies would then, in effect, create a group institutional structure where none existed before. In this situation the remedy creates an institutional structure upon which to build a legal fiction of a collective entity.

Of course, judiciaries do not operate in a political vacuum, but this analysis could help remove at least some of the conceptual clutter impeding construction of adjudicatory mechanisms. I do not want to stand accused of being a politically naive cheerleader for the courts. Alternatively, we should not overlook the possibilities found in adjudicatory mechanisms. Reorienting judicial focus toward group harm has important repercussions for international law and politics. It advances the agenda of human rights by providing a workable framework for dealing with claims of group injustice. It promotes collectivist concerns by providing mechanisms for warding off group harms.

Group Harm

So far I have contrasted group harm with culture, but my charges against Kymlicka's use of *culture* seem applicable to my reliance on *harm*. Here I will add a few admittedly sketchy comments about group harm per se.[46] Physical and psychological senses of pain have social aspects. Individuals can feel a form of pain that has a great deal to do with their perceived social status. Their social status, their group identity, further sets the threshold of vulnerability to pain. Certain group identities not only enhance the vulnerability to pain but also have an experiential component. If we see pain as a social phenomenon and if we acknowledge the strong role that group dynamics play in shaping suffering, then group harm begins to make more sense. Social suffering includes vulnerability and a type of experience. Since individual physical suffering serves as the paradigm of suffering, it is difficult to accept the more subtle and cruel social variety as a type of suffering. Although people do not generally writhe in physical agony over their group identity, they do experience a type of suffering that directly connects to their group identity.

The latent form of social suffering resembles a disposition such as brittle. An object such as glass is brittle in the following sense: if an object hit the glass with a certain force, the glass would break. Similarly, an individual socially suffers in the following sense: if certain conditions developed, then the individual would suffer in more manifest ways. Still, social suffering is more than a disposition, more than a potentiality waiting activation. Social suffering has an experiential component. Social pain is like a background noise, similar to a low, throbbing pain about to burst into a debilitating migraine headache. Some South Americans call social pain *violencia blanca* (white violence), associating it with background white noise. The symptoms of social suffering are often subtle and hidden. Social suffering eludes the confines of a crisp analysis. It is more amenable to metaphoric description. Nonetheless, social suffering does exist despite its elusive character. Social suffering has another experiential side. Members of the group often live in horrid conditions, particularly compared with the dominant group. The literature on indigenous peoples abounds with discussions of culture but contains few references to their everyday living conditions.

No one can deny that harms befall individuals, but group harms seem mysterious. How can a group become harmed? The critic would contend that groups operate similarly to corporations and do not suffer. Individual corporate executives or workers may suffer, but not the corporation. Likewise, individual North American Indians can suffer harm, as many have, without harm coming to the social group. Despite such protestations, it does make sense to speak of group harm. A group becomes harmed when (group-related) individual harms lower the threshold of vulnerability for other group members. To take a simple but obvious situation, if private individuals or authorities of the state brutalize an individual primarily because of the perceived or actual group affiliation of that individual, then other individuals associated with that group become more vulnerable to harm. By focusing on indirect harms, I do not want to belittle the effects of direct harm to an individual occasioned by group membership. Lowering the threshold of protection of others from possible harm often pales in comparison to actual harm to a single individual. Some members of a social group may experience group harm indirectly, through association with the group, and the harms they experience may look slight compared with those who directly experience the brunt of group harm. Conversely, direct harm should not overshadow completely the effects of indirect harm. Not all members of the group experience the same lowering of the threshold of vulnerability, but all experience it to some degree or another.

Group harm makes sense. At one extreme, we find a large number of examples of genocide, where group vulnerability to harm is obvious. Jewish people living today are still vulnerable because of the Holocaust. Toward the other end of the spectrum we find incidents of hate speech. Direct harm increases social suffering when group members become more vulnerable and experience more suffering because of a hate-speech incident.

Conclusion

Rather than revert to a pre-Cleisthenes sense of tribal groups, the proposal made here fully acknowledges group harm without falling into the trap of reifying groups. Culture does not adequately capture what needs protecting under the rubric of minority rights. By pointing out the inadequate characterizations of culture and the inappropriateness of using culture as a theoretical foundation stone, I do not thereby intend to belittle attempts by insiders and outsiders to find ways to positively value, whatever they might mean by, "cultural activities." However, I object to treating culture as the definitive background condition and not looking to the economic and political background that provides the context for culture itself. A political theory about groups must first address the lingering and current affects wrought by the forces of prejudice and discrimination. Harms, and not culture, must become a central focus for political theory and action to address critical group-differentiated issues tearing apart the world today.

Notes

1. Josiah Ober, *Mass and Elites in Democratic Athens* (Princeton, N.J.: Princeton University Press, 1989).

2. Some of the opposition appears disingenuous in that the critics couch their rejection of group rights in philosophical terms when their real grounds for dismissal are political. The critics disfavor the social groups currently vying for enhanced status. Their vocal opposition to the status of social groups does not extend to corporations, states, interest groups, and the many other collectivities. Even if we confine this analysis to the philosophical, we should not lose sight of the underlying political dynamics.

3. For purposes of this chapter, I do not need to differentiate ethnic minorities, national minorities, and indigenous peoples. There are, of course, important differences.

4. Lawrence W. Beer, "Introduction," in *Constitutional Systems in Late Twentieth-Century Asia* (Seattle: University of Washington Press, 1992), 8.

5. The award for the longest list goes to Galtung and Wirak, who propose the following: the right to sleep, the right not to be exposed to excessively and unnecessary heavy, degrading, dirty, and boring work, the right to identify with one's work product, individually or collectively (as opposed to anonymity), the right to be a member of some primary group (not necessarily the family), and the right to be a member of a secondary group (not necessarily the nation). Galtung and Wirak, "On the Relationship Between Human Rights and Human Needs," UNESCO Doc. SS-78/CONF. 630/4 (1978), 48. Philip Alston warns against the undue proliferation of rights. See Alston, "Conjuring Up New Human Rights: A Proposal for Quality Control," *American Journal of International Law* 28 (1984): 607.

6. Almost all of the legal examples used in this chapter come from international and Canadian law. I use the latter because Kymlicka, the main object of my criticisms, emphasizes Canadian cases. I use the former because any theory, especially Kymlicka's, should apply to the international sphere.

7. See Mark Tushnet, "An Essay on Rights," *Texas Law Review* 62 (1984): 1363; Tushnet, "The Critique of Rights," *Southern Methodist Law Review* 47 (1993): 23.

8. Catherine A. MacKinnon, "Reflections on Sex Equality Under Law," *Yale Law Journal* 100 (1991): 4281.

9. See J. M. Zvobgo, "A Third World View," in *Human Rights and American Foreign Policy*, ed. Donald P. Kommers and Gilbert D. Loescher (Notre Dame, Ind.: University of Notre Dame Press, 1979), 92–103.

10. Not all collective rights fall under the category of group rights. The collective right to the common heritage of humanity, found in treaties and commentaries on the international law of the sea, provides a challenging example of a collectivist right.

11. UN Doc. E/CN.4/1988/36, para. 16.

12. See Ronald Dworkin, "Liberal Community," *California Law Review* 77 (1989): 494; Jan Narveson, "Collective Rights?" *Canadian Journal of Law and Jurisprudence* 4 (1991): 329.

13. See Michael McDonald, "Should Communities Have Rights?" *Canadian Journal of Law and Jurisprudence* 4 (1991): 217; Ronald Garet, "Community and Existence: The Rights of Groups," *Southern California Law Review* 56 (1983): 1001.

14. Michael Hartney, "Some Confusions Concerning Collective Rights," *Canadian Journal of Law and Jurisprudence* 4 (1991): 293–314.

15. Marlis Galenkamp, *Individualism Versus Collectivism: The Concept of Group Rights* (Rotterdam: Rotterdamse Filosofische Studies, 1993) ("in order to be really innovative, the issue of collective rights has to exceed this fictitious level"), 109.

16. These corporate rights include the Fourth Amendment freedom from unreasonable warrantless searches; the Fifth Amendment right of due process, protection against

double jeopardy, and right of just compensation (takings clause); the Sixth Amendment right to jury trial in a criminal case; and the Seventh Amendment right to jury trial in a civil case. Scott R. Bowman, *The Modern Corporation and American Political Thought* (University Park: Pennsylvania State University Press, 1996), 362 n. 79.

17. I will say more about a group-harm analysis in the final sections of this chapter.

18. I owe this objection to Allen Buchanan.

19. Will Kymlicka, *Multicultural Citizenship: A Liberal Theory of Minority Rights* (Oxford: Clarendon Press, 1995), 7, 35–48.

20. Will Kymlicka, "Individual and Community Rights," in *Group Rights*, ed. Judith Baker (Toronto: University of Toronto Press, 1994). An excellent example of the problem of internal dissent in aboriginal cultures is *Thomas v. Norris*, 2 C.N.I.R. 139 (1992), a case involving a member of the Lyackson Band of British Columbia who was forced to participate in an initiation ceremony for spirit dancing.

21. Kymlicka, *Multicultural Citizenship*,18. Kymlicka elaborates on his definition of *societal culture* on page 76.

22. Ibid., 18. Kymlicka elaborates on his definition of *societal culture* on page 76.

23. For a brief history of attempts to create international political structures for the Romani, see Ian Hancock, "The East European Roots of Romani Nationalism," in *The Gypsies of Eastern Europe*, ed. David Crowe and John Kolsti (London: M. E. Sharpe, 1991), 139–49.

24. Avishai Margalit and Joseph Raz, "National Self-Determination," in *The Rights of Minority Cultures*, ed. Will Kymlicka (Oxford: Oxford University Press, 1995), 86.

25. Will Kymlicka, *Liberalism, Community and Culture* (Oxford: Clarendon Press, 1989), 165.

26. See Jeremy Waldron, "Minority Cultures and the Cosmopolitan Alternative," in *The Rights of Minority Cultures*, ed. Will Kymlicka (Oxford: Oxford University Press, 1995), 105–10, who makes similar criticisms, except that he concedes too much by admitting that "we need cultural meanings, but we do not need homogeneous cultural frameworks." Why do we need any cultural frameworks?

27. Although Kymlicka mentions "economic life" in characterizing culture, he does little or nothing with it. Kymlicka, *Multicultural Citizenship*, 76.

28. Kymlicka, *Liberalism, Community and Culture*, 166.

29. For a similar analysis, see John Tomasi, "Kymlicka, Liberalism, and Respect for Cultural Minorities," *Ethics* 105 (April 1995): 580–603. My analysis differs from Tomasi's in that he does not question the viability of the notion of culture, whereas I do.

30. Allen Buchanan, "Liberalism and Group Rights," in *In Harm's Way*, ed. Jules Coleman (Cambridge: Cambridge University Press, 1994), 9.

31. Kymlicka, *Multicultural Citizenship*, 60.

32. John Rawls, *A Theory of Justice* (London: Oxford University Press, 1971), p. 178.

33. Kymlicka, *Liberalism, Community and Culture*, 146.

34. Jorge Noriega, "American Indian Education in the United States: Indoctrination for Subordination to Colonialism," in *The State of Native America*, ed. M. Annette Jaimes (Boston: South End Press, 1992), 375–83.

35. Kymlicka, *Liberalism, Community and Culture*, chap. 9.

36. Ibid., 190.

37. T. S. Eliot, *Notes Towards the Definition of Culture* (London: Faber, 1962), 93. I owe the reference to Chandran Kukathas, "Are There Any Cultural Rights?" in *The Rights of Minority Cultures*, ed. Will Kymlicka (Oxford: Oxford University Press, 1995), who is more concerned with culture's being interpreted as untainted from politics. He provides an excellent critique of Kymlicka's position but leaves the term *culture* largely unanalyzed.

38. For a discussion about adoption of the frozen rights theory, see *Simon v. The Queen* 23 C.C.C. (3d) 238.

39. This scheme offers an acknowledgment of the special *bumiputra* entitlements of historic rulers, who were Malay sultans, but it is not precisely the same as group rights of all Malays. However, it serves the purpose of illustrating one way of institutionalizing group claims.

40. I have discussed the Slovak case in detail in *Democracy and Social Injustice* (Lanham, Md.: Rowman and Littlefield, 1995), chap. 4.

41. Iris Marion Young, "Deferring Group Representation," in *Ethnicity and Group Rights*, ed. Ian Shapiro and Will Kymlicka (New York: New York University Press, 1996), 349–76. Young has tempered her previous enthusiasm for group representation.

42. See Kent Roach, "Remedies for Violations of Aboriginal Rights," *Manitoba Law Journal* 10 (1991) 499–543.

43. *Mahe v. Alberta* (1990) 68 D.L.R. (4th) 69 at 106 (S.C.C.).

44. Here I am not playing fast and loose with the idea of structure, a problem I previously found with Kymlicka's analysis. In the context of judicial remedies, structure, in the sense of institutional rules, has a fairly clear meaning.

45. *Marchand v. Simcoe County Board of Education* (1986) 55 O.R. (2d) 638 (H.C.).

46. For a more complete analysis, see my "Group Harm," *Journal of Social Philosophy* 26, no. 3 (winter 1995): 123–38.

Part II

Groups and Democratic Theory

Introduction

Groups and Democratic Theory

Larry May

What do members of a majority owe to various minority and disadvantaged groups in democratic societies? How sensitive should majorities be to the interests of minorities? The authors of the chapters in this part examine various ways to answer these questions. The chapters that follow embody five principles for the sensitive treatment of minority and disadvantaged groups in democratic societies. I will briefly discuss each of their views, explaining the general issues at stake, as well as some potential criticisms.

The five principles employed by the authors in articulating what minorities or disadvantaged groups are owed are these: (1) that minorities should have their voices heard; (2) that minorities should have their needs heeded; (3) that minorities should not have their basic liberties infringed; (4) that minorities should be treated according to justice as fairness; and (5) that minorities should be treated according to justice as reciprocity. While most of the authors hold some combination of these views, it is worth considering them in isolation in order to determine their strengths and weaknesses. These principles seemingly proceed along a continuum from least stringent to most stringent, and they are representative of most of the major philosophical work on what majorities owe to minorities and their members in a liberal, democratic society.

Steven Lee's chapter, "Democracy and the Problem of Persistent Minorities," discusses the principle that the minority's voice be heard. In the case of so-called persistent minorities, the problem is that a strong and coherent majority can run roughshod over any minority group simply by consistently outvoting the minority even concerning issues that are of core concern to that minority. Since at least the founding of the American Constitution, this problem has been recognized as the possible "tyranny of the majority." To avoid such a tyrannical possibility, and to be true to the goal of not arbitrarily excluding any group from democratic decision making, the minority must have a way to express its views and be heard by the majority, thereby giving the minority a chance of changing the views of the majority.[1]

The main problem with this view is that merely letting a minority have its voice be heard does little for the status of the minority if its voice is not taken seriously. The way in which a minority is regarded by a majority is key here. If the majority members disregard or discount the voice of the minority, because the majority holds stereotyped attitudes or blatantly racist beliefs, then letting the minority have its voice be heard will amount to little or nothing. There is no reason to think that a need that is voiced will indeed be given any uptake, and less reason still to think that it will be acted upon. What is important is that the voice of the minority be heard in an efficacious manner. This means that it be given uptake, that is, that it count in the deliberations of the majority, but not necessarily that it be acted upon. The problem, then, is that there are various forms that uptake can have, where it is often hard to distinguish legitimate uptake from lip service being paid to the expressed needs of a minority group.

Emily Gill's chapter, "Recognition, Identity, and the Accommodation of Differences: Groups in the Liberal State," explores the principle that a minority group have its needs and interests heeded, not merely its voice heard. To heed the needs or interests of a minority group, the minority group must be afforded widespread respect in a given society. Such respect will mean that the minority's voice is not merely heard and then disregarded or discounted. Rather, widespread respect for a minority will mean that significant, although not necessarily overriding, weight is attached to what is said by the minority members about their needs or interests. According to this view, the minority's interests should not be afforded overriding weight because the majority has to balance the demands of the minority with other important goals of the larger society.[2]

The main difficulty with this second position is that respecting minority members in this way does not necessarily mean that they will emerge from the shadow of the old problem of the possible tyranny of the majority. For the majority could decide, in every case, that satisfying the needs and interests of the minority demanded more than the society could bear. After all, as Gill reminds us, no "culture can celebrate or even tolerate all practices." The minority may demand that it be allowed to engage in practices that the majority finds abhorrent, that it be allowed to speak a separate language or even have a separate state for its people. The disruptions of the larger society would be massive if such demands were given overriding importance in the society. But it can also be said that if respecting a minority does not at least mean that certain core practices of that minority are tolerated, then the notion of respect is quite hollow, for when a majority acts intolerantly toward the core interests and practices of a minority, it is at least prima facie evident that the majority does not respect that minority. This is because most groups, especially minority groups, are constituted by certain core interests and practices, so failing to be tolerant toward those core interests and practices just is failing to be tolerant toward the minority group.

Joan McGregor's chapter, "Group Values and Liberal Democracy," explores the third position, that minorities not have their basic liberties infringed, with emphasis on the difference between mere preference satisfaction and protection of basic liberties. McGregor tries to identify a set of basic liberties or rights that must be afforded to any minority group for that group to be truly shown respect by the majority. The basic liberties or rights that must not be infringed are generally thought to include the rights to speak, to participate in the political process, and to conduct their affairs in a way they see fit, as long as they do not harm anyone else. These basic liberties and rights are not merely what the members of the minority group prefer, and are hence different from the minority group's core interests, but are thought to be necessary for the livelihood of any person or group.[3] By protecting these liberties, the majority in effect says that there are some things they will refrain from doing to the minority to show that they are acting in a respectful way toward the members of the minority.

There is an interesting question about whether it is better to grant to minorities what the majority members believe to be the minority's basic liberties and rights, or whether it is better merely to let the minority pursue whatever its strongest expressed preferences are. Indeed, some theorists would deny that we can make sense of the notion of basic liberties and rights independently of what particular people prefer at any given time. But this move is not fully plausible, for it ignores the many commonalities among peoples over time and ignores important normative arguments that have been advanced to show that respecting people as equals demands a minimum level of protection of liberties.

The most problematic case is of a minority group that has a preference for renouncing a basic liberty in exchange for something else preferred more strongly, such as in the case of American Indians who agreed to give up certain basic liberties in exchange for the guarantee of religious or cultural autonomy on their tribal reservations. How should these preferences be treated by the majority? One of the problems here is that a majority may have stereotyped views of what is preferred by the minority and may overestimate what that minority cares about. Alternatively, the majority may feel overprotective of the minority because of a perception that the minority members are inferior in reasoning capacities or some other important basis of reaching decisions for themselves. The emphasis on basic liberties and rights, rather than on preferences, may make headway in overcoming the biases that could influence how majorities view minority liberties. For instance, both what was taken from the American Indians and also what conditions were established for their tribal autonomy reflected stereotyped views of Indians that meant that they were not treated as fully rational human beings. The main problem with the third position (protecting basic liberties or rights) is that it may not go far enough; something more may be owed to minority groups in addition to protecting minority liberties that are basic.

Rex Martin's chapter, "Rights, Democracy, and Distribution: Economic Justice," illustrates the fourth position as it tries to overcome the difficulty of the third position by proposing that minorities should be treated according to the principle of distributive justice understood in terms of justice as fairness. Consider one disadvantaged group, the poor. In trying to determine what the majority owes to this disadvantaged group, one cannot rely only on what are the basic liberties or rights of this group, since it is highly controversial that anyone has a basic right to a particular level of economic well-being. Yet it is precisely by virtue of having a (much) lower economic status than the majority in a society that some economically disadvantaged groups, like the poor, are disadvantaged. If such disadvantaged groups are owed anything by the majority, it is not by virtue of having been denied basic liberties or rights.[4]

What some economically disadvantaged groups, like the poor, are owed, if they are owed anything, is best captured by appealing to a principle of distributive justice that goes beyond the protection of basic liberties and rights. One way to formulate a principle of distributive justice that goes beyond mere protection of basic liberties or rights is as follows: no group should be made worse off so that another group can benefit. According to this principle, or variations on it, distributive justice requires a certain kind of fairness where no group is forced to pay for benefits that accrue only to others. Such a principle states a claim to a relative distribution of beneficial treatment that cannot be understood independently of the specifics of particular societies. It is for this reason that the principle is different from one that appeals to basic rights or liberties, since the latter is meant to tell us how to treat one another regardless of the differences among groups.

The principle of justice as fairness is best seen within the context of a contractarian model of moral and political obligation. What is fair is what would be accepted by everyone who is affected by a certain policy. This preserves an egalitarian dimension at the root of the idea of distributive justice in that each person, in effect, can veto a particular policy, and no one else can override this veto. But since the "contract" is between people who "would" accept, rather than those who "do" accept, a given policy, it is not likely that a minority group would get more than a decent minimum of economic goods. Most of what comes out of this principle of fairness will involve negative liberties and rights, and it is for this reason that some have wondered whether such a fairness principle is sufficient for giving to minorities what they are owed.

Patricia Smith's chapter, "Duties of Group Membership: Justice as Reciprocity and Liberal Democratic Institutions," illustrates the final principle, justice as reciprocity. This principle does not proceed from what people would agree to but rather starts from what obligations people have by virtue of being in relationships where they must cooperate with each other to accomplish common goals.[5] It is odd to start by assuming that people actually could or would consent or not consent to existing social arrangements, for in most cases we are simply thrust into those arrangements. Instead, we should start by considering what is owed to people who are already in ongoing relationships that provide mutual benefit for each other.

According to this fifth view, what majorities owe minorities will have to do with the contributions made by both minority members and majority members to the ongoing practices that produce benefit in their societies. What one group owes another is to be based on the contributions made by each. Out of such mutuality is supposed to flow a trust that will be productive of increased social interaction and stability. Such trust will be the basis for mutual aid, not mere protection from possible harm. Reciprocity is one of the main bases for community, and it supports the notion that what groups owe each other is based on membership within a given community. Specifically, what is owed is what other members deserve based on their roles and contributions in the larger ongoing activities of the society in which both minority and majority groups live.

The principle of justice as reciprocity seems to demand the most from majorities in their treatment of minorities; but this is somewhat illusory. For if it is judged that minority members have not contributed much to the common endeavors of the society, then it will turn out that these minorities are not owed much either. And without some sense of basic rights or a negative moral minimum to fall back on, "unproductive" or "uncooperative" minorities may fail to get even basic respect by the members of the majority group(s). Think of how the current debate about welfare is proceeding. Those members of the nonworking poor who have been granted Medicaid, Aid to Families with Dependent Children, or other forms of welfare are castigated for being a drain on the resources of the society. They are in effect being told: until you make a contribution to the society, that society owes you nothing. Yet it may be that there simply are no jobs that these people could secure; and it is surely true that the children who benefit most from welfare programs are not yet in a position to have made such a contribution. Considerations such as these should lead us to wonder whether the principle of justice as reciprocity really is indeed more stringent than the other principles we have considered.

In democracies, majority groups owe minority groups more than that the minority be merely heard or even heeded. There is no intrinsic basis for valuing a group, and hence no intrinsic value in having more than one social group in a society. Yet once there is more than one group, then in democracies no group should be able to silence or tyrannize another group, thereby excluding that group from the processes of discussion, debate, and voting. In democratic societies the interests and preferences of minority groups should be given uptake as a sign that they are respected participants in these democratic processes. Most especially, the basic rights and liberties of the minority members need protection as a sign of this respect.

In those societies where a minority group has been the subject of historically disadvantaged treatment, more is owed than mere respect of preferences or interests. Where historical disadvantage has occurred, then justice enters the picture for groups just as it does for individuals. As with individuals, groups have obligations and are owed certain things, such as reparations, due to various injustices. The best way to conceptualize the demands of justice between groups is with an amalgamation of the concepts of fairness and reciprocity. We rely on the concept of fairness when one group has done harm to another; and we rely on the concept of reciprocity when there are inequalities between groups that adversely affect their cooperative relations.

To be morally sensitive to one another, groups need to do more than merely follow various principles as conceptual guides, although doing so is indeed important for being morally sensitive. In addition, groups must care about each other. Given the metaphysically problematic nature of groups, groups need not (indeed, probably cannot) have the same kind of care toward each other that individuals need to have in order to be morally sensitive. Majority groups owe minority groups a certain amount of sensitivity to the interests and needs of that minority or disadvantaged group. This is especially true when the majority group is responsible for the plight of the minority, although, as we have seen, even where this is not true there is sometimes still a sufficient basis for demanding that majorities be sensitive to minorities.

Notes

1. See Thomas Christiano, *The Rule of the Many* (Boulder, Colo.: Westview Press, 1996).

2. See Will Kymlicka, *Multicultural Citizenship: A Liberal Theory of Minority Rights* (Oxford: Clarendon Press, 1995).

3. See Elizabeth Anderson, *Value in Ethics and Economics* (Cambridge, Mass.: Harvard University Press, 1993).

4. See Lawrence C. Becker, *Reciprocity* (New York: Routledge and Kegan Paul, 1986).

5. On this point, see Hugh LaFollette and Larry May, "Suffer the Little Children," in *World Hunger and Morality*, 2d ed., ed. W. Aiken and Hugh LaFollette (Upper Saddle River, N.J.: Prentice-Hall, 1996).

Chapter 6

Democracy and the Problem
of Persistent Minorities

Steven Lee

In a democracy, there are two kinds of groups: groups *in* the democracy and
groups *of* the democracy, we might say. The first kind, groups in democracy,
are groups that have their foundation outside government, often in civil
society. Given the heterogeneity of any human society, a society with a
democratic government is composed of a variety of groups that exist at least
partly independently of the political operations of the government. These
groups, often referred to, in the context of democratic governance, as *inter-*
est groups, include various ethnic, racial, and economic-class groups, as well
as groups united, as the label suggests, simply by a common interest. What
members of these groups have in common are characteristics they have
independently of their participation in the political process. While it is
often as a result of their members' participation in the political process that
such groups are organized and self-conscious, the basis of the groupings is
not itself a function of the governing process. To take an example, the
Sierra Club, though partly a creature of the political process, is based on a
characteristic its members share independently of that process, namely, an
interest in the environment.

Groups of the second kind, groups of democracy, are those wholly
brought into being by the operations of democratic governance, those
whose membership is determined by the rules of the political system. The
most important of these groups are the majorities and minorities created
through the voting process. Also, in the case of representative democracy,
there are often, as in the United States and its federal subdivisions, groups
defined by geographic voting districts. I will refer to groups of the second
kind as *political groups*, and those of the first kind as *social groups*. While
social groups, as indicated, often have a political dimension, they are not
purely political, as are political groups such as voting majorities and

124

minorities. The distinction between these two kinds of groups is not completely sharp. For example, political parties, at least those without a strong ideological base, may be an intermediate case. But the distinction is clear enough to work with.

My thesis is that the relation between these two kinds of groups may create a problem for the theory of democracy. My intention in this chapter is primarily to explain what that problem is; a solution to the problem is a more difficult matter. The name often given to it is the *problem of persistent minorities*. The general situation out of which it arises is that in a majoritarian democracy, some individuals may constantly be in the voting minority and, as a result, never have a real opportunity, through their votes, to influence policy. But not all cases in which individuals are constantly in the voting minority turn out to be problematic for democratic theory. The problem of persistent minorities refers at most to a subclass of such cases. By thinking in terms of the distinction between social and political groups, we can come to understand both when this situation is problematic and why it may be problematic. I will begin by considering why the situation may be problematic, later turning to the question of when it is problematic.

I

A situation that arises through the operations of democracy will be problematic for the theory of democracy if situations of that sort are defective in terms of the moral principles by which democracy is justified. How is democracy justified? Most of the justificatory theories for democracy that have been proposed fall into two categories: theories that regard democracy as instrumentally justifiable by the good results of its practice in a society and theories that regard democracy as intrinsically justifiable by its embodiment of a fundamental principle of equality.

Can instrumentalist theories explain why individuals' constant membership in a voting minority may be problematic? Consider, briefly, three prominent instrumentalist theories: first, one that sees democratic governance as the way to maximize satisfactions in a population; second, one that sees democracy as the best way to arrive at good governmental policy; and third, one that regards democracy as the best means to achieve social and political stability. It seems that proponents of the first two theories would not be troubled by a situation in which individuals were constantly in the voting minority. Maximization theories do not care who has satisfactions, so long as they are maximized, so some individuals constantly having lesser satisfactions out of the political process is no problem. In the case of best-policy theories, it seems that those who, for whatever reason, are poor choosers of policy should constantly be in the minority, so some individuals being constantly in the minority would be expected by, not incompatible with, the theory. In regard to the third kind of instrumentalist theory, Lani Guinier argues that "political stability depends on the perception that the system is fair to induce losers to continue to work within the system rather than to try to overthrow it."[1] So, those constantly in the voting minority might not regard the system as fair, and hence threaten stability. But such arguments depend on a variety of empirical assumptions and cannot be taken as conclusive.

Consider now the intrinsic justification for democracy based on its embodiment of a principle of equality. The idea of equality inherent in democracy is often represented by the phrase "one person, one vote," but we need to look deeper to understand what the basis of democratic equality is. The principle of equality justifying democracy is that the lives of all individuals should be treated as of equal importance. This is often expressed by a quotation from Thomas Rainsborough: "The poorest he that is in England has a life to live as the greatest he."[2] A society's political system should embody this principle. The justification of democracy is that it does embody this principle, specifically in the form the equal consideration of interests. If the lives of all individuals should be treated as of equal importance, and government is a scheme for the promotion of its members' interests, then government ought to be organized under a principle that accords equal consideration to each member's interests. "Each person has an equally important life to live, so there is a strong presumption in favor of his or her interests being given equal consideration." Democracy embodies this idea because "it gives each person the same chance as every other to affect the outcome."[3] Peter Jones observes, "To allow the will of the minority to prevail would be to give greater weight to the vote of each member of the minority than to the vote of each member of the majority, thus violating political equality."[4] The principle of equal consideration of interests is not satisfied in virtue of certain outcomes, such as equality of welfare, though outcomes may be relevant to assessing whether it has been satisfied.[5] Since democracy is a decision-making procedure, the equality embodied in democracy is an equality in the process of decision making, and as such it is an equality among individuals in the decision-making resources they may command in pursuit of their interests.[6] The equality embodied in democracy is an equality of resources rather than an equality of welfare. The principle of equal consideration of interests requires that all individuals have an equal opportunity in the communal decision-making process to promote their own interests.

What are the implications of this idea of equality for the situation in which individuals are constantly in the voting minority? We should ask, with Jones, whether such individuals "should regard their position as unfair or merely unfortunate."[7] The question is whether those who are constantly in the voting minority can be said to be participating in a political system that considers their interests equally. When what is being considered is a single vote on a single issue, in isolation from other votes, it is indeed always fair to give the decision to the majority, for to give the decision to the minority, as we have seen, would be treating the votes, hence the interests, of the minority as of greater value than those of the majority. But individuals who are constantly in the minority are in the minority on a series of votes, and it is this fact that may introduce an inequality in the consideration of their interests. An aggregation of votes may possess a property, being unfair to the minority, that is not possessed by any one of those votes considered by itself. This is where the phrase "one person, one vote" may be an inadequate representation of the equality that should be embodied in democracy. In the context of a series of votes, "one person, one vote" may represent an inadequate notion of equality in the same way that Bentham's notion of equality, that each should count for one and no more than one, may be inadequate.[8] Bentham's notion is inadequate, on a deontological critique, because, while ostensibly considering the interests of each equally, it allows one's interests to be completely subordinated to those of others, given that the others are more numerous. Likewise, if one is constantly in the voting minority, "one person, one vote" allows that person's interests to be completely submerged, in the sense that they are never determinative of policy.

The inequality involved in "one person, one vote" is, as Lani Guinier points out, analogous to that involved when individuals participating in a common practice ignore the principle of "taking turns."[9] Imagine a group of children playing a series of games in the days of summer vacation. If a bare majority of those children always prefer baseball to soccer, and the rest always prefer soccer to baseball, the majoritarian decision procedure of "one person, one vote" would determine that the group would always play baseball and never play soccer. In such a situation, those preferring soccer could legitimately complain that the decision procedure had not been fair to them, and that the fair thing to do would be to play soccer at least some of the time. This sort of complaint could not legitimately arise if the children were deciding for a single game. But when those preferring soccer constantly lose the vote, they may legitimately complain that they have been treated unfairly, that their interests have not been equally considered.

This line of reasoning may be criticized on the ground that it misunderstands what equal consideration of interests amounts to. One version of this criticism is suggested by Charles Beitz.[10] In discussing certain distortions that may arise in representative legislatures, distortions related to the problem of persistent minorities, he asserts that they are not inconsistent with equality when this is understood as each voter having "an equal a priori probability of influencing any particular legislative choice." The assumption involved in this understanding is that each voter "is equally likely to take any available position" on the vote in question.[11] In other words, the equality here is an equality of *potential influence* rather than of *actual influence*. Under "one person, one vote," individuals who are constantly in the voting minority do indeed have an equality of potential influence, in the sense that, independent of knowledge of the constellation of interests among voters, they would be seen as as likely to cast the deciding vote as anyone else. But, given the particular constellation of interests among voters that results in certain individuals being constantly in the voting minority, the actual influence of those individuals is clearly not equal. The question, then, is whether the notion of equal consideration of interests is better understood as involving the notion of merely potential influence or that of actual influence. Here it seems that the analogy with Bentham's notion of equality is helpful. Bentham's notion provides a potential equality among people in the sense that it guarantees that in the abstract all individuals' interests will be taken into account in the utilitarian calculus. But its shortcoming is that in actuality it is consistent with some individuals becoming means to the benefit of others. To avoid a similar shortcoming, the principle of equal consideration of interests should be interpreted so that it ensures actual, not merely potential, influence in the determination of policy.

Thus, the answer to the question of whether individuals constantly in the voting minority should regard their situation as merely unfortunate or as unfair is that, in at least some cases, they should regard it as unfair. Those who are constantly members of a voting minority are members of a social group, at least in virtue of their sharing the same perspective on the issues that the voting is about. Consequently, on at least some occasions in which political groups, specifically, voting minorities, are identical with social groups, there is an unfairness in democratic procedure, a failure of democracy to satisfy the principle of equality in terms of which it is justified. Persistent minorities thus pose a problem for democratic theory. The principle of equal consideration of interests seems to require that we move beyond the idea of equality in decision-making resources, at least as this is embodied in the phrase "one person, one vote."[12]

The problem of persistent minorities sometimes becomes the perennial concern about the tyranny of the majority, for it is when voting majorities and minorities are fixed by the fact that some individuals are constantly in the minority that the majorities have an opportunity to tyrannize.[13] If the memberships of voting majorities and minorities were in constant flux, as Madison thought they would be, then neither persistent minorities nor majority tyranny arises as a problem for democratic theory. But if Madison's expectations are wrong, the problem may be with us. It is important to note, by the way, that this problem is not solved (though it is made less severe) by the existence of a set of constitutionally guaranteed rights, often called *minority rights*, that can trump majority decisions, for such rights represent, and hence guarantee, the consideration of only a portion of individuals' interests. Individuals also have interests in the distribution of resources and in the nature and extent of governmental intervention to solve public-goods problems, issues decided by majority rule even when civil and political rights are respected. These interests may not be equally considered for members of voting minorities when those minorities are persistent.

II

Now the second question. Given the why, we must investigate the when. Given that persistent minorities may be a problem for democracy, we need to know under what circumstances they are in fact a problem. Here is where my thesis becomes more modest. In most cases the existence of persistent voting minorities does not raise problems for democratic theory. The reason is that voting is not the only dimension of democratic decision making or the only activity through which individuals participate in the democratic process, and hence it is not the only activity in terms of which to judge whether the democratic process is satisfying the principle of equal consideration of interests.

Consider again the Sierra Club. While environmentalists are now often in the voting majority in regard to environmental issues and candidates, for a long time this was not the case. Prior to 1970, environmentalists were in the political wilderness. During that time, when they had a persistent minority status, was the political system treating them unfairly, not giving their interests equal consideration? Our intuitive answer is no. The reason is that during their time in the political wilderness, environmentalists were allowed to engage in the activity of educating the public and seeking to build a pro-environment political coalition. (That activity, by the way, eventually brought them to majority status, but it is not this fact that leads us to regard their treatment prior to 1970 as not unfair; members of the Socialist Workers Party may never achieve majority status, but still we do not view their treatment as unfair.) During their time in the political wilderness, groups like the Sierra Club doubtless saw their prime task not as voting for pro-environment issues and candidates, since they recognized their persistent minority status, but as education and coalition building. Because the democratic system allowed them to engage in these activities, because their being allowed to do so was seen as an inherent aspect of the democratic system, the system treated them fairly, giving equal consideration to their interests, despite their persistent minority status. Prior to 1970, the Sierra Club had actual influence through its public educational and coalition-building activity, even while its influence through voting was merely potential.

In short, what allows us to say that members of the Sierra Club were given equal consideration, despite their persistent minority status, was their ability to participate in the public debate. The status of a social group as a persistent minority provides only a prima facie case that its members are not being afforded equal consideration, a case that can be successfully rebutted by its being shown that the group was allowed to participate in the public debate. In accord with this line of thought, Thomas Christiano distinguishes between two dimensions of the democratic process, the adversarial dimension, which involves voting, and the deliberative dimension, which involves public discussion and debate.[14] The equality of decision-making resources derived from the principle of equal consideration of interests is an equal right of participation in both of these dimensions. Moreover, these two dimensions must be understood as interrelated. The interests or preferences of individuals should be seen not as fixed but as amenable to change through activities in the deliberative dimension. Thus, Christiano writes, "It is important for [individuals] to reflect critically on and improve their preferences so as to have a sophisticated appreciation of their interests and ideals," and it is in the deliberative dimension where this happens, where "beliefs and convictions are formed, changed, elaborated, and given final articulation."[15] This is why individuals may be members of a persistent minority without their being treated unfairly. Their interests are being given equal consideration if they have the opportunity to participate in the public debate, because through that debate voters' perception of their interests can change so that a voting minority can become a voting majority. Through participation in the public debate, through efforts to educate other voters, through coalition building, the influence of members of persistent minorities can be real, not merely potential, because an avenue is provided by which they can achieve majority status.

This line of argument applies most clearly when the issue up for public discussion and voting is one that is more a matter of judgment than of preference, because it is matters of judgment to which public debate has a direct implication. But it applies as well when the issues are more matters of preference, because of the indirect effect public debate can have on preferences. Consider again environmental issues. Many specific environmental issues seem to be more matters of judgment, for example, the effect of the concentration of greenhouse gases on human society. Here the environmentalists' empirical case about the negative impact of global warming can lead directly to a change in voters' perceptions of their interests away from their initial preference for cheap energy. But other environmental issues seem more a matter of preference, for example, the extent to which wilderness should be preserved.

Consider another example of this sort suggested by Peter Jones.[16] Residents of a street vote on three aspects of the built environment of their neighborhood: asphalt or paved sidewalks; gas lighting or electric lighting; and planting or not planting trees. The "economizers," two-thirds of the population, vote in each case for the cheaper, less attractive alternative, while the "aesthetes," one-third of the population, vote in each case for the more expensive, more attractive alternative. Jones uses this example to argue that persistent minorities present a problem for the democratic principle of equality. But this ignores the role of the deliberative dimension: the aesthetes have an opportunity to persuade the economizers to see things their way. Jones responds that the divide in question is not one where the opposing sides would be open to mutual persuasion.[17] This suggests that he views the issue as one of mere preference, involving no matter of judgment that could lead to a change in preferences. But there are plenty of matters of judgment that the aesthetes could raise in arguing for their choice, even if these reasons are not their main reasons for favoring the policies. For example, trees reduce air-conditioning costs, and paved sidewalks and gas lighting raise property values. Moreover, preferences can be educated through discussion in a variety of ways that blur the sharp dichotomy between preferences and judgments.

At this point, the tendency of the argument seems to leave little room for the original thesis that persistent minorities are a problem for democratic theory. But this perception is misleading. The implication of the role of the deliberative dimension is that when social groups are persistent minorities, their members are being treated with equal consideration so long as they have a real opportunity to persuade members of the majority to vote their way, and that they often have such an opportunity even when the issue in question is primarily a matter of preference. But there are some cases where a majority's perception of its interests or its preferences is not amenable to change in the arena of public debate. If there are social groups that are persistent minorities in such cases, the prima facie case for their members not being afforded equal consideration would not be successfully rebutted by the argument that they have the opportunity to make a case for their interests in the public arena, because, by our hypothesis about the nature of the majority's preferences, this opportunity provides the minority with no real influence on policy choices. So the question of whether the existence of persistent minorities poses a problem for democratic theory turns on the question of whether there are cases where persistent minorities face majorities whose members' attitudes are such as to make their perceptions of their interests, in regard to the matter on which the majority and minority differ, immune to change by public debate. Unfortunately, there are sometimes such cases. They occur when the attitudes of the majority are a function of implacable prejudice, as is the case, for example, with racist attitudes.

Consider a distinction between two different kinds of social groups, namely, interest groups and identity groups. While interest groups often come together "around some temporary unifying concern," identity groups are "linked by a common culture, a common experience, a common language," and feel joined by a common experience of "oppression and exclusion." Members of identity groups are typically linked, Anne Phillips asserts, by "a past experience of being excluded."[18] When a social group is an identity group, it frequently has been subject over a long stretch of time to exclusion by other social groups, and one of the forms this persistent exclusion takes in a democracy is the group's persistent status as a voting minority. Moreover, it is a sad but familiar truth that the basis of the group's exclusion is often prejudice founded on the deeply rooted attitudes of other social groups (groups constituting a persistent voting majority) that are largely unamenable to alteration by public discussion. In the case of interest groups, as we have seen, the deliberative dimension of democracy shows that the existence of persistent minorities need not be a problem for democratic theory. But at least sometimes in the case of identity groups, when attitudes that form the basis for the majority's voting behavior are unamenable to alternation by public discussion, the deliberative dimension of democracy becomes moribund, and the prima facie case that persistent minorities represent a failure of equal consideration is unrebutted. Thus, when the attitudes of a voting majority are based on deep-seated prejudice, the members of the social group, the identity group, against whom those attitudes are directed, when that group is a persistent minority, are not being treated with equal consideration. So, when a social group is also a persistent voting minority under these conditions, there is a problem for democratic theory.

The extent to which the voting behavior of a majority is determined by prejudicial attitudes toward members of the minority is often difficult to determine and is, of course, a matter of degree. So there is a vigorous debate about the extent to which, for example, racism in the United States causes the democratic system's apparent lack of attention to the interests of African-Americans. But it seems clear that a significant level of racism exists in American society, and to the extent that it does, the persistent voting minority that is the result of this racism pose a fundamental problem for democratic theory. The underlying question is whether democracy is morally compatible with the existence in a society of prejudicial attitudes like racism, for when such attitudes cause persistent voting minorities, the political system has lost the moral justification, its ability to provide equal consideration for the interests of all.[19] Given the demise of the Soviet Union and other global political trends, the question of the material and cultural conditions for democracy has been much discussed. But equally worthy of attention is the question one aspect of which I have tried to raise in this chapter: What are the moral conditions of democracy? Can a morally justifiable form of democracy be practiced in societies, such as the United States, in which majorities allow deep-seated prejudices against minorities to determine their voting behavior?

III

Many would find in this last question a challenge to institutional design and seek in institutional design a solution to the problem that persistent minorities pose for democracy. The task is to design a form of democracy, going beyond "one person, one vote," that provides equal consideration for the interests of all, even members of minorities subject to prejudicial attitudes on the part of majorities. I can speak on solutions only briefly. In representative democracy, members of persistent minorities are unable to elect representatives who would promote their interests. Members of an identity group may be spread through the general population in such a way that they do not constitute a majority in any legislative district, so that, if the majority were strongly prejudiced against the interests of the group, candidates representing those interests (who would often be themselves members of the group) would never win an election, so that the legislature would be composed of no one who would represent those interests. One institutional solution to this problem is to draw district lines so as to create districts in which members of the identity group constitute a majority, and indeed, until recent Supreme Court decisions, this has been a path taken by the federal government in fulfillment of Section 2 of the Voting Rights Act, as amended in 1982. The logical extension of this solution would be the adoption of a system of proportional representation, which would allow social groups to be represented in the legislature roughly in proportion to their numbers in the general population. The legislature would then be "a replica of the realm."

But this cannot be the whole solution, for it simply allows the whole problem to be replicated at the legislative level, where the persistent minority status of the identity group will be embodied in that group's representatives being persistently in the legislative minority. Can the problem be solved at the legislative level? Guinier has labeled attention to the problem at this level as a "third-generation" civil rights concern, requiring efforts "to police the legislative voting rules," and she has made some proposals. These include proposals for cumulative voting, where each person has multiple votes, and for supermajority voting.[20] Supermajority voting, however, violates the principle of equal consideration, since it treats the votes of members of the (simple) minority, in their ability to veto measures approved of by a (simple) majority, as of greater importance than those of that majority. But a more interesting observation about Guinier's proposals concerns the direction in which she argues they tend, namely, toward a "restructuring [of] the legislative decisionmaking process on the model of jury deliberation," that is, toward a consensus model rather than an adversarial model of decision making.[21] If she is right in this, it may be not be possible to solve the problem of persistent minorities without radically restructuring democracy away from majoritarianism and toward consensus decision making, a model of democracy that some feminists and others have advocated on different grounds. But this may convert our difficulties from the moral problem I have been discussing to a problem of political feasibility: if there are deep-seated prejudices in a society, unamenable to alternation through the deliberative dimension of democracy, there is little reason to think that consensus can be achieved.

Notes

1. Lani Guinier, *The Tyranny of the Majority* (New York: Free Press, 1994), 9.

2. Quoted in Thomas Christiano, *The Rule of the Many* (Boulder, Colo.: Westview Press, 1996), 53.

3. Ibid., 54, 55.

4. Peter Jones, "Political Equality and Majority Rule," in *Democracy: Theory and Practice*, ed. John Arthur (Belmont, Calif.: Wadsworth, 1992), 211.

5. Indeed, if the principle of equal consideration of interests were understood as applying to outcomes, it is not even clear that it would justify democracy, as opposed to some nondemocratic form of government, for ordinary people may not be the best judges of their own interests.

6. Christiano, *Rule of the Many*, 56–71.

7. Jones, "Political Equality," 209.

8. Ibid., 216.

9. Guinier, *Tyranny of the Majority*, 2ff.

10. Charles Beitz, "Procedural Equality in Democratic Theory: A Preliminary Inquiry," in *Liberal Democracy*, Nomos XXV, ed. J. Roland Pennock and John Chapman (New York: New York University Press, 1983), 72–74.

11. Ibid., 89 n. 8.

12. Thomas Christiano, "Democratic Equality and the Problem of Persistent Minorities," *Philosophical Papers* 23, no. 3 (1994): 186–89.

13. Thomas Christiano distinguishes between the problem of persistent minorities and the problem of the tyranny of the majority, which makes clear that the problem of

persistent minorities can arise even when the persistent majority does not use its power to tyrannize over the minority. "Democratic Equality and the Problem of Persistent Minorities," 174. In this regard, see my comments at the end of the text paragraph.

14. Christiano, *Rule of the Many*, chap. 2.

15. Ibid., 48, 87.

16. Jones, "Political Equality," 215.

17. Ibid., 217.

18. Anne Phillips, *Democracy and Difference* (University Park: Pennsylvania State University Press, 1993), 146–47.

19. There are other kinds of attitudes besides prejudice that are unamenable to change through public debate and that affect voting behavior so as to create persistent minorities, such as occur, for example, in societies deeply divided along religious lines. The argument in this chapter would apply in these cases as well. But it seems as a matter of practice that such attitudes are almost always accompanied by prejudice as well.

20. Guinier, *Tyranny of the Majority*, 8, 14–17.

21. Ibid., 8, 106–9.

Chapter 7

Group Values and Liberal Democracy

Joan L. McGregor

There is much discussion today about different kinds of groups and about their roles and function in democracy. Some of these discussions focus on the question of what constitutes a group. Some groups, for instance, racial minorities, are made up of members none of whom choose to possess the defining characteristic of that group.[1] Group membership, then, is involuntary. Other groups are to varying degrees voluntary, some formed around shared ideals or conceptions of good. For instance, if one was raised a Baptist, then one did not choose to be Baptist but found oneself in a Baptist environment. Nevertheless, if one remains in the church as an adult, then one has voluntarily chosen to be a member of that group. There are some associations or groups—for example, the National Rifle Association or the Sierra Club—that one is not brought up in, and hence we might say they are more voluntary, since one adopts or joins them as an adult. Nothing for the purposes of this chapter hinges on what type of group I am discussing. I am interested in thinking through how groups' interests get expressed in the democratic process and what role groups play in the democratic process. My intention is that this exploration have relevance to many kinds of groups, particularly groups that share ideals or goals for society. I want to know how those groups function within a liberal democracy. In this discussion environmental groups will function as a token of a particular type of group found within democratic institutions. How, then, should liberal democracies handle the values advocated for legislation from groups such as environmentalists? Environmental legislation appeals to, what environmentalists will argue, are shared public values about the following issues: what kind of world we want to live in, what kind of world we want to leave for future generations, what kind of people we want to be, and what we think is of intrinsic value. Policies about air and water quality, natural resources, species and their habitats, and wilderness rely upon shared public values.

137

What I am interested in knowing is whether a liberal democracy can consistently enact and impose these environmental rules and policies. Some environmental legislation fits easily into the liberal framework because that legislation fits squarely within the cornerstone of liberalism—the harm principle. Liberals are eager to support legislation with the end of preventing harm to others. But whether a liberal democracy can support a more robust environmental agenda, going beyond the prevention of harm to present or even future generations, is in dispute. My worry is that, since many theorists conceptualize democracy simply as the aggregation of the existing unexamined preferences of individuals, ideals for the society will unlikely result from such a process. These same theorists rely on market choices to reveal the true preferences of individuals. Out of that cataloging of preferences, it seems unlikely that we would arrive at a rich environmental agenda, or get to other shared goals as a society. Another worry comes from the nature of liberalism. There may be even more difficulty for liberals to support an environmental agenda, since most liberals argue that the state must be neutral among competing conceptions of the good. Given that the advancement of environmental goals involves a conception of the good, it may then be antithetical to that foundational principle of liberalism.

It is because of some of the prevalent models of democracy and liberalism that the worries about groups' interests have arisen. The idea that conceptions of the good have no place in legislation in a liberal democracy closes the door on the kind of political action for groups with a conception of the good. The notion that what democracies do is sum up the preferences of individuals and express them as a social choice denies the relevance of groups' ideals and the role of deliberation, discussion, and compromise. These conceptions of liberalism and democracy make it seem unlikely that ideals for the society will emerge from the process or that those ideals, even if they did emerge, would be legitimate. Given the constraints on length, I can only briefly explore some of these issues. I am, as I said at the outset, mainly interested in how a liberal democracy can enact and enforce a group's conception of the good for society.

Democracy as Satisfying the Preferences of the People

The slogan about democracy is that it is government "of the people, by the people, and for the people." Many theorists have argued that democracy is special because it is a form of government whereby the people, or at least the majority of the people, get what they want. The role and purpose of government are to promote the welfare of the people, and the best way to do that, so the argument goes, is to aggregate their preferences into a social choice. Democracy is justified on instrumental grounds as having the best consequences because it maximizes social welfare. The results of democracy reflect the preferences of the majority or what sometimes is referred to as the will of the people.[2]

For many theorists, the conception of democracy as satisfying existing preferences is the only rationally defensible one.[3] If democracy is justified because it maximizes social welfare, then how is it best to determine what is social welfare? The best way to do this, it is argued, is to aggregate the preferences of individuals, and the legislation that arises out of this process is the "winner." This theory is exceptionally influential; many forms of utilitarianism, some versions of Paretian efficiency, politics as bargaining theory, welfare economics, public choice theory, and some forms of libertarianism all subscribe to this view. What the democratic process is about is aggregating individual preferences into a societal preference or choice. The theory assumes that individuals know their own welfare and that their preferences are an indication of their welfare; hence, the aggregation of individuals' preferences is the social welfare. Social welfare determined by aggregating individuals' preferences gained momentum with the perceived difficulties of making interpersonal comparisons of utility. The stumbling block to making interpersonal utility comparisons throws into question the possibility of saying that some particular state of affairs is better for one person over another state of affairs for another person. To make those comparisons, we would have to be able to compare one person's welfare or happiness with another person's welfare or happiness. Many have argued that it is impossible to make such comparisons. Another general worry for political theory is the epistemological one of knowing whether the individual's preferences are in fact in the individual's true welfare. On the view considered here, sometimes referred to as *subjective welfarism*,[4] the term *welfare* just means satisfaction of preferences, thereby avoiding the epistemological problems. No objective determination of "true" welfare need be made by the government. Having the government make such decisions raises its own dangers.

Imported from economics, we get the assumption that welfare is based upon satisfying the existing preferences of individuals. Economists determine what individuals prefer by what individuals choose in the market—

in other words, by noting what they are willing to pay for. The strengths or intensities of the preferences are determined by how much individuals are willing to pay for something. A further assumption of most economists is that agents are self-interested (*homo economicus*); in other words, they are motivated by maximizing their own expected utility. Their preferences are for their own private interests rather than public ones. The role of the state is to maximize the welfare of the citizens, and if you assume that individuals' preferences are for their own private interests, then the social welfare function will reflect that. The state is to satisfy the preferences that agents happen to have rather than shaping the preferences along the lines of some ideal or conception of the good. The subjective welfarist model does not require that the preferences which get counted satisfy some minimal constraints such as, for example, deliberation. Value, for many theorists who subscribe to this view, just *is* satisfying preferences. That the assessment or evaluation of preferences involves illegitimate judgments about the conceptions of the good or worse is utterly incoherent. And, so the argument goes, it is not the job of the state to make those judgments. Preference satisfaction is the sine qua non of democracy.

This model of the democratic state maps easily upon the assumptions of value used by many economists that underlie the cost-benefit or efficiency criterion in public policy. In designing public policy, government need only refer to cost-benefit analysis and it will arrive at the outcome that will maximize welfare. Government is mimicking the outcomes that could have been arrived at in the market (under ideal conditions). The normative assumption, on this model, is that the personal wants of the individuals in the society should guide the use of resources in production, distribution, and exchange.[5] Market choices are treated as normative for public policy. Rational choice for society is the one that maximizes value, and value is defined in terms of individual preferences as exemplified by their willingness to pay. Many of the theories that adopt this model suppose that individuals in their market roles express "all or the most important motivations and attitudes they have, and perhaps even express the fundamental truth about human nature."[6] And thus these theories entail the idea that market norms are appropriate for all social contexts, including democracy. Cost-benefit analysis is seen as a perfect example of giving people what they desire, what they truly value. Adherents thus argue that the use of cost-benefit analysis for making social policy enables democratic political institutions to be more responsive to citizens' values. This view of democracy sees social regulations based upon the welfare of the individual to be the major desideratum of public policy.

Liberalism and Democracy

What is implied by liberalism for the structure of government is first the limitation of government by stringent rules. Liberal government must be limited government, since all strands within the liberal tradition confer upon persons rights or claims in justice that the government must acknowledge and respect and that, indeed, may be invoked against government. Limited government does not, however, necessarily require, as some libertarians suppose, the minimal state. Nevertheless, unlimited democratic authority cannot be liberal government, since it respects no domain of independence or liberty as immune to an invasion by governmental authority. No government in which basic liberties are open to revision by temporary majorities can be regarded as satisfying liberal requirements. Individuals, according to liberals such as John Stuart Mill, are the best judges of what is in their own welfare, so individuals should be granted the widest possible range of liberty. Some liberals have understood this to mean that government should stay out of most affairs of its citizens, except those involving harm to others. Each individual is sovereign over his or her domain, and the state should recognize his or her right to be left alone. Liberalism, then, particularly classical liberalism, was committed to individualism.

A main tenet of liberalism is that each individual ought to be at liberty to develop and act on his or her own conception of the good. Mill claims "the free development of individuality is one of the leading essentials of well-being."[7] The state must be, according to prominent liberal thinkers such as John Rawls[8] and Ronald Dworkin,[9] neutral between competing and possibly incompatible conceptions of the good. Rawls argues that our essential interests are harmed by attempting to enforce a particular view of the good life. The neutral state, Rawls argues, is one that does not justify its actions or policies on the basis of the intrinsic superiority of one conception of the good, nor does it deliberately attempt to influence individuals' adoption of a particular vision of the good life.

The picture we get of democracy aggregating individuals' preferences and liberalism's focus on individuals' having control over their own domain, developing their own conception of the good, and being left alone by government leads to a political theory that is only interested in the personal preferences or wants of the individuals in the society. This view may regard public ideals or values as a peculiar kind of personal desire. Whether the preference is for personal benefit or social benefit, it goes into the calculus the same. Given the individualism of many versions of liberalism, the democratic process may dismiss idealistic, impersonal, or community values as illegitimate meddling in other people's affairs. "What underlies this is a rejection of any suggestion that an ideal-regarding judgement," as Brian Barry calls it, "should be treated as anything other than a peculiar kind of want."[10] Barry supplies the following example: "If Jones believes that people would get more out of life if they developed a taste for, say, the theatre, this can be translated for purposes of the political calculus into 'Jones wants people to go to the theatre.' Once the translation has been made along these lines the question immediately presents itself: Why should people be encouraged to go to the theatre just because Jones wants them to?"[11] Even Dworkin has suggested that we exclude ideal-regarding judgments as "external" preferences; to include them would be unfair, since it would count the preferences of theatergoers twice, once to please them and a second time to please Jones.[12] Lawmakers may view Jones's preference as expressing a "moralistic" value and thereby construe it as failing on grounds of neutrality.

Aggregating Individual Preferences into Social Welfare

The model of a liberal democracy as suggested here is open to a number of serious objections. One major objection and an embarrassment to this account of democracy, that is, democracy as the aggregation of preferences into a social welfare choice, was raised by Kenneth Arrow. He showed, in what came to be known as Arrow's impossibility theorem, that it was not possible to translate the will of the people, to aggregate the preferences of the people, into consistent social policy. In other words, it is not possible to derive a formula for aggregating individual preferences regarding states of affairs in society into collective preferences, such that the formula always yields determinate (transitive) social preferences. Arrow gave the following example: "There are three alternatives, A, B, and C, among which choice is made. One-third of the voters prefer A to B and B to C, one-third prefer B to C and C to A, and one-third prefer C to A and A to B. Then A will be preferred to B by a majority, B to C by a majority, and C to A by a majority."[13] Notice it is not that the government cannot get the will of the people right, but rather the content of the popular will itself may not be determinate all the time. The popular will does not necessarily yield preferences that are transitive. What is the government to do in those instances where there is no will of the people? If one thought that the will of the people was the aggregation of preferences and the defining characteristic of democracy, then Arrow's conclusion might shake one's faith and make one rethink one's theory.

Arrow's proof relies upon a number of normative principles, most of which were thought to be noncontroversial. These principles rest upon value assumptions that, in light of the problem of indeterminacy, we need to question. One basic value assumption at work is that "social action should be designed to maximize or at any rate increase the satisfactions of the members of the society, irrespective of the state of affairs, events, or activities from which they derive these satisfactions."[14] Citizens' sovereignty is accounted for by this assumption. Without it we might want to exclude some citizens' preferences from the social ranking. With the assumption, the racist's preference to wreak havoc on people of his despised minority group has as much weight as the citizen who is concerned about improving the opportunities of minorities in society. If we excluded some individuals' preferences, by relaxing citizen sovereignty, then a consistent social welfare might be possible.

Why do theorists like Arrow argue that all preferences, regardless of their content, are included in the social welfare function? Arrow held this view because he was skeptical about knowing what welfare was independently of individuals' preferences, and he was skeptical about the possibility of doing interpersonal comparisons of utility. Are there good reasons to share these worries, or have they been exaggerated? The points have been greatly overstated. There are indeed problems with making cardinal comparisons or even comparing the intensity of preferences (although even those can be meaningful). Nevertheless, it is clear that some kinds of comparisons are possible. Individuals living near polluted rivers are, all things considered, less well off than individuals living by unpolluted rivers.

Additionally, if we are not so skeptical about knowing, independent from individuals' preferences, what true welfare is (at least some aspects of it), and if we suppose that there are other values that we are interested in protecting, for example, rights and justice, then we will not worry so much about excluding some preferences from the social welfare calculation. We will exclude, for example, discriminatory preferences based upon racial animus because those preferences are antithetical to other values that we want to protect in democracy. Presumably, one way to view the importance of a constitution is that it rules out certain preferences from the social welfare function. A constitution embodies other values than maximizing individuals' preferences. If individuals have preferences to deny opportunities to others in society based on race, ethnicity, gender, and other irrelevant characteristics, then those preferences should not be counted the same as other preferences. The reason for the exclusion is that democracy makes sense as a preferred form of government because we care about equal citizenship and the equal value of each person. Preferences that undermine others' ability to be equal citizens should be excluded from the calculus. We may be able to avoid the embarrassment and catastrophe of Arrow's proof if we change how we understand his principles, and then, as part of that change, we will change what goes into the calculus. We still may not always get a determinate outcome, but we may not worry about it so much once we realize that there are other values that can guide government officials in their determination about policy, for example, values that come out of our Constitution or deeply entrenched public values.

More generally, there are a number of reasons for questioning whether we want to wholeheartedly subscribe to the assumption that we must maximize individuals' preferences. Although it may be thought generally to be good thing to aim at satisfying individuals' preferences in a liberal democracy, is it also important in a liberal democracy to question the content of those preferences. The fact that a preference is directed to diminish the welfare of another group when, for example, that preference is based upon merely ill will provides a liberal democrat with no reason to think that preference ought to be part of social welfare. Racist preferences, for example, have as their object denying opportunities and benefits to members of a despised group. Democracy need not, indeed ought not, without some compelling reason, treat those preferences analogously with other preferences.

Liberals have traditionally been eager to exclude another set of preferences, for example, those whose object is restricting other people's freedom of conscience or religious beliefs. Additionally, liberals have thought it important to exclude preferences whose objects are the private behavior of others when that behavior does not involve harm to others. When aggregating preferences, democratic procedure should exclude, as illegitimate, preferences about others' behavior that is done in private and does not harm others. Liberals suppose individuals ought to have an opportunity to have a sphere of private influence to develop their own conception of the good life unfettered by the preoccupations of others. Private homosexual behavior is an example of behavior that ought to be tolerated regardless of the preferences of others. Of course, it is not easy to draw a sharp line between what is private behavior and what is not.[15] Liberals themselves have very different views about this matter. Millian liberals, interpreting *private* broadly, argue for the largest possible range of choice for the individual. Other liberals, who are suspicious of this view, suppose that some preferences and choices are constitutive of an autonomous life and others are not, making them less interested in merely expanding the range of choices and more interested in the quality of those choices.[16] For example, laws that prevent individuals from using drugs are argued for on the grounds that those preferences do not promote the autonomy of the agent.

What lies behind the claim that democratic governments ought to promote the welfare of their citizens when what is meant by that is maximizing the existing preferences of the individuals in society? On that account, no question about the content, character, or intensity of the preferences is warranted. What is avoided on this account is any determination of the legitimacy of the preferences. No one has to judge which preferences are appropriate or legitimate, and hence, whether they should or should not be a part of the social welfare function. On the other hand, in not determining or ruling out as illegitimate at least some preferences, one runs the danger of indeterminacy (Arrow's problem) and, I believe more crucially, of not having a system that is justified. If all preferences get the same weight, the government is suggesting that they are all equally legitimate. Ultimately, this undermines the legitimacy of the outcomes of the process. Individuals might agree to go along with the outcome of democratic processes even if it was not their own preferred outcome, but only if they thought that the content of the preferences that go into the process is itself legitimate.

It is important to remember that when we say that government ought to maximize the welfare of its citizens and yet what is meant by welfare is what economists mean, the preceding claim may not be so obvious. For the economist the term *welfare* is unpacked solely in terms of preferences. *Preference* also has a specific technical meaning for economists: the order of priority in which a person chooses from a given set of alternatives (without questioning the reasons behind the preferences). For instance, on this analysis, the brother of the suspected Uni-bomber chose to turn in his brother, recognizing that he will likely be convicted and serve a long prison sentence (or, worse, be executed). The economist would say that he prefers the alternative of his brother going to jail over the alternative of his brother not going to jail, whereas ordinarily we would say he is driven by his moral convictions to choose to turn his brother in, not that he prefers that outcome. We ordinarily distinguish choices made from preferences from choices made from moral or religious convictions.

Along these same lines, in ordinary usage the term *welfare* means in a person's interests, advantage, or benefit. We suppose that we can know a person's welfare, at least some of the time, independently of a person's preferences or choices. There are things that are thought to be in everyone's interest, for instance, health, wealth, security, education, an unpolluted environment. The point is that what the economist means by *preference* and *welfare* is not necessarily what we ordinarily mean. The underlying support for the claim that government ought to maximize welfare needs to be questioned when we are using *welfare* in the economist's sense.

Preferences as Changeable

Another objection to the subjective welfarist's view of democracy is that it assumes that preferences are constant and not susceptible to easy alteration. Preferences are formed in a context, a particular society, with particular social attitudes. John Stuart Mill and Harriet Taylor commented on this phenomenon in "On the Subjection of Women." The preference structure of nineteenth-century women, they argued, was formed by the social environment in which they lived. The fact that many women did not appear to want equal status with men could not by itself be taken as an argument that it would be wrong for society to provide those opportunities and benefits to women. Preferences, particularly what are known as *revealed preferences* by economists, are not fixed but are susceptible to change from a large number of outside influences. This is, of course, why advertising works so well. Some preferences derived from advertising have what some call a "fetish" character. In the owner's mind they take on the character of a need, yet they have been wholly generated and reinforced by market advertising. The suasions that can affect preferences range from reasoned arguments to subtle propaganda.

The allocation and distribution of commodities or entitlements by the government can themselves shape individuals' preferences. This is known as the *endowment effect*. The legal rules that *ex ante* establish the allocation of goods in society affect people's preferences about those things.[17] This suggests that any initial allocation of an entitlement—and government cannot refuse to make an initial allocation—may well have effects on preferences.[18] For example, in a study about accepting degradation of visibility, the participants required payments to accept the degradation in the range of five to sixteen times higher than their valuations based on their willingness to pay.[19] In other words, if the good was theirs, their preferences about it were different from what they were if the good was not theirs. If the legal rules can shape the preferences of individuals, why suppose that government ought to take individual preferences as given and having normative force? This fact undermines the claim that preferences *ought* to be the basis of social welfare.

Are Preferences Sovereign?

Again, if we had some reason for supposing that treating all preferences as sovereign was likely to promote individual welfare and/or social welfare, then the argument that they should be the basis for legislation might be compelling. But we have already established that the notion of welfare at work in these models may not be worth promoting. Preferences based on hatred or envy are not justifiably part of the social welfare. Preferences created through media or by government distribution of rights seem poor candidates for forming new legislation. Is it merely satisfaction of individuals' preferences, regardless of the content or basis of those preferences, that we are interested in, or are we interested in cultivating informed, reasoned, autonomous choices? We know that when individuals have adequate information about their options, their choices often change. In a liberal democracy, we might think that some preferences are justifiably discouraged through legal rules, for instance, preferences for self-destructive behavior. Presumably, liberal democratic societies are interested in encouraging and supporting choices that are based on deliberation and adequate information, not merely on satisfying any unexamined preference. Since liberal democratic governments are interested in promoting autonomous lives, they are going to support educational programs and methods for individuals to secure information upon which to make fully informed decisions. The justification for those regulations would be based on the argument that doing so would promote individuals' welfare (in the nontechnical sense). Governmental action requiring that individuals save for their retirement through the Social Security system or the government's giving tax advantages for retirement savings is justified on the basis that these programs are advantageous to individuals' welfare. Some governmental programs, for example, the establishment of national parks and support for the arts, might be argued for on the grounds that individuals will have the opportunity to formulate new preferences for those things and having those preferences increase individuals' welfare. Individuals' lives are enriched by experiencing the marvels of the natural world and cultivating their taste for the arts.

Considered Choices Versus Revealed Preferences

Many preferences that individuals have, for example, preferences for cigarettes or preferences based on envy, hatred, or spite, are in no obvious way of moral value. Why should society see it as a goal to maximize those preferences? Kant, among others, was critical of preferences as the basis of moral choice because he thought they were mere "inclination," which may be arbitrary or contingent from a moral point of view, and thus the satisfaction of which per se has no value or moral significance.[20] There appears to be no greater support for them as the sole basis of political choice.

I have been assuming that there is one way in which individuals value things and that what they value can be captured by preferences revealed in the market. The discussion of the subjective welfarist's view has progressed without a simple distinction between choices based on moral or religious or aesthetic values and choices based on unexamined preferences or tastes (often the latter form the basis for our consumer preferences). Moral values, for instance, are open to rational evaluation and discussion in a way that mere tastes or inclinations are not; for example, "I like chocolate ice cream" is not open is evaluation. We should note, nevertheless, that often consumer preferences are more complicated than so-called mere tastes. Consumer preferences are often based on economic values, making them susceptible to assessment from an economic point of view.

Another way of capturing that difference is by distinguishing between our choices in our role as consumers and our choices in our role as citizens.[21] When we make choices as consumers, we often choose on the basis of our "tastes" and to suit our own self-interest, whereas our choices as citizens may involve ideals or goals for the society in which we live—collective goods for everyone in society. These ideals may come from our moral, religious, or even aesthetic values. Our consumer choices are hence not always compatible with our citizen choices. One may vote for more public transportation and for tougher emission standards for automobiles but still buy a gas-guzzling car.

Economists determine what people value by considering their preferences, and preferences, in turn, are determined by what people are willing to pay for. The subjective welfarist thinks that by deciding all policy in democracy by what people are willing to pay for, he is thereby giving people what they value. But if our distinction correctly points out at least two logically discrete ways people value, then the market preferences are not exhaustive of individuals' values. Hence the subjective welfarist's argument fails. Not all of what we value is expressed in the choices we make in the market. In fact, many of us will make consumer choices that run counter to our considered citizen choices. We buy nonbiodegradable laundry soap because it is cheaper, even though we value protecting the environment more than saving money. The same person who bought the polluting soap might happily support legislation requiring only the sale of biodegradable soap. Most of us have ideals about what kind of society we think is good, what kind of life is worth living. These values may or may not get expressed in the market. Individuals may prefer to go to ball games on the weekends but vote to have the government support the arts. An individual might watch sitcoms and yet advocate that the government support educational television. Merely looking at market choices will not provide an accurate picture of what people value; it will merely tell the consumer preferences of individuals.[22] It should be noted that some consumer choices are reflective of an individual's values: the person deliberated about options and chose according to his or her considered moral values. It is no guarantee, nevertheless, that because a person chooses something in the market that choice reflects that person's deep, reflective moral values. Because the subjective welfarist is interested in mere preferences expressed, this in essence leaves an important place in the political sphere neither for the reasons behind individuals' preferences nor for the values behind them. An individual's unexamined preference receives the same consideration as the choice based on well-reasoned arguments and articulated values.

Why do individuals' consumer choices not accurately reflect their ideals or principles? First, many people simply lack the requisite knowledge about their consumer choices. None of us knows all the ramifications of all of our market choices—that the clothes we buy are made by children working in hazardous conditions or that the produce we eat has dangerous pesticides used in its production.

Second, collective action raises a thorny problem. An individual may want a particular outcome that is collectively desirable. That outcome can be achieved only if most, if not all, individuals choose the desired outcome, but choosing the collectively desirable outcome has costs associated with it. Everyone must sacrifice to get the collectively desirable outcome. But without coercion, there is no guarantee that everyone will contribute, making it unlikely that the optimal outcome will be achieved. Individuals may each reason that it is rational not to contribute unless they get a guarantee that others will contribute. All of us would be better off buying cars that do not pollute the air we breathe. Getting clean air requires that almost everyone drive a "clean" car, yet each individual may reason that he or she is only going to buy a "clean" vehicle if others do so. Of course, without government intervention, we do not achieve the collectively optimal outcome. Hence, we cannot infer from the fact that individuals buy big, polluting automobiles that they do not want or value clean air.

A third reason that may account for the fact that not all market choices reflect individuals' values is that not all options are available in the market. An individual may prefer a world where only solar-powered or electric automobiles are sold, but since there are none available in the market, he purchases what is available. He values products that will have the least impact on natural resources and the rest of the environment, but he must choose among the available alternatives. Through democratic collective action, he might be able to force the market to bring forth the options that he seeks. (Examples of this abound. In California there have been strict emission standards for years that have effectively forced auto manufacturers to build autos that meet the new standards. Federal regulations have also pushed automobile manufacturers to make more fuel-efficient, less polluting, and safer autos.)

A fourth reason for the distortion between market preferences and considered choices is that preferences in the market are determined by willingness to pay, and willingness to pay is a function of ability to pay. Since individuals have radically different abilities to pay, this measure tells us little about social utility or social welfare. The preferences of more affluent individuals will count for more because they have a greater ability to pay; this further erodes the democratic commitment to equal citizenship.

Deliberative Democracy

Democracy is the proper place for individuals to express their citizen values, their ideals, and their goals for society. It provides a place for public discussion and debate about the reasons, including the moral reasons, behind proposed public policies. Groups that are formed around shared values come into the political process to express their ideals and try to convince others of the merits of their goals. It diminishes groups and individuals to treat their moral views and ideals as if they were consumer choices susceptible to change for the right price. Many of the things that people value as citizens are not up for sale; in other words, individuals will not trade them for other states of the world for the "right" price (individuals are not only motivated by personal utility and characterized by indifference).[23] Market choices tend not to reflect social welfare (in the nontechnical sense) or the common good; rather, they reflect the individual's own wants and interests. Politics should encourage deliberation about the common good. It should foster reasoned debate and discussion, and base policy on emerging consensus around those deliberations. It is the proper role of the liberal democratic state to adopt policies that promote citizens' freedom and autonomy; hence, the types of policies it will adopt will not necessarily mimic the market. Since practices in the market may undermine freedom and autonomy, it is acceptable for the government to limit those practices, to change the background conditions within which individuals exercise their freedom in the market. Laws may require that individuals' preferences in the marketplace sometimes be frustrated in order to achieve a larger societal goal. That practice is permissible because we recognize that individuals' consumptive preferences are not always consistent with their aspirations and ideals for society as a whole. Further, the government may see that supporting certain programs or projects, for example, the arts and sciences, will play an important role in enhancing autonomy by opening up areas of endeavor in which individuals can learn, grow, and transform themselves. If these pursuits were not funded by the state and were left to the market for support, they would be undersupplied.

The term *deliberation* is important. To deliberate means to discuss the reasons for and against the suggested policy, and it means that one might change one's views and choices after the deliberative process. Deliberative democracy recognizes that individuals' and groups' ideals for their society, particularly in modern pluralistic societies, will differ. The deliberative democratic process requires that citizens or representatives should continue to work together until they can reach mutually acceptable decisions.[24] Deliberative democracy wants to support and enhance opportunities for individuals to live autonomous lives, and part of doing so will involve enacting laws on the basis of widely held social ideals or goals. Government values autonomy by valuing choices of individuals. The choices that are constitutive of autonomy are not our "consumer preferences" but the thought-out ones that are derived from our deeply held values or arrived at through deliberation with others.

Groups' Goals and Liberal Democracy

I have discussed a vision of democracy that can consistently support the interests of groups that form around goals and ideals such as environmental goals and ideals. I have not, however, shown whether the advancement of ideals of groups, into legislation, is consistent with liberalism. Let us consider the case of environmentalism. An environmental agenda that reaches beyond the protection of harm to others—one that protects species, biological communities, and wilderness—involves a conception of the good. How can the environmentalist's conception of the good be consistent with the liberal's commitment to neutrality? Liberals mean various things by *neutrality*.[25] The most defensible approach, I believe, is to view liberalism's commitment to neutrality as a theory about the basic structure of society, namely, the basic structure of society cannot be biased in favor of a particular group's conception of the good. The structure of the institutions themselves must be neutral among the different and sometimes incompatible comprehensive conceptions of the good. Rawls attempts to sort out a number of meanings of neutrality. He first distinguishes between procedural neutrality and neutrality of aim. He argues that justice as fairness is not procedurally neutral because its principles of justice are substantive. Rather, "justice as fairness has neutrality of aim."[26] Political liberalism does not aim at any conception of the good, and it is not biased in favor of one conception of the good. The basic structure should be designed so that groups or individuals with different comprehensive conceptions of the good can participate in the democracy and be treated with equality and respect.

As part of the democratic process, groups and individuals will present arguments for various kinds of legislation and public policies, often based upon their own ideals and ideas about the good for the public. In a deliberative democracy, those with the best reasons will ideally be successful. They will try to convince others to share their values and their ideals about the society in which they live, or they will deliberate and work toward mutually acceptable decisions. In a *liberal* democracy, we will want to know whether the policy advocated involves a restriction on freedom that is consistent with the due consideration and respect owed to each individual. Giving due consideration and respect to each individual is ensured by prohibiting policies that undermine one of our basic liberties without good reason. Some liberties are more important or basic for treating individuals with concern and respect. The liberty to collect postage stamps is not a basic liberty, but the liberty to express oneself is. The liberal will have stricter guidelines about what constitutes a good reason for a restriction on a basic liberty.[27] Only certain kinds of reasons will be successfully mounted in favor of restricting a basic liberty. For instance, in order to restrict freedom of expression, only certain reasons will count as good ones (and even then they may not be weighty enough). Outside that domain, however, there is room for citizens or their representatives to deliberate about the collective goals for society.

For a liberal democracy it is essential that the state leave enough room for each individual to decide about his or her personal, intimate associations, private conscience, and political views. It is not proper for the state to coerce individuals in these areas. Outside the area of basic liberties, groups or individuals in a liberal democracy may put forth reasons and try to implement legislation that supports their ideals or vision of the good for society.

Advocating a rich environmental agenda, restricting pollution, using natural resources responsibly, establishing wilderness areas, and protecting species and habitats must be argued for on the grounds that the restrictions on freedom are consistent with treating individuals with concern and respect and do not undermine the basic liberties of individuals. Some of these regulations come out of a properly deliberated view about harm to present generations. Many health and safety regulations need to be reviewed in light of the values involved: What levels of risk are acceptable for human health and safety? These considerations need to go beyond the market norms, since, as I have shown, other factors bear on individuals' choices there. The fact that a person will take a job in a hazardous chemical plant is not good evidence that she values the money more than the risks to her life. The upshot of this deliberation in democracy is that we have an enriched conception of harm to others. Individuals recognize that they cannot bring about changes through the market without collective action through democratic processes. The next step is to go beyond enriching our conception of harm to present generations to deliberating about the rights or interests of future generations. Through legislation we will express our concern for the quality of life for future generations.[28] Other environmental policies cannot merely be argued for on the basis of harm to others; they involve a commitment to the intrinsic value of nature. This is a conception of the good or, at least, part of a conception of the good. An alternative justification for a rich environmental agenda is to focus on the human traits and attributes toward the environment that we admire and believe are morally important. What kind of people do we want to be: destroyers of the natural world, a people who think their own wants and interests are more important than those of others, or caretakers and stewards of the natural world?[29] Different individuals in the deliberative process might accept different reasons for particular public policies.

Environmental regulations do entail certain restrictions on individuals' liberty, but since these normally consist of restrictions on the uses of property, and since particular property rights are not a basic liberty, environmental policies are consistent with liberalism. For some liberal theorists, however, such as subjective welfarists and libertarians, liberty is conceived as economic freedom. They do, therefore, conceive of property as a basic liberty. Individuals are free if they are allowed to express their preferences in using and exchanging their private property without having to respond to the values and preferences of others. For those theorists, freedom enhancement comes by restricting the state from regulating property. If freedom is the right to exclude others from participating in decisions about one's private property, then the conception of deliberative democracy mapped out here will not be sound. But why conceptualize freedom so narrowly in terms of exclusive control over private property? Indeed, since much of the distribution of property is arbitrary, one wonders why so much should hinge on it. This is not to undermine the importance of a stable and reliable institution of property. If a particular piece of environmental legislation was to do away with private property altogether, then the argument that having some control over objects in the external world is necessary for personhood would be cogent against it.[30] Prohibiting all private property would, I believe, constitute restricting a basic liberty. Nevertheless, too much emphasis on liberty as control of property may cheapen the conditions in which everyone is able to live autonomous lives. It constrains the sphere of democratic decision making too much, thereby constraining important opportunities for individuals to express their autonomy.

Democratic institutions are not designed to merely sum up the uncritical preferences of individuals. Groups bring to the political table their interests and through the deliberative process attempt to get others to share in their vision of the goals of their society. Legislation that does not infringe upon the basic liberties of individuals can involve shared ideals or a conception of the good. Nothing in liberalism precludes this. Since environmental policies do not intrude upon one's private or personal decisions about one's life or upon one's religious beliefs, they are consistent with liberalism. In fact, since a significant part of the environmental agenda has to do with preventing harm to current and future generations, liberals would be compelled to support those policies. Other groups that advocate government support for the arts and sciences also bring to the deliberative process a vision about a good for society. Democracy needs to be conceptualized such that it is not merely adding the consumer preferences of individuals but rather is engaged in a critical discussion of the values that groups of individuals bring to the process.

Notes

1. Many theorists are questioning whether racial membership is involuntary; see David Goldberg, *Racial Subjects: Writing on Race in America* (New York: Routledge, 1997).

2. A version of this view was supported by James Mill, father of John Stuart Mill. It is interesting to note that John Stuart Mill disagreed with this view, thinking that preferences could be influenced by many outside factors and hence were not worthy of wholehearted inclusion into legislation. See *Mill on Bentham and Coleridge*, ed. F. R. Leavis (London: Chatto and Windus, 1950), 68, 70, 71. In fact Mill believed, what sounds very undemocratic, that some people, the educated and intelligent, should be given more than one vote each. See *Considerations on Representative Government* (New York: Harper, 1862), 283.

3. See Kenneth Arrow, *Social Choice and Individual Values* (New Haven, Conn.: Yale University Press, 1951); I. M. D. Little, "Social Choice and Individual Values," *Journal of Political Economy* 60 (1952): 422–32; A. K. Sen, *Collective Choice and Social Welfare* (San Francisco: Holden-Day, 1970); Russell Hardin, "Social Choice and Democracy," in *The Idea of Democracy*, ed. David Copp, Jean Hampton, and John Roemer (Cambridge: Cambridge University Press, 1993).

4. This usage originally comes from Amartya Sen.

5. See Allen Kneese and Blair Bower, *Environmental Quality and Residuals Management* (Baltimore: John Hopkins University Press, 1979), 4–5.

6. Elizabeth Anderson, *Value in Ethics and Economics* (Cambridge, Mass.: Harvard University Press, 1993), 219.

7. John Stuart Mill, *On Liberty*, in *Utilitarianism and Other Writings*, ed. Mary Warnock (Glasgow: Collins, 1962), 185.

8. John Rawls, *A Theory of Justice* (Cambridge, Mass.: Harvard University Press, 1971).

9. Ronald Dworkin, "Liberalism," in *Taking Rights Seriously* (Cambridge, Mass.: Harvard University Press, 1977), 234ff.

10. Brian Barry, *Political Argument* (Berkeley: University of California Press, 1990), 71.

11. Ibid., 72.

12. Dworkin, "Liberalism."

13. Arrow, *Social Choice and Individual Values*, 27.

14. Kurt Bair, "Welfare and Preference," in *Rational Man and Irrational Society*, ed. Brian Barry and Russell Hardin (London: Sage, 1982), 288.

15. I should mention that many feminist theorists have argued that this distinction between public and private behavior has worked against women's interests. This makes for a more complicated view for liberal feminism.

16. Cass Sustein, "Democracy and Shifting Preferences," in *The Idea of Democracy*, ed. David Copp, Jean Hampton, and John Roemer (Cambridge: Cambridge University Press, 1993), 196–229.

17. See ibid.

18. Ibid., 199. See also D. Kahneman, J. Knetsch, and R. Thaler, "Experimental Tests of the Endowment Effect and the Coase Theorem," *Journal of Political Economics* 98 (1990): 35.

19. Robert Rowes, Ralph d'Arge, and David Brookshire, "An Experiment on the Economic Value of Visibility," *Journal of Environmental Economics and Management* 7 (1980): 1.

20. Immanuel Kant, *Critique of Practical Reason*, trans. Lewis White Beck (Indianapolis: Macmillan, 1956), esp. 18–20.

21. See Mark Sagoff, *The Economy of the Earth* (Cambridge: Cambridge University Press, 1988), 51ff; and Anderson, *Value in Ethics and Economics*, 203ff. for this distinction.

22. See Anderson's discussion of the different ways of valuing in *Value in Ethics and Economics*.

23. There have been many studies by economists asking how much individuals would demand in compensation to accept pollution. Many respondents reject the concept that they can be bought off to accept pollution. See Rowe, D'Arge, and Brookshire, "An Experiment on the Economic Value of Visibility," 1; and Steven Kelman, *What Price Incentives? Economists and the Environment* (Boston: Auburn House, 1981).

24. See Amy Gutmann and Dennis Thompson, *Democracy and Disagreement* (Cambridge, Mass.: Harvard University Press, 1996).

25. See John Rawls, "The Domain of the Political and Overlapping Consensus," Joshua Cohen, "Moral Pluralism and Political Consensus," Jean Hampton, "The Moral Commitments of Liberalism," and David Gauthier, "Constituting Democracy" all in *The Idea of Democracy*, ed. David Copp, Jean Hampton, and John Roemer (Cambridge: Cambridge University Press, 1993).

26. John Rawls, *Political Liberalism* (New York: Columbia University Press, 1993), 193–94.

27. See Rawls's discussion of public reason, where he argues that public reason is necessary for restricting a basic liberty. *Political Liberalism*, 213.

28. See Joel Feinberg, "The Rights of Animals and Unborn Generations," in *Philosophy and Environmental Crisis*, ed. William T. Blackstone (Athens: University of Georgia Press, 1974).

29. See Tom Hill's essay "Ideals of Human Excellence and Preserving the Natural Environment," *Environmental Ethics* 5 (fall 1983) 17.

30. See Margaret Radin, "Property and Personhood," in her *Reinterpreting Property* (Chicago: University of Chicago Press, 1993); and Hegel *Philosophy of Right*, trans. T. M. Knox (Oxford: Clarendon Press, 1952).

Chapter 8

Rights, Democracy, and Distribution: Economic Justice

Rex Martin

Basic Rights in a Democratic System

Active civil rights are beneficial ways of acting, or ways of being treated, that are specifically recognized and affirmed in law for every citizen within a given political society and are actively promoted there. Existing legal rights, universal within a given society, could be regarded as justified insofar as they identify ways of acting (or ways of being acted toward) that actually did satisfy this initial supposition of mutual and general benefit.

The setting required by civil rights can be provided by democratic majority-rule government. Or, at least, I would want to argue this. Democracy, in its turn, needs a justification, and this can be provided by giving priority to preferences that include universal political (or civil) rights. More specifically, the ordering of permissible options, put in terms of the interests involved, would be as follows: (1) the interests of each and all over (2) the good of the corporate whole and either or both of these over (3) a mere majority interest. The crucial priority, in (1), does not arise from the idea of universal rights (which are a proper subset of the interests identified there) but, rather, from the idea of democratic institutions, as justified.

What were initially two quite independent elements—civil rights and democratic procedures—have been systematically brought together and connected by the brief line of argument just sketched. Our two key notions (established civil rights—of individual persons—and justified democratic government) are mutually supportive.

A simple, basic idea underlies the notion of a democratic system of rights: the idea that the respective justifications of its two main elements— civil rights and democratic political institutions—stem from the same source. For each of the two key elements is grounded in the same justificatory pattern, in the idea of mutual and general benefit. Thus, these elements, as so grounded and as mutually supportive of one another, can form the central undergirding of a distinctive political system, one in which civil rights are accorded priority.

One final point. The relation between the nondefective operation of democratic institutions, on the one hand, and the production of civil rights laws, on the other, is at best only probabilistic. I have merely identified a tendency here.

Even so, although we might never be in a position to say that literally all civil rights policies are actually in the interest of each and all, we do have adequate evidence for saying, for example, that long-established civil rights, assuming here that a highly concurrent favorable social opinion exists in their case, are justifiable on the regulative standard of mutual and general benefit. Such well-accredited rights are the basic rights in a democratic system of rights, and they have a peculiar title to be regarded as constitutional essentials there.

Distributive Economic Justice

I next want to direct attention to the place of social justice within a democratic system of rights. This is an issue that, up to now, has not been effectively dealt with within the frame of this particular set of ideas.

Let us begin with a straightforward claim. Many issues of justice are captured, more or less adequately, through an analysis of the rights (in particular, the basic rights) involved. But it appears that not all issues of justice can be handled in this way. For example, standard defenses of affirmative action (as it is called in the United States) are characteristically put in terms of justice—in terms of compensatory justice or of distributive justice. But, arguably, a policy of affirmative action, even when justified on such grounds, does not reduce to a question of basic rights. Why not?

For one thing, such policies are understood to be temporary. More important, they are not ways of being treated that are a means to (or parts of) the good of *each and all*. Rather, they are policies that benefit some individuals (members of some groups) but, unlike basic rights, do not benefit all individual citizens.

The issue, then, is whether economic justice fits this particular pattern: where it is understood to be a matter of justice but not one readily resolvable into a question of basic rights. In order to focus discussion here, let us put one well-known contemporary theory of economic justice, that of John Rawls, under the magnifying glass.

Rawls claims that inequalities among persons stem in important ways from differences in people's natural endowments and in their initial social circumstances. He claims as well that in a just or well-ordered society, resultant inequalities in positions and in income and wealth can be allowed—indeed, should be allowed—subject to certain conditions. One of these conditions is that the basic political and social and economic arrangements are such that goods and services are so distributed as to improve over time the level of income and wealth of the various income groups involved. A society that met this standard would be "thoroughly just" in Rawls's view. But to be "perfectly just," it would also have to *maximize* the level of income and wealth of the least well-off group in particular.

This last point is not intended to identify a benefit for everyone but only for those in the bottom group. Moreover, the distributive effects enjoined by the overall operation of this principle (often called the *maximin principle*) are not the same for everyone; they are not even the same for everyone in the target group, say, the bottom one-fifth. The relevant effects here, rather, are the effects on a "representative" person within that target group; they are effects on an ideal-type *average* individual in the bottom group.

Unlike the case with basic rights, then, the benefits required by economic justice cannot be reduced to a *rule* that specifies an identical way of acting or of being treated and proclaims that way as an equal matter for everyone. (Or, at least, it cannot be reduced to such a rule for everyone *if* their incomes were above a certain level.) The guarantee of a minimum income level can attach over a given period only to some. And over a lifetime only some—but not likely each and every one—can have the benefit of this guarantee.

Such restricted beneficial effects are not appropriate to basic rights, Rawls believes. He concludes, then, that the result required by his principle of distributive economic justice—in particular, in its maximizing version—is not, properly speaking, itself a basic right.

Another point is worth making here as well. It could be argued that, even if the result required by "perfect" Rawlsian economic justice *could* be a basic right, it is not *in fact* one in Great Britain or in the rest of Europe or in the United States. Now, granted, in many European countries (e.g., Denmark or Sweden) there is an extensive "safety net" or social minimum in place concerning such matters as health care, public schooling, housing, unemployment, and retirement income. My point, though, is that this social minimum does not conform to the requirements of Rawls's maximizing principle, for it does not typically pitch things at that high a level. Hence, it is fair to say that the maximin standard is not recognized and maintained in any of these places as a basic right.

Indeed, it could be further argued (as Rawls himself does) that the required result *should* not, given the precise character of the American political system, be recognized and maintained there as a basic constitutional right; instead, the required result should properly be a legitimate object of legislative policy but *not* a feature of the fundamental constitution itself. Rawls's reason for saying that the maximin principle should not be incorporated as a feature of the text (or of the understood text) of the U.S. Constitution is that he does not want that principle to become an object of interpretation by American courts. Rather, he wants the basic determinations and principal implementations of policy to remain within the province of the legislature (in this case, of the U.S. Congress). The debate is by no means closed on this matter, but I think enough has been said to suggest that distributive economic justice (at least as Rawls conceived things) may not be a matter of basic rights at all.

If distributive economic justice is to be fitted into our account of a democratic system of rights, we should begin by assuming, if only for the sake of argument, that it is not itself a matter of basic rights. And we must try to fit it into our account of a democratic system of rights on some other basis.

Let me suggest how it might be accommodated there on some such basis. In my previous account of a democratic system of rights, two quite distinct elements—civil rights and democratic procedures—were brought together and connected to one another by an argument sketch. This particular systematic connection was underwritten by the intrinsic affinity each element exhibited (under analysis) for the other, based on their shared justification by the standard of mutual and general benefit. By the same token, if distributive economic justice could itself be shown to be a matter of *everyone's* benefit—or, at least, of every income group's benefit—then it might plausibly come within that same orbit.

Thus, distributive economic justice might enter the political space appropriate to a democratic system of rights on this very basis. In being concordant with the notion of mutual and general benefit, distributive economic justice shares an important feature with the main elements of that system—with basic rights and democratic political institutions, as justified.

The question is whether this particular notion of distributive economic justice is one that could gain wide acceptance or whether it is, on the contrary, simply one person's idea (say, Rawls's or mine). I think this notion could command a surprisingly wide assent; it is deeply rooted in existing theory. There is in effect already a consensus about economic justice. For we can point to a single, common, underlying idea of economic justice (or, better, to an element within that idea) that can be found in Locke, in Adam Smith, in Marx, and in much recent contractarian theory—in Rawls, as I have already indicated, but also in Gauthier and in Nozick, if we count Nozick as a contractarian of sorts, though more Hobbesian than Lockean in certain respects.

The root idea here is that the arrangement of economic institutions, where we are concerned with justice, will include—as an important part of the story—the idea that all contributors benefit or, at least, that none are to be left worse off. In a just scheme the root idea is that, if some individuals (say, those in the top 20 percent) improve their standard of living (measured in terms of real income and wealth), others should do so as well; no group, not even those least well-off (say, those in the bottom 20 percent), should be left behind. All should continually improve their lot in life together. None at least are to be left worse off.

Of course, important differences come in the way each thinker embeds this root idea in an overall theory. Locke puts it in a state of nature, and thus within the context of a theory of natural rights; Smith lodges it in an open and competitive market and then puts that ultimately within the confines of a rather utilitarian scheme of justification; and Marx embeds it in a system of proper social ownership of the means of production, and that, in turn, is set within his theory of historical materialism. I have already indicated that the root idea is also one we can plausibly ascribe to Rawls. For he seems committed to the principle that every income group is to benefit or, at least, that none is allowed to become worse off. Indeed, Rawls says this, quite explicitly, at a number of points.

To sum up: I have made a quick but plausible case, ultimately on inductive grounds, for saying that there is a root idea of distributive economic justice. This root idea can be stated, in simplest terms, as "every income group benefits, or, at least, none is to become worse off." And I have suggested that this root idea is not in any way idiosyncratic; for historically, it has been incorporated into one or another distinctive conception of justice on natural rights, utilitarian, Marxist, and contractarian grounds.

Finally, I have suggested that mutual and general benefit (an idea central to the theme of justification within a democratic system of rights) can plausibly be regarded as overlapping, in important respects, this root idea and, thus, as connected with the root idea of economic justice, historically conceived. Given this connection, we have a presumptive case for making the issue of justice so conceived a matter of public political policy in a democratic system of rights.

I say presumptive here, for more than this simple connection would likely be at stake before policies of economic justice took hold as a vital concern in such a system. Such policies might be driven by the concern that concentration of wealth and of the management of firms (and even industries) in a few hands would have an adverse effect on basic democratic institutions (on one person, one vote, on contested elections, on majority rule). Or it might be that a given democratic society took the view that the economy was a *political* economy—that it was set within a whole host of political and social arrangements, with reciprocal effects all around—and that the economy ought to give results that were for the general welfare, or for the benefit of each and all. Or it might be, most likely it would be, that some ideal of citizenship was at work. That ideal might be reflected in and play out in a variety of ways, in the complex notion that the lives of citizens needed a certain wherewithal, a certain level of income and services and social capital, in order for citizens to be fully flourishing members of a democratic social order; or in order for citizens to be able to have and use their rights effectively; or in order for citizens to possess the grounds of dignity and mutual respect that citizenship in a democracy ordained, or that the responsible exercise of the right to vote and the right to free speech called for. With these sorts of considerations in view, then, we might be able to fill in on the case for making the issue of distributive economic justice, as I have been conceiving it, a matter of public political policy in a democratic system of rights.

This being so, let us next try to determine what might be a likely shape for policies of economic justice to take in such a system. The root idea (that every wage-earning group benefits, over time) will, of course, be present. Thus, people in a given democratic society are justified in moving from one set of economic arrangements to another (say, to a new tax law and attendant scheme of expenditures) if all income groups benefit (or at least none are left worse off). The root idea, when carefully stated, becomes the principle of (Pareto) efficiency. Often, though, several such efficient arrangements are feasible, given a single determinate starting point. What then?

In such an event, that arrangement (among those available) which minimizes the difference in income between the topmost and the least well-off group should be selected and implemented. This constraint at least seems a plausible one to add here—that is, in the context of a democratic system of rights. For it has the merit of recommending the selection of that one alternative that minimizes the necessary inequality required to be imposed, consistent with satisfaction of the root idea that every group is to be benefited.

Thus, an "everybody benefits" or efficiency principle constrained by some form of egalitarianism emerges as a likely, perhaps even the preferable, account of distributive economic justice when seen from the perspective of contemporary democratic theory (as given in the account of a democratic system of rights). For the root idea of economic justice—(1) that every group is to benefit—as constrained (2) by a reasonably vigorous egalitarianism would appeal, in *each* of these crucial emphases, to values already central to the idea of a democratic system of rights. Hence, it could suitably direct democratic decision making there.

My guiding intuition throughout this section has been that setting the root idea of economic justice within a democratic framework should yield a distinctive principle of economic justice, one that is peculiarly appropriate to elements within that framework. What counts in a democratic system of rights is what is compatible, in particular, what is integral, with the leading ideas of that system. Accordingly, I have tried to show that it would make good sense to incorporate an efficiency-cum-egalitarian theory of distributive economic justice into the theory of democracy, to set this theory within the justifying network that connects basic rights and the democratic political institutions (i.e., the institutions of one person, one vote, of regular and contested elections and parliamentary voting, of majority rule).

Now, as I have already noted throughout, economic justice (historically conceived) is an aggregative notion and best attaches to groups; moreover, such justice, even with the so-called egalitarian constraint, exhibits no real commitment to the strict equality of all citizens. For it does not require that economic benefits or offices of ownership be identically or even substantially the same for each and every citizen (except, perhaps, at some minimum level). Thus, on this understanding, the conception of economic justice I have recommended is, in important respects, *unlike* the case with basic rights.

Accordingly, the demands of this particular conception of economic justice will probably not count as among the institutional essentials of a democratic system of rights nor be accorded the highest priority there. For economic justice, as here conceived, is neither a basic right nor a corporate good (such as one finds, for example, in providing for a suitable level of gross national product). Even so, the claims of economic justice should have a reasonably high profile in such a system (given the close kinship—indeed, the overlap—of the root idea of economic justice with the formative notion of mutual and general benefit, the notion that does in fact justify the institutional essentials in that system).

Here, then, appropriate political policies that are themselves democratically developed would have to be designed to achieve such justice. These policies would be, if properly constructed, policies that made every income group better off (or at least none worse off) over some reasonably determinate period of time, subject (of course) to the egalitarian constraint. And the policies we are interested in would have to be policies that when properly constructed did not supersede or violate existing basic rights in the particular country in question. Or at least these are the main results I have argued for.

The various norms I have emphasized in this brief summary are norms appropriate to distributive economic justice when conceived within the framework of a democratic system of rights. Achieving economic justice, in this manner, is part of the democratic project. It is part of the project of identifying and then implementing policies that serve interests common to the voters.

Distributive economic justice (on the efficiency-cum-egalitarianism principle) is a standard for achievement, a standard for assessing policies in a democratic system of rights. And the goal it invokes should be part of the public understanding of such a system and should inform debate there. For distributive economic justice, as here conceived, is the kind of thing we would expect a rights-respecting democratic government and electorate to be specially concerned with. To provide economic justice (on the efficiency-cum-egalitarianism model) is one of the things such a democracy should be doing, given its character and its justifying norms.

Achieving distributive economic justice is a matter of democratic majority rule, but it is not a matter of *mere* majority rule. For it is never a matter of sheer indifference how policies turn out as to their impact on distributive economic justice in a democratic system.

Thus, we should expect to find in the typical operation of a democratic system such things as policies of job creation and job training, redistributive taxation and income transfers and various subsidies at the lower income levels, and, finally, controls on campaign spending and policies designed to give more or less equal empowerment to voters at all income levels. For the idea here is that the total set of policies in a country modeled on a democratic system of rights should be geared to achieve distributive economic justice, as understood in the idea that everybody benefits (as constrained by egalitarianism).

A Reflection and Assessment

In concluding the argument of this chapter, and as a main part of my assessment of the project it proposes, I think it important to establish one point in particular, one that may not be, as yet, wholly clear. The argument I have conducted here is intended to show two things merely: that the meeting of the criterion set by the everybody benefits-cum-egalitarian principle has been developed as a *sufficient* condition for distributive economic justice and that the criterion, so understood, would be both acceptable and integral within a democratic system of rights.

Let me put this point a bit more precisely here. The criterion would be a sufficient condition for distributive economic justice, if certain preconditions were met. Some of these conditions are already familiar to us; they pertain to the notion of a democratic system of rights itself and were mentioned at the end of the previous section. I mean such things as the priority of basic rights and the need to rely on democratically derived policies and on democratic scrutiny in meeting the "everybody benefits" goal. And some of these preconditions belong to the theory of justice itself. Perhaps most important here would be the meeting of the standard of fair equality of opportunity at a suitable level.

My claim, then, is that if the criterion (as just elaborated) is actually met in a country modeled on a democratic system of rights, that fact would be a sufficient condition for saying that the distributive economic arrangements there were just; for rebutting claims (should such be made) that they were *unjust*. The satisfaction of the criterion marks a sufficient condition for saying that the various levels of income and wealth for representative groups (say, the top 20 percent of wage earners on down through the bottom 20 percent) in that country were not contrary to justice.

I have not argued, however, that the meeting of this criterion is a *necessary* condition for distributive economic justice in such a system. More specifically, I have not argued that meeting the "everybody benefits" part of this criterion is a necessary condition there. In other words, if the criterion is *not* being met in a country modeled on a democratic system of rights, or not being met on the point that every income group benefits, it does not follow (from that fact alone) that the distributive economic arrangements there are positively *un*just. Or so my argument is meant to suggest.

On one reading at least, the point just made is perfectly obvious. For where it is assumed that past injustices have occurred and that rectification or redress of these defective patterns is thereby in order, Marx and Rawls (and I am sure many others) would insist that a pattern of reciprocal benefit is *not* required while the maldistribution is being corrected. Clearly, then, in cases such as this, we cannot regard satisfaction of the "everybody benefits" principle (or, more generally, the standard of Pareto efficiency) as itself a *necessary* condition of distributive economic justice.

Even if we stayed with favored cases—where mutual improvement is possible (up to some optimal point) and where we were considering only standard or normal distributions (and not those designed to correct previous maldistributions)—we would still encounter reasons for thinking that satisfying the relevant criterion (the criterion set by the everybody benefits-cum-egalitarian principle) should not be a *necessary* condition for distributive economic justice.

At least four such reasons could plausibly be advanced. They could, for purposes of reference and ready recall, be identified as (1) historical reasons, based on interpreting the various theories of economic justice (those of Locke et al.) briefly mentioned in the previous section, (2) reasons of limited knowledge and of reliance on shared normative intuitions and of the indeterminacies these introduce, (3) reasons of conceptual indeterminacy in the efficiency-cum-egalitarianism criterion itself, and (4) reasons of democracy. Only the last of these crucially concerns the argument of the present chapter. Let me turn, briefly then, to this particular argument from democracy.

Consistent and determined adherence to a necessary condition requirement would be inappropriate within a democratic system of rights. For to insist on such adherence would be inconsistent with the institutional essentials—in particular, those identified with basic rights and with democracy (such things as contested voting, majority rule)—that constitute the theoretical system of political institutions and ideas which we must rely on to ground the notion of distributive economic justice, justificatorily, in the first place.

In a democratic system of rights, one is committed to the notion that majority rule decision making, so long as it conforms to the main priorities established there, is itself decisive and determinative. Distributive economic justice (as I have conceived it) does not have the status of a democratically derived basic right or set of such rights in the theoretic system I am discussing. Nor is it a corporate good there. Thus it cannot control democratic decision making in the way that these main concerns do. Indeed, a creditable profile of economic justice in such a system must itself conform, in appropriate ways, to democratic norms, norms that include (as I have noted) contested voting and majority decision among their crucial and defining features.

Consistent and determined adherence to a necessary condition requirement would take us *outside* our justifying net and cause us to lose our moorings in the very system of institutions and ideas whence we had begun. And we would have surreptitiously turned what had been a mere free-floating normative consideration, inductively generalized from the basis provided by modern discourse about distributive economic justice (as captured in the root—or everybody benefits—idea and its obvious importance), into an absolute, into *the* governing norm, into the very idea of justice.

The view I am disputing, that the criterion of efficiency-cum-egalitarianism is a necessary condition of economic justice, suffers from a serious flaw. It fails to see that *injustice*, like the idea of justice itself, is something that requires political interpretation. It fails to see that neither injustice nor justice is a simple, clear-cut idea. Instead it assumes without further ado that the sufficient criterion here is also a necessary one and that—within relevant parameters—all failures to satisfy it are per se unjust. In this respect, it dogmatically begs the very question we are here concerned with.

The fact is, people may well think that not all failures to meet the criterion are unjust. And if they do think that, and if the grounds for so thinking can be made out in a principled way (and, in particular, one fully consistent with the justifying norms and the network of institutions of a democratic system of rights), then we have in hand all that is needed to settle the matter at issue.

Consider here the following two cases, which we can call paradigm case A and paradigm case B. Let us begin with A. Here all indicators (in all expert hands) show both that some groups are actually worse off (in particular, those in the bottom group, who are now much worse off) and that the disparity between top and bottom has actually significantly increased over time. Both these results are permanently irreversible.

Surely, we have here a presumptive case for saying that the distributive arrangements implicated herein are *unjust*. I would agree. But the case can be conclusively made only *within* the actual operation of a democratic system of rights. Thus, public debate and the ensuing votes would actually have to *reach* this very judgment, over time and given experience, for it to count as a fully conclusive one within a given democratic state.

In sum, when we say that some such judgments or conclusions are to be drawn over time and given experience, we mean they are to be drawn *upon reflection*. And the reflection we have in mind is found in free public discourse, in contested voting, in majority decisions, in confirmation through the checking devices (such as subsequent judicial decisions), and in established public consensus within an ongoing democratic polity over time. Such reflective conclusions as these are authoritative in a given democratic polity and, under the conditions identified, serve to resolve otherwise ineradicable indeterminacies in the inbuilt criterion of distributive economic justice, as (for example) in determining what is positively *un*just.

Let us consider next, in concluding the argument of this section and of the chapter, a somewhat different case from paradigm A. We can call it paradigm case B. Here all indicators (in all expert hands) show both that some groups are actually worse off (in particular, those in the top group, who are now marginally worse off) and that the disparity between top and bottom has actually significantly decreased over time. The first result (expected to last, let us say, for a decade) is not permanently irreversible, though the second may well be.

These two cases, A and B, are different in many relevant respects, but they are alike in one: each represents a failure of satisfaction of the efficiency-cum-egalitarianism criterion at a crucial point, at the point of the so-called root idea (as given in the "everybody benefits" principle). Given this important point of similarity between A and B, do we have a presumptive case (as we did in A) for saying that the distributive arrangements implicated in case B are *unjust*?

My own intuition in the matter—shared with many other people, I would suspect—is that we do not. But, under the terms of the present analysis, this is at best only a presumptive conclusion. Suppose, now, this very conclusion—the conclusion that such arrangements are not unjust— was in effect drawn within a democratic polity (under the same conditions as in case A: free public discussion, etc.). Such a conclusion-in-effect would be drawn when democratic policy produced or endorsed such a result under those conditions.

The argument of this section would lead us to endorse this conclusion, from within the confines of a given democratic polity (and ultimately from within the idea of a democratic system of rights)—to endorse it as authoritative, as reflectively sound, as a practical and principled way of resolving one of the otherwise ineradicable indeterminacies in the inbuilt criterion of distributive economic justice I have identified, that of efficiency-cum-egalitarianism. If one accepts this overall conclusion—that the result given in paradigm case B is not presumptively unjust and would not be decided to be, given time and reflection, in a polity modeled on a democratic system of rights—then one cannot consistently believe that satisfaction of the governing criterion is a *necessary* condition of distributive economic justice in such a system. Or, to put the matter here somewhat differently, if one thinks the overall conclusion to be based on sound reasons, then one would not take the criterion to be a necessary condition (in the sense that any failure to satisfy the criterion is, under plausible circumstances, *un*just as such).

A Conclusion and a Further Thought

The question of distributive economic justice is one of the fundamental issues that all democratic countries face today. The present chapter has suggested that this issue can be confronted within the frame already established by basic rights and by the democratic institutions. Social justice for the different income groups (i.e., social justice as given in the criterion of efficiency-cum-egalitarianism) can be on the agenda for political programs within a democratic system of rights. And it is important to be clear in our understanding of the criterion I have tried to establish: it is understood to be a sufficient, but not a necessary, condition for distributive economic justice within any given polity modeled on a democratic system of rights.

One further observation. It is, I think, important to see that the income groups here are real social groups and not arbitrary or merely statistically constructed groups (such as, for example, the group constituted by people in a given year who have missed two consecutive days of work due to head colds). To see this, let us return briefly to the issue of the Rawlsian sources of inequality.

It is often taken for granted, and was by Rawls, that the people who are initially advantaged (in respect of their natural endowment and social circumstances) end up in the better positions, the positions affording greater income and wealth, and that the people who are disadvantaged in these respects end up less well-off. It is, in short, usually merely assumed that a connection exists between one's starting point and one's ending point.

Now, curiously, we know this assumption to be incorrect in given individual cases. For example, a person who has suffered a disabling childhood illness or who has come from very poor circumstances could end up in a favored position, which yielded a better than average income. Another person, seemingly favored by factors of health and family wealth, might do *less* well and fall below the average, far below that person's starting point. How, then, can we support the assumption in the face of these counterexamples?

The assumption rests, we could say, on a fundamental law of social science: that there is a probabilistic or *statistical* connection between a person's having been strongly initially disadvantaged (in terms of natural endowment or social circumstance) and that person's ending up in a lower income group or a less-satisfying or less-skill-requiring job. Correspondingly, there is a reliable probabilistic connection between a person's having been strongly initially advantaged and that person's ending up in a higher income group or in a more-satisfying or more-skill-requiring job.

In sum, the various income groups here—as sorted by quintiles, say—are real social groups (most conspicuously so, the top 20 percent and the bottom 20 percent). And the argument of this chapter has concerned the question of distributive economic justice among such income groups within a context of democratic institutions. One interesting feature of this argument is that the point about justice has been made without assuming that these groups, though real social groups, have group rights—without assuming, that is, that these groups or the persons within them have a basic right to the levels of income identified as appropriate by the standard of distributive economic justice endorsed, in the present chapter, for a democratic system of rights: the standard of efficiency-cum-egalitarianism.*

---

*For a convenient elaboration of the main argument in the first section, see my short essay "Basic Rights," *Rechtstheorie* 15 (1993): 191–201. The simple, basic idea mentioned there (as the main idea of the first section) is developed and argued for, at considerably greater length, in my book *A System of Rights* (Oxford: Clarendon Press, 1993) esp. chaps. 6, 7, 12, and the appendix. An earlier version of the second sections of the present chapter can be found in a paper I published in *Analyse & Kritik* 17 (1995): 35–51. A somewhat longer version of the present chapter can be found in *Social Justice*, ed. David Boucher and Paul Kelly (London, Routledge, 1998).

Chapter 9

Duties of Group Membership: Justice as Reciprocity and Liberal Democratic Institutions

Patricia Smith

The notions of group membership and group rights have been the object of considerable recent interest. Much of the discussion has been focused on minority groups, oppressed or disadvantaged groups, and how such groups should be regarded within the context of a larger and mainstream society.[1] Some philosophers have begun to examine how group membership may generate rights or obligations.[2] I would like to suggest that group membership is central to all social obligation and has the potential to explain fundamental mainstream institutions of liberal democratic society, despite its focus on individualism. To pursue this thought I will outline how group membership is related to an aspect of justice that I call *justice as reciprocity*. I contend that justice as reciprocity is necessary to understand obligations recognized as intrinsic to basic liberal institutions such as the family and professions, which are traditionally viewed as based on natural and contractual relations.

To explain and justify moral and political obligations in liberal democratic society, liberal theory has focused strongly on the concept of justice as respect for persons. A duty of respect responds to the individual need to be recognized as a separate entity of worth. It reflects the dignity of human beings as individuals, each one unique and intrinsically valuable in her own right. It is premised on the value of the human capacity for self-legislation and consequently protects the integrity of rational agency in the form of free, autonomous choice. These are all significant values and are crucial for liberal democratic institutions, but they are inadequate to account for all the needs of human life or even for all the requirements of justice. Not all duties of justice are alike. Not all duties of justice are negative, or based on respect for individuals as unique and autonomous.

Special positive duties are also duties of justice. Like universal negative duties, they are perfect duties—specifiable obligations owed to particular

172

individuals. Failing to meet them violates the rights of those individuals to whom they are owed. Unlike universal negative duties, special positive duties are limited in scope and affirmative. They are generally thought to be based on natural or contractual relations. While contractual obligations are thought to fit the liberal paradigm of obligations based on consent, natural obligations (i.e., family obligations), although acknowledged as central to liberal democratic society, were assumed to be derived from biology and otherwise traditionally ignored in liberal theory, and ignored for good reason. Basing obligations on biology directly and obviously contradicts basic liberal presumptions of individual freedom and autonomy. Biological obligations can only be viewed as exceptions to liberal principles. I have argued that the best liberal justification for these affirmative obligations in the context of family relations is mutual reliance in a cooperative endeavor with which one is (partly) identified. These, I have suggested, might be called *duties of membership*. While not based on consent, they are more compatible with liberal principles and liberal democratic institutions than obligations of biology could ever be.[3] The aspect of these duties that needs to be highlighted here is their connection to the notion of fairness in terms of mutual contribution to cooperative endeavor. Because of this, I would like to explore the possible connection between these ideas and the concept of justice as reciprocity.

Justice as reciprocity is an ancient idea; in fact, it has been argued that reciprocity is actually the oldest of all concepts of justice.[4] It is without question much older than its individualistic Kantian counterpart, but although there are exceptions,[5] it is not widely discussed in contemporary literature except in its negative form as retribution.[6] Aristotle considered it the appropriate form of justice in matters of exchange:

> In associations for exchange this sort of justice does hold men together—reciprocity in accordance with a proportion and not on the basis of precisely equal return. For it is by proportionate requital that the city holds together. Men seek to return either evil for evil—and if they cannot do so, think their position mere slavery—or good for good—and if they cannot do so there is no exchange, but it is by exchange that they hold together.[7]

Reciprocity is concerned with the idea of appropriate return—the notion of like for like; good for good; and, traditionally, evil for evil. (At least one contemporary philosopher has argued that the virtue of reciprocity does not entail returning evil for evil,[8] and virtually all moral traditions have treated this relation as more complex than strict retaliation in kind, whether affirmative or negative.) In any case, in its affirmative mode, the general idea embodied in reciprocity is the idea of mutual and fair or proportional contribution. From reciprocity is derived the notion of desert, a central moral concept that is directly connected to fairness—the idea that people should receive what they deserve. Within the context of cooperative endeavor, if people should receive what they deserve, they also should contribute their fair share.[9] As Aristotle treats it, reciprocity reflects the human need to interact socially and cooperate, to transact business in terms of mutual exchange, or even to foster relationships of mutual advantage.[10] This form of justice, he claims, holds people together and responds to a basic inclination to return like for like.

Consequently, the ideas of mutual reliance and cooperative support, which are central to duties of membership, fall, I believe, within this general domain of justice. The idea behind such duties is not self-sacrifice or altruism, nor respect for individual integrity as such, but mutuality of contribution and collateral trustworthiness.[11] They are, consequently, the basis for building relationships of cooperation and responsibility as well as mutual respect. Most important, perhaps, these ideas of mutual reliance and cooperative support as reciprocity are inherently social concepts that apply to all transactions but are especially conducive to the promotion of ongoing relationships. They provide the basis for reliable human cooperation and the ground rules of social intercourse and interrelation.[12]

Thus, unlike duties of respect, which focus on and protect the autonomy, individuality, and separateness of persons, duties of reciprocity are the building blocks of social interaction and personal interdependence. Although they have not been featured in liberal theory for the most part, being overshadowed by an emphasis on duties of respect, these duties of interaction have always been acknowledged in liberal theory and are central to liberal democratic social practice. Of course, duties of reciprocity are in no way incompatible with liberalism, and they can (as I have argued elsewhere)[13] provide a better explanation of natural duties (i.e., family obligations) as duties of membership in the form of mutual reliance and cooperative support. I think that it is time to reorient the focus of liberal theory to highlight these neglected duties of reciprocity that in fact have always been so central to cooperative liberal institutions and practices. Family obligation is a good beginning point for this project, since family relations are paradigmatic of ongoing, cooperative endeavor. Construing family duties as obligations of membership, necessary for continuing and cooperative communal association at an intimate level that is fundamental to liberal democratic society, provides a grounding for setting boundaries on individual freedom that is compatible with liberal presumptions in a way that was never true of traditional ideas of natural duty based on biology.[14]

The idea of reciprocity also helps to provide a better explanation of some contractual obligations. In fact, the traditional contractual model of professional obligation based on explicit consent or agreement must be complicated a great deal if it is to account for actual practices of employment or profession. Ideas of consent and reliance as a foundation for contractual obligation in this context are not entirely distinct and exclusive of one another.[15] Both play a part in explaining complex obligations that together constitute an occupational role, which one accepts as a package under a variety of conditions, ranging from fully free to severely constrained. Consent in this context is like joining a team. It is consenting to play a part, and to be a part, that is, to be a member, of an ongoing enterprise over which one does not have full control. It is also consenting to allow others to rely on one to fulfill the obligations attached to that role.[16]

Obviously, then, the idea of role is crucial to these explanations, and yet it is not clear that either consent or reliance can adequately accommodate that concept. Role, as a concept, is extraneous to the notion of contract. Standard theories of contract cannot account for it. Yet it is central to obligations of profession or occupation. The question is, How do the ideas of consent and role interact within a professional context, and can the formal structure of liberal theory provide a framework for accommodating these interactions? I believe that it is helpful to consider these obligations as incorporating elements of group membership as well as contract. Let me sketch briefly an outline of how these elements might fit together within the occupational or professional context.

Within the professional context a contract is a minimally consensual relationship of mutual reliance or cooperative commitment for reciprocal benefit (frequently between parties with different ends).[17] At least that is a reasonable preliminary statement that follows from considerations of the history of contract law, as well as the interactions of consent and reliance reflected in the traditional debate over the foundations of contractual obligation.[18] It also distinguishes a contractual obligation from an obligation of membership.

Obligations of membership are duties of connection in a common pursuit or relationship by parties with a common source of identification (i.e., a group). These duties are derived from connection: from being part of something with which one is partly identified (one's family, nation, or profession, for example); they are fleshed out or developed and defined by the reasonable expectations (or common assumptions and beliefs) of the community over time; and they are justified if the institution or practice they constitute is justified, all things considered.[19]

Duties of contract, by contrast, are duties of cooperative interaction by parties of any sort, frequently (but not necessarily) with different ends, and usually (but not necessarily) with different connections. There is no intrinsic connection between contracting parties, as there is with members of a common institution or practice. Very often contractors may have nothing apparent in common other than the contract. In fact, one useful way to view a contract (or contract law) is as a device that extends the range of rational reliance or cooperation to strangers. On the other hand, this point should not be overstated, since contracting strangers do have more connections than meet the eye. They are not totally disconnected, since all contracting takes place within contexts that provide rules and practices that enable such transactions to take place. (Commercial [or social or political] interaction in a state of nature composed of totally disconnected individuals would actually be bizarre, when you think about it.) All contracting takes place within a complex, and at this point highly developed, structure of legal, social, and commercial practice or custom that actually makes contractors rather connected indeed, even if they are strangers to one another. These connections form the background conditions that make the contracts possible.

Yet the difference (between a duty of membership and a duty of contract) is that preserving or supporting these background connections is not the object of the contract, nor the point of the obligations that follow from it, whereas the common connection or relation of membership is itself a part of the object of obligations of membership. One object of family obligation, for example, is or may often be supporting and nurturing the family itself. Furthermore, the interests, values, and even the identity of the members are not always clearly separable (which is not to say they are not separable at all) from the well-being, the values, and the identity of what they are members of. But the identity and interests of contractors are surely separable from the background conditions and connections that make their contracts possible. Suppose we represent this difference by referring to duties of membership as duties of common connection and duties of contract as duties of individual cooperation.[20] This represents what distinguishes them. What they have in common is the value of reciprocal reliance.

Duties of membership and contract are both founded (at least in part) on reliance, since both participation in a common relation and cooperative interaction by diverse parties require it. *Webster's* defines *reliance* as "trust." To be reliable is to be trustworthy. Conversely, the *Oxford English Dictionary* defines the verb *to trust* as "to rely or depend upon." Yet, oddly, this close association of the two terms is not always noted. Charles Fried, for example, in arguing against reliance as a foundation of contractual obligation and for the strength of promising in that capacity, repeatedly refers to the value of trust to justify his promise principle.[21] But why doesn't that just reintroduce reliance under another name? It may be that he has in mind a focus on honesty, and that is indeed an important aspect of trust. There is no question that deception in the form of fraud or false promise undermines trust. But what does that amount to other than the fact that people cannot rely on the deceiver? Of course, there are various ways of being unreliable. Dishonesty is only one of them. So it might be assumed that reliance is a broader category than trust, and so, perhaps, includes too much. But that is incorrect, for all the ways in which it is possible to be unreliable are the same ways in which it is possible to be untrustworthy. For example, one can be negligent and therefore unreliable or untrustworthy, but not dishonest. Honesty is a narrower concept, but trust is essentially synonymous with reliance, and so I will use them interchangeably. Virginia Held has used the concept of trust in approximately the way I intend to use it here, I believe.[22] Trust, she argues, is a social value that must be supported by a proper environment. At least minimal social conditions must be met, since trusting the untrustworthy is not virtuous, or even rational. Trust is an interactive value. It must be fostered. It is for this reason that it is best captured as a form of justice as reciprocity in cooperative interactions. To be a value at all (rather than a pious hope), it must be reciprocated. The more it is undermined socially, the harder it is to maintain individually. Even individually (i.e., between two individuals alone), trust must be built. It must be earned over time by mutual adherence to standards of reliability. It must be deserved. The more untrustworthy the general environment, the harder it is to accomplish this. If community standards of honesty are strong, for example, each individual within the community has an easier burden of proof. If members of a society are normally scrupulous about telling the truth, then it is not unreasonable to assume that a particular individual within it is also likely to be truthful. But if there is no such community standard, then each individual bears the entire burden of providing evidence of trustworthiness alone. If the environment is bad enough, it may not be clear how to get that started at all. Thus, reliability must be reciprocal in order to produce trust.

Trust is absolutely crucial for cooperation, which in turn is critical for either contractual or membership relations. Since cooperation is not possible without trust, the virtue of trustworthiness must be cultivated. And if trust is needed for cooperation, how much more is it needed for relationships of common membership? Thus, we can characterize both duties of membership and duties of contract as duties of trust or reciprocal reliance. We might construe this as two forms of trust: the trust required for common connection, and the trust required for individual cooperation.[23]

Both of these can be distinguished from negative duties, in that negative duties are founded on respect for other individuals as unique and significant in their own right. They are commonly characterized as duties of noninterference, and thus can reasonably be described as duties of separation, as well as respect. Duties of respect protect individuals as such from the harm or interference of others. We can think of them as forming a shield around each person, enclosing each individual within a protective barrier that no one else is entitled to penetrate. Thus, negative duties are duties of separation.

This provides a clear contrast with duties of trust, as duties of connection and cooperation. Negative duties of respect for persons protect the integrity of separate individuals; positive duties of trust or reciprocal reliance form the groundwork of human interaction and social cooperation. Yet all three appear to be derived from justice: based on respect for persons as autonomous individuals, on the one hand, and on mutual trust or reciprocal reliance, on the other. While duties of respect and noninterference have been a powerful focus of liberal theory, duties of reciprocity, especially in the form of mutual trust, have been much less considered. Yet there is no question that these are values based on the requirements of justice. It is justice that requires us to pay our debts and keep our promises. But it is not the justice of noninterference and respect for autonomy. It is not the justice of separation, but the justice of interaction. Some theories have tried to explain these duties of promising and paying debts in terms of the duty of noninterference, but these accounts are always awkward. And that is because noninterference is the wrong aspect of justice with which to explain positive duties. These duties are founded on the affirmative aspect of justice: the justice of interactions, of reciprocity and reliance and trust. But they are nonetheless duties of justice for that. This affirmative side of justice is badly in need of further analysis. We need to understand the weight and scope of duties of reciprocal reliance. This brief sketch at least explains how the duties are related to and distinguished from one another.

Let me sum up briefly the points made here. Family (or natural) obligations are better explained on liberal grounds as obligations of membership (i.e., as obligations implied in communal cooperative endeavor that can be institutionally justified) than by traditional notions of biology or consent alone. Professional obligations are traditionally considered contractual and thus justified by consent. Yet in circumstances of general responsibility of profession or employment, the appeal to voluntariness or autonomy tells us less than one might hope. When one holds a responsible position (as in profession or employment), the position itself is constituted as a set of obligations in the form of a role. Since others must, and do, reasonably rely on occupational specialists to meet the responsibilities associated with their positions, whether or not they freely choose the position or its full complement of attendant obligations, the idea of reliance must be included in any adequate explanation and justification of occupational obligation. This is not to say that consent is not relevant. The nature of the consent component in employment is usually that of agreeing to be a participant in an ongoing venture over which one does not have full control, like joining a team. Ordinarily, what you consent to is a role or position composed of certain duties or general responsibilities within a larger entity. That is to say, you consent to become a member of that larger entity and in a particular capacity or role. You consent to play a part that you yourself do not get to define. All this shows that the ideas of role and membership are crucial elements in an adequate account of occupational obligation. But how do consent and role (or contract and membership) interact within the context of professional obligation? They combine the following elements:

1. Duties of contract, which I construe as obligations of cooperative commitment for reciprocal benefit by otherwise unrelated parties, perform a central explanatory function.

2. Duties of membership, which are obligations of common connection by parties ordinarily identified with one another by role or objective, are also necessary factors.
3. Both of the preceding are based on mutual reliance and common contribution, which I develop as two elements of justice as reciprocity in cooperative interaction.
4. Both can be distinguished from negative duties as duties of separation or respect for individuals as such.
5. While negative duties protect individual integrity, positive duties of reciprocity or mutual trust form the groundwork of personal connection, human interaction, and social cooperation.
6. Finally, despite their differences, all these duties are derived from justice, based either on respect for persons or on reciprocal reliance and mutual trust. Thus, to account for basic liberal democratic institutions of family and contract, the concept of justice must include justice as reciprocity, as well as justice as respect for persons as individuals.

Acknowledging this analysis of professional (or occupational) obligation also reinforces the view that an adequate liberal theory cannot rely on an atomistic social vision, even as the basis of contractual obligation, the paradigm of traditional liberal theory. Simple models of consent alone are much too narrow to accommodate the complex features of any ongoing contractual relations (which is to say, most actual contracts) as the long-standing debate over consent and reliance in legal theory attests. And when we move to the context of professional or occupational obligation (surely a very large component of contractual obligation), we find that these cannot be explained without reference to some account of cooperative communal interaction such as that provided by analysis in terms of group membership and/or role relations. I have suggested one such analysis here. Adopting it or anything like it "socializes" liberal individualism just as incorporating a serious liberal account of family obligations will do.

Thus, providing even the beginnings of an account of special positive duties in terms of the traditional categories of natural and contractual relations that attempts to accommodate actual liberal social practices and institutions requires a cooperative social vision that eliminates atomistic individualism as a viable foundation and broadens the concept of justice to include ideas of reciprocity as well as noninterference. This is an important point. It shows that standard traditional liberal categories of affirmative obligation (namely, natural and contractual relations) cannot account for special positive duties if they are construed in traditionally narrow terms. Now these categories can easily be, and often are, interpreted more broadly just as I have interpreted them more broadly here. My way is surely not the only way to do this, but however it is done, it will require a liberal foundation that relies on a cooperative rather than an atomistic vision of social life and human nature, as well as a concept of justice that explicitly includes the requirements of cooperative social interaction.

The positive side of justice and the cooperative element of special positive duty that I have been discussing here have been much neglected by the liberal tradition, and this causes a gap in the ability of liberal theory to account adequately for obligations that are in fact commonly recognized and relied upon in liberal societies, including familial and contractual duties. It also has affected the liberal analysis and understanding of obligations that are more controversial than those I have been discussing here, namely, political obligations. Developing that theme, however, is a topic for another time.

Notes

1. See, e.g., Will Kymlicka, *Multicultural Citizenship: A Liberal Theory of Minority Rights* (Oxford: Clarendon Press, 1995); Alan Buchanan, *Succession* (Boulder, Colo.: Westview Press, 1991).

2. E.g., Carol Gould, *Rethinking Democracy* (New York: Cambridge University Press, 1988); Larry May, *Sharing Responsibility* (Lawrence: University Press of Kansas, 1992).

3. See Patricia Smith, "Family Responsibility and the Nature of Obligation," in *Kindred Matters: A Reconsideration of the Family*, ed. Diana Meyers, Ken Kipnis, and Cornelius Murphy (Ithaca, N.Y.: Cornell University Press, 1994); Smith, *Liberalism and Affirmative Obligation* (New York: Oxford University Press, 1997).

4. Peter Singer, *The Widening Circle: Ethics and Sociobiology* (New York: Farrar, Straus and Giroux, 1981).

5. E.g., John Rawls, *A Theory of Justice* (Cambridge, Mass.: Harvard University Press, 1971); Gould, *Rethinking Democracy*.

6. See, e.g., Jeffrie G. Murphy, *Retribution, Justice and Therapy* (Dordrecht: Reidol, 1979).

7. Aristotle, *Nicomachean Ethics*, trans. T. Irwin (New York: Hackett, 1985).

8. See Laurence Becker, *Reciprocity* (New York: Routledge and Kegan Paul, 1986).

9. For discussion and analysis, see Gould, *Rethinking Democracy*.

10. Aristotle, *Nichomachean Ethics*.

11. Cf. Virginia Held, *Rights and Goods: Justifying Social Action* (New York: Free Press, 1984).

12. See Smith, *Liberalism and Affirmative Action*.

13. See ibid.

14. See ibid., chap. 4.

15. See, e.g., P. S. Atiyah, *Essays on Contracts* (Oxford: Oxford University Press, 1986); see also Atiyah, *Promises, Morals, and the Law* (Oxford: Oxford University Press, 1981).

16. For fuller discussion see Smith, *Liberalism and Affirmative Obligation*, esp. chaps. 6, 7.

17. As with the consent element, the reciprocity of the benefit may be minimal, that is, very unequal, perhaps even unfair. Yet there will always be some mutual benefit for both parties.

18. See Atiyah, *Promises, Morals, and the Law*; Smith, *Liberalism and Affirmative Obligation*.

19. See Smith, *Liberalism and Affirmative Obligation*, chap. 7.

20. This distinction is not captured necessarily by any single interpretation of the terms I selected. We can only use them stipulatively to represent the distinction.

21. Charles Fried, *Contract as Promise: A Theory of Contractual Obligation* (Cambridge, Mass.: Harvard University Press, 1981).

22. Held, *Rights and Goods*.

23. See Smith, "Family Responsibility and the Nature of Obligation," in *Kindred Matters: A Reconsideration of the Family*.

Chapter 10

Recognition, Identity, and the Accommodation of Differences: Groups in the Liberal State

Emily R. Gill

Even casual acquaintance with current events in the 1990s demonstrates the fact that individuals and groups are not assimilating into a common culture, in spite of the reciprocal interdependence supposedly promoted by global networks of information and transportation. Instead, individuals and groups are asserting or reasserting their particularist identities, be these ethnic, religious, cultural, or national. In the politics of multiculturalism, writes Charles Taylor, "The thesis is that our identity is partly shaped by recognition or its absence. . . . Nonrecognition or misrecognition can inflict harm, can be a form of oppression, imprisoning someone in a false, distorted, and reduced mode of being."[1] The genesis of the human mind and of human agency is through interaction and interchange with others, giving human life "its fundamentally *dialogical* character."[2] That is, one's identity is defined and worked out in dialogue with others, even when the dialogue is hypothetical and internal. Individuality is developed, then, within a particular framework. Yael Tamir's concept of the contextual individual "portrays an autonomous person who can reflect on, evaluate, and choose his conception of the good, his ends, and his cultural and national affiliations, but is capable of such choices because he is situated in a particular social and cultural environment that offers him evaluative criteria."[3]

Too often, however, these evaluative criteria have been interpreted to minimize or suppress differences among individuals and groups. As Thomas Bridges asserts, the Enlightenment denigrated cultural particularism by elevating universalism. And it is true that citizens of the liberal democratic polity each "must develop and cultivate not only an identity shaped by the values and ranking systems of some particularistic cultural community, but also the identity of a free and equal individual (i.e., an identity defined by a certain kind of independence from any particularistic set of values),"[4] if they are to exhibit civic virtues such as tolerance and the rational resolution of disputes. The problem, in Bridges's view, is that modern liberal theory has portrayed the individual's former, particularistic or *communitarian* identity as an obstacle to the development of the latter, *civic* identity, rather than as a building block in its formation. According to Bridges, "Modernist liberalism represented the standpoint of citizenship as a standpoint stripped of all particularistic cultural attributes. The process of developing a civic identity was thereby defined as a process of stripping away the culturally accidental in order to arrive at a supposedly culture-neutral, natural, and universal standpoint."[5] Civic identity appeared to be one's primary identity, developed through "an inward search for a 'true' self."[6] William Connolly makes a similar point: although "a politics of the common good is essential" both to collective identity and to collective action, "the very success in defining and enacting commonalities tends to naturalize them, to make them appear as unambiguous goods lodged in nature or consent or reason or the universal character of the normal individual or ideal dialogue or a higher direction in being."[7]

A viable postmodernist liberalism, in Bridges's view, must reverse the relationship between civic and communitarian identity and culture: "Civic culture has but one function. It must provide the cultural resources sufficient to render intelligible the liberal democratic moral ideals of individual freedom and equality, and to motivate citizens to pursue these ideals."[8] More specifically, "Civic culture, then, as a partial and countervailing culture, presupposes and remains dependent upon communitarian culture. It cannot stand by itself."[9] Abstract ideals of natural freedom and equality or of autonomous reason cannot alone motivate individuals, grounded in particularistic cultural identities, to develop civic identities. "Liberal political institutions can flourish only where the particularistic cultural communities subject to them can find a basis within their particular traditions for an affirmation of civic freedom and civic equality."[10]

In this chapter, I propose to examine the relationship between communitarian and civic identities. First, I shall examine the role of particularistic cultural identity in the development of civic identity. If situation within a particular social and cultural environment is a precondition of individual autonomy, individuals can interpret and reinterpret their cultural identities in ways that exert a direct impact on their civic identities. Second, I shall examine instances of conflict between communitarian and civic identities. Whether we endeavor to protect whole cultures or only given cultural practices, there are limits on the degree to which communitarian identity *should* function as the basis of civic identity. Finally, I shall argue that although consensus should be contestable, it is also a necessary component of liberal politics. I agree with Bridges that the civic culture of liberalism requires the development of narrative imagination, of the capacity to view the goods constitutive of particularistic identity as provisional objects of allegiance. Although this capacity does not require a universalist or essentialist stance, it does require an attitude shared by all liberal citizens.

I

In line with Taylor's view of the dialogical character of the self, Will Kymlicka holds that cultural membership is a primary good, and that its recognition contributes to and expands individual choice: "Cultural membership is not a means used in the pursuit of one's ends. It is rather the context within which we choose our ends, and come to see their value, and this is a precondition of self-respect, of the sense that one's ends are worth pursuing."[11] In line with her own view that the contextual individual is both a situated and a choosing self, Yael Tamir argues that "culture can be a precondition of reflective thinking and the exercise of choice, while in itself remaining an object of choice."[12] Cultural particularism appears desirable in two respects. First, without a plurality of cultures, individuals cannot make choices among cultures. "Cultural plurality ensures that reflections about one's own culture take place within a genuine context, one offering models for imitation and even options for assimilation."[13] One's cultural context, then, denotes not only a primary communal membership from within which one makes choices about one's moral identity but also a culturally plural environment from within which one may make cultural choices. Thus cultural pluralism benefits the members of or participants in given cultural groups, those who may borrow from or even assimilate into a particular culture from outside, and, finally, everyone else "for whom the existence of any culture enriches their own experience of what it means to be human."[14]

Although cultural particularism possesses an instrumental value, its second claim to desirability lies in its intrinsic value. To expand Tamir's focus on nations, I suggest that cultural communities as well as nations meet the test in which "recognition of fellow-members, the drawing of boundaries between members and nonmembers, . . . becomes a product of human imagination, contingent on the belief that there are similarities among members."[15] Cultural self-determination, like national self-determination, would entail the public expression of identity, or "the right of individuals to a public sphere, thus implying that individuals are entitled to establish institutions and manage their communal life in ways that reflect their communal values, traditions, and history—in short, their culture."[16] For Tamir, the right to adhere to a particular culture is an individual right and interest, and overall it is the individual to whom the value of membership accrues. The communal domain, however, is not only an arena for the pursuit of individual interests but also "a space where one's communal identity finds expression."[17] That is, individuals enjoy a type of self-fulfillment in interacting with others that they cannot experience in isolation; the members of such an expressive association experience a belief in the existence of special and constitutive ties and obligations. Particularistic ties, then, are not parochial attachments to be transcended in the course of individual moral development. Instead, they fulfill a need which is part of the human condition: "Individuals are better off when they are able to share their lives with some particular others they care about and see as their partners in a life-project."[18]

The celebration of particularistic ties is indeed compatible with liberal political thought. Following the recent writings of John Rawls, Donald Moon suggests that because political liberalism focuses on politics, or the organization and aims of public power, it is necessarily limited in scope: "Political liberalism differs from other forms of liberalism because it takes political community itself as an aim, and not the realization of a particular vision of human flourishing or human excellence."[19] Bridges also describes political liberalism as partial rather than totalizing in the way it functions. Any civic culture must both render intelligible the values and standpoint necessary for citizenship and also provide motivation for the development of the requisite moral capacities.[20] The civic culture of liberalism is no exception in this regard. But, Bridges notes,

> First, while metaphysical liberalism was [a] universalist and essentialist doctrine—a doctrine claiming to pronounce the truth about the very essence of political morality—political or rhetorical liberalism is a particularistic cultural doctrine, defining only the norms proper to one particular and contingent form of political association. Second, while metaphysical liberalism, in its universalism and essentialism, was a comprehensive or totalizing doctrine, a doctrine applying to the whole of life, political or rhetorical liberalism is a doctrine that applies to only a part of

life, the part concerned with the capacities and norms proper to liberal democratic citizenship.[21]

Instead of a theory of justice to which truth claims are attached, political liberalism instead offers "a statement of the principles of justice that might win the uncoerced adherence of the reasonable citizens of a modern constitutional democracy."[22] Because the goal of this project is the consensus of a specific audience, a rhetorical strategy of persuasion is essential. In addition, "Because a rhetorical concept of reason views critical reasoning as an activity that is always culturally and historically situated, it is not inclined to view as rationally defective the particularistic cultural supports of civic values."[23] If particularistic ties are central to and constitutive of human identity, and if communitarian identity is a potential bulwark of the civic culture of liberalism, how might recognition of the legitimacy of particularistic attachments work out in practice?

According to Jeff Spinner, "Liberalism is a political theory that is concerned with giving people power over their own lives and an equal say in how government is run."[24] One way of giving people power over their lives is by allowing them to define and interpret for themselves their particularistic identities. They should not face a forced choice between defining themselves solely or primarily by their communitarian or private identities, on the one hand, and embracing cultural conformity or public identity at the expense of their communitarian identities, on the other. Spinner is concerned with the ways in which public and private identity affect each other. Liberalism deals with public institutions but "is also a prescription for how people ought to act when they meet their fellow citizens in civil society and in the public square. In many different settings liberal citizens may see others whom they dislike, but liberalism calls on them to control their feelings."[25] We must treat others as equals even when we do not think that they really are equals. But our behavior affects our thoughts: "Habituated to treat others equally or at least civilly, liberal citizens may begin to look upon others equally or civilly."[26] These demands mean that virtues of liberal citizenship exist that keep liberalism from moral agnosticism on the character of citizens and that render liberal citizenship more robust in content than critics acknowledge.

Liberal limits on the scope of authority, suggests Moon, are intended "to create a moral space within which individuals and groups can freely pursue their ends and ideals without having to seek approval from others, or suffer serious legal liabilities for their choices."[27] Although Spinner does not require approval of others' practices, he does believe that liberal citizenship requires more than toleration: "When ethnic groups become accepted in the United States, their practices become part of the larger community."[28] The liberal polity has not always reflected this hope. For example, "Black Americans have cultural practices that others do not share, but members of mainstream culture sometimes demand cultural conformity before they give Black people a chance to succeed in many mainstream institutions."[29] With respect to immigrants, "Too often citizens demand complete conformity from immigrants; at other times, citizens grant that they will merely tolerate others. Both of these attitudes enable citizens to escape the hard work that should be done by liberal society in accepting immigrants."[30] That is, "Liberalism calls upon citizens to revamp their image of the citizens of their state as the state gains new members or as old members take on new practices. Liberalism constantly makes new demands on citizens; it calls upon citizens to consider and accept new practices as they arise and as long as they are not illiberal."[31] The purportedly neutral state is not neutral among cultural groups. But in the course of what Spinner calls pluralistic integration, public institutions can teach about and celebrate ethnic values and practices in ways that encourage citizens to develop a more inclusive image of their fellows. "Once particular ethnics and their practices are accepted, then their ethnicity need not be a public concern. Until this happens, however, the social pressure on ethnics to conform must be fought."[32] Otherwise, as Connolly notes more generally, "The pretense to neutrality functions to maintain established settlements below the threshold of public discourse. The issue must be politicized rather than neutralized, even though that response too contains its dangers."[33]

Social interaction with others may weaken the existence of robust ethnic and cultural identities as readily as social pressure does. Yet the virtues of liberal citizenship allow individuals, even when constituted by their particular "istic" ties, to interpret their communitarian identities in various ways, accepting some values and practices and rejecting others. In other words, public recognition of the legitimacy of communitarian identity broadens the ways in which individuals may understand and interpret themselves. For example, "Jews can now interpret their own identity; they can decide for themselves what it means to be Jewish. . . . Liberal citizenship does not mean the inevitable end of Jewish identity, but it does mean that Jews can drop, add, and combine cultural practices in ways that will transform Jewish identity."[34] Similarly, "Denied the right to define themselves," the claim by some African-Americans to nationhood "can be seen as an attempt for them to become self-interpreting."[35] Traditionally, culture and communitarian identity were private matters. "When one version of citizenship (a white version) is the norm in society, however, the relegation of Black identity to the private realm denies equal citizenship to Blacks by perpetuating an exclusive version of citizenship." Recognizing African-American culture and institutions as legitimate shows "that there is more than one way to be an American citizen and that there is more than one set of cultural institutions and practices worthy of American citizens."[36]

In Spinner's sketch of pluralistic integration, liberal citizens' acceptance of ethnic practices compatible with liberalism means that ethnic or cultural groups can preserve their differences.[37] "Pluralistic integration means—or should mean—that different cultural practices become diffuse, spreading out across the population." Although the desire for equal citizenship leads to the initial quest for public recognition, this recognition will also begin to break down distinctive and particularistic identities, the "integrative" aspect of pluralistic integration. "Without this recognition, however, many ethnics will be denied equal citizenship. This is the dilemma that many ethnics face in liberal states, a dilemma that cannot be fully resolved."[38] Accordingly, some groups have attempted to preserve their differences by *resisting* the diffusion of their cultural practices. They have established boundaries between themselves and others, creating a public space with public sanction within which a particular group's identity can flourish because it is the dominant group. Liberals eschew restrictions on choice. But "choice . . . is restricted not only by official state policies; a decision by the state to avoid involvement would also restrict choices, but it would restrict the choices of a different set of people."[39] Greater opportunities for some groups result in more restricted opportunities for others. Communitarian and civic identities may reinforce each other in some circumstances, but they may conflict in others. It is to the latter circumstances that I now turn.

II

The example of bounded cultures such as Quebec serves to demonstrate "that characterizing the 'identity' of a culture is itself a politically and ideologically charged issue." According to Amelie Rorty, the arguments of those like Taylor and, by extension, Tamir suggest that "because individuals are, at least in part, essentially constituted and sustained by their cultural identities, . . . their basic protection extends to the protection of their cultures." Furthermore, "The claim to the right of cultural survival and of cultural self-determination . . . appears to derive from the right accorded to the citizens in a liberal state actively to pursue their conceptions of a good life. If the state legitimately promotes the self-defining activities of individuals—centrally, for instance, assuring their basic education—it also is charged with promoting the self-defining activities of its constitutive cultural groups."[40]

In other words, matters of culture and identity are not simply private affairs. Spinner notes that the survival of distinct cultures is difficult in the liberal state, both because illiberal practices are discouraged or forbidden and because the diffusion of cultural practices across the population weakens the connection between practice and identity. Moreover, as we have seen, pressure to conform to the dominant culture betrays "implicit cultural norms that typically exist in liberal states."[41] Finally, the argument that cultural practices are private matters "does not recognize the differences between what liberals tolerate and what they want. Although liberals often emphasize laws and procedures, there is a liberalism of tendencies, a liberalism that encourages certain values and practices and discourages others. Liberalism puts obstacles in front of some life choices."[42] Thus, the right to a cultural context involves not only a cultural claim but also a political one, a facet of cultural identity not always recognized by such defenders as Taylor and Tamir.[43] Communitarian identity may function as a potential support for the civic culture of liberalism. But whether this relationship between cultural and civic identities so evolves is often shaped by political decisions.

Contrasting models for the interface between particularistic and civic identities can be found in the work of Will Kymlicka and Chandran Kukathas. Kymlicka defends the rights of cultural minorities who desire legal recognition as a distinct cultural community, such as aboriginal peoples in Canada. We are "dependent on a cultural community for our self-development and for our context of choice," yet we may rightly claim independence, "as self-directed beings, from any of the specific roles and relationships that exist in the community."[44] On the one hand, because cultural membership should not disadvantage or impose costs on individuals as a result of unchosen constituents of their identities, certain groups need special political rights "to remove inequalities in the context of choice which arise before people even make their choices."[45] On the other hand, the recognition of a cultural structure "should not be used to protect a particular preferred vision of what sort of *character* the community should have."[46] In Kymlicka's view, "The cultural community continues to exist even when its members are free to modify the character of the culture, should they find its traditional ways of life no longer worthwhile."[47] Moreover, "On a liberal theory of equality, the very reasons to respect a principle affirming the importance of cultural membership to minority groups is also a reason to respect a principle affirming the rights of individual members of those groups."[48]

To Kukathas, on the other hand, it is the right of association, not the right of a cultural community, that is fundamental. The former is a right of individuals, but nevertheless "it gives considerable power to the group, denying others the right to intervene in its practices—whether in the name of liberalism or any other moral ideal."[49] Although cultural rights should protect autonomy, in a cultural structure where autonomy and critical reflection are *not* valued, Kymlicka privileges individual autonomy over cultural integrity, undermining the cultural rights he purports to defend. Kukathas suggests, by contrast, that social unions that make up a liberal society are those of individuals, and that "for each social union to have any significant measure of integrity, it must *to some extent* be impervious to the values of the wider liberal society." Since those disenchanted with the cultural character of a community may leave, "what matters most when assessing whether a way of life is legitimate is whether the individuals taking part in it are prepared to acquiesce in it."[50] Yet Kukathas's formulation is also problematic. A liberal conception of minority rights cannot "justify . . . special rights for a culture against its own members. . . . Liberals are committed to supporting the rights of individuals to decide for themselves which aspects of their cultural heritage are worth passing on."[51] Overall, where Kymlicka's liberal society champions the substantive values of equality and individual autonomy, Kukathas defends "one in which different ways of life can coexist even if some of those ways of life do not value equality and autonomy."[52]

Contemporary liberals like Bridges and Moon, we saw earlier, reject the universalistic, totalizing, or essentialist claims of earlier liberal theories in favor of a particularistic and partial interpretation. From Moon's perspective, "Rather the discourse of political liberalism must be contextualized to particular historical settings, governed by a particular set of normative understandings, which can then be called into question." More specifically, "Each 'we' must remain alive to the possibility that what 'we' consider reasonable may be experienced by others as a form of opposition."[53] Kymlicka's attempt to protect and sustain minority cultures might be interpreted as an effort to contextualize political discourse to particular types of historical settings, those in which individuals' communitarian identities, in Bridges's terms, are in danger of being swallowed up by their civic identities as members of the larger political community. For Kymlicka, "A liberal needs to know whether a request for special rights or resources is grounded in differential choices or unequal circumstances." With respect to the latter, as with Canadian aborigines, cultural minorities "have to spend their resources on securing the cultural membership which makes sense of their lives, something which nonaboriginal people get for free."[54]

If, as Spinner suggests, liberalism presents obstacles to some life choices, either through pressure to conform to the dominant culture or through cultural diffusion, certainly "enforcing the authority of . . . 'cultural' groups can contribute to their survival by making it costly for individuals to abandon them, and by strengthening the ties of members of the group to each other and the salience of one's identity as a member of the group."[55] On the other hand, the effort to respond to differences may lead "to a false imputation of essentialist qualities to the members of some group, ignoring important variations within groups."[56] Or, as Tamir explains, "The right to culture is interpreted as the right to preserve the culture in its 'authentic' form,"[57] even if this violates individual rights in some cases. Essentialist or totalizing claims, then, may be made not only at the expense of groups within the whole but also at that of individuals within a particular group, a point recognized by Kymlicka in his refusal to sanction the preservation of any given cultural character.

We may avoid this sort of essentialism by recognizing, with Tamir, that "respect is due to cultural preferences not by virtue of their intrinsic contents, but because they reflect autonomous choices." Each of us is born with a particularistic identity, but this does not preclude our moving beyond that identity. "Having discovered the cultural and national frameworks we were born into, we can reflect on them critically and exercise choices regarding our future commitments and affiliations. . . . Furthermore, . . . [individuals] should also have the right to define the meanings attached to this membership, that is, they should be the ones to decide on the cultural practices they wish to adopt, and on the ways of expressing them."[58] Because affirming one's identity with one's native culture and choosing a different cultural identity are equally matters of choice, both options should be subsidized, on Tamir's view, by the according of special rights if identity with one's chosen culture results in unequal circumstances compared with membership in other cultures. "Membership in a cultural community is a matter of personal choice, but this does not imply that members have chosen to be a minority."[59] Moreover, once cultural membership is recognized, Tamir, like Spinner, holds that individuals should interpret for themselves the meanings of their cultural identities. Her overall approach gains support in the light of Connolly's inverse observation that some contingent elements of identity are branded or entrenched, and thus resistant to modification even when a will to change is present.[60] Thus the distinction between choice and circumstance may be a specious one.

Although Tamir and Kymlicka diverge in their views of the extent to which the affirmation of unchosen constituents of one's identity is a matter of choice, both avoid essentialist or totalizing claims, believing that the members of a cultural community should be free to define for themselves the meaning of their membership and, in Spinner's words, "to become self-interpreting."[61] Yet Spinner, like Kukathas, disagrees with Kymlicka "that liberal rights transcend cultures." Focusing on cultural structure over content or practice, Kymlicka suggests individual choice both in maintaining and in changing culture. But the net effect is that "Kymlicka allows his liberalism to run amuck, destroying the very cultures he wants to protect. . . . In other words, the liberal state should protect minority cultures in its midst—as long as they are liberal!"[62] Spinner's perspective is that of one who champions the right of cultural communities like the Amish to seek exclusion, not inclusion, as a means of cultural survival. If those who would reinterpret Amish practices may do so while remaining in the Amish community, the resulting dilution of cultural homogeneity may cause these communities to disappear, actually allowing for less choice among distinctive cultures. As Spinner explains, "This shows a paradox of liberal theory; liberalism allows people to reject liberal values. The liberal state cannot insist that its citizens embrace liberalism. Liberalism allows people to think for themselves, to make their own decisions—or even to decide not to think for themselves."[63]

On the other hand, Spinner disagrees with Kukathas that a cultural community is purely a private association, and that as such it must therefore possess a high degree of internal autonomy. First, cultures change over time; a particular interpretation of cultural identity should not be entrenched for all time. "Second, not all cultural practices should be protected simply because they are someone's cultural practices. Illiberal practices should not be protected."[64] Finally, cultural diversity can coexist with the economic subordination of some groups to others, and celebration of the former should not be allowed to eclipse the presence of the latter. We may infer not only that cultural identity is not merely a private affair but also that the degree to which it *is* a private affair is publicly determined and is therefore a public concern. By discouraging or forbidding illiberal practices and by emphasizing specific practices rather than cultures, Spinner's model of "pluralistic integration rejects the idea that cultures are somehow sacrosanct and need to be protected at all costs."[65]

The point is that although we may disagree about the value of given practices, no culture can celebrate or even tolerate all practices, not even the civic culture of liberalism. According to Moon, "We may all agree that certain drives, certain desires, ought to be repressed, even while we strive to remain open to the possibility that our judgments in this regard are mistaken."[66] As for those who disagree, according to Charles Larmore, "A liberal political system need not feel obliged to reason with fanatics; it must simply take the necessary precautions to guard against them."[67] And for Rawls, the fact that doctrines exist which reject democratic freedoms "gives us the practical task of containing them—like war and disease—so that they do not overturn political justice."[68] Moreover, the determination of which practices are incompatible with liberalism, which groups are peopled by fanatics, and which doctrines reject democratic freedoms will be made by the dominant culture within the liberal polity. Although Spinner's focus on cultural practices rather than cultural structure may grant legitimacy to a large number of practices, the larger community decides on the legitimacy of given cultural practices, thus still controlling the content of cultural identity by extending or withdrawing its protection.

Another way to put this is that the liberal polity itself is the legal expression of a particular cultural structure. Although in Bridges's terms the civic culture of political liberalism is partial rather than totalizing in its function, allegiance to this civic culture is *itself* a type of particularistic or communitarian identity. On this view, the liberal polity is a voluntary association with substantive purposes, or "not merely . . . a gathering of individuals striving to improve their lot, but rather . . . a community struggling to preserve its distinctive character."[69] The question is that of how this distinctive character, however defined, may be expressed in both its commonalities and its diversities without, in Connolly's terms, "normalization through a nonpolitics of gentle assimilation."[70]

III

For addressing diversity, Rawls's conception of an overlapping consensus of reasonable religious, philosophical, and moral doctrines may itself be a controversial view, avoiding deep disagreement and conflict simply by removing it from political deliberation.[71] Socially recognized differences are essential to identity, which "converts difference into otherness in order to secure its own self-certainty."[72] But too often, a particular identity defines certain differences as evil, abnormal, or dangerous, in order to paint itself as good or rational. According to Connolly, "This constellation of constructed others now becomes both essential to the truth of the powerful identity and a threat to it."[73] Although identity is developed dialogically, then, opposition emerges from this process as surely as consensus. How might we achieve consensus sufficient for the practice of politics without suppressing the differences without which identity cannot exist? Let me make two brief suggestions.

First, although multicultural activists often understand liberal toleration as insufficiently sensitive to difference or tending toward the co-optation of minorities,[74] liberalism need not be practiced in this manner. Bridges suggests that "citizens must identify and strengthen the doctrines, themes, and practices within their local cultural traditions that can provide additional normative and persuasive resources in support of liberal moral ideals."[75] Brian Walker argues that a public culture or common citizenship is created by "individuals who strive to open up a position of tolerance within whichever culture they find themselves."[76] An overlapping consensus does not precede but instead results from this process. As Walker explains, "Fighting for toleration is not a matter of attempting to align other groups with a preexisting order, but a form of dialogue in the course of which the picture of what toleration is and requires gradually becomes clear. By attempting to build my idea of toleration on the terrain of the other, I am myself affected by new and alien ideas, and perhaps my own view is changed."[77] In what Melissa Williams calls a political rather than a juridical approach, "Standards of justice can only avoid reproducing inequality if they are defined *within* a political process that provides the opportunity for marginalized groups' perspectives to be expressed and heeded."[78]

In short, not only should liberal society as a whole exhibit diversity, but so also should individuals, as it were, through their intersubjective awareness of and thoughtfulness about various alternatives. As Walker states, when we relinquish the view of cultures and individuals as "sealed unities,"[79] we may realize "that doctrines can take either tolerant or intolerant forms and the goal is to encourage the former,"[80] even when this means challenging the nontolerant to modify their own interpretations of their beliefs. As a situated cultural agent, I must possess the ability to move beyond or outside my own tradition, to perceive the potential in diverse ideas for the creation of a common citizenship, and to be open to changing my views, in Spinner's terms, of what it means to be an American citizen or a citizen of a liberal democratic polity.

Second, even amid the recognition of diversity, some consensus is a necessary component of liberal politics, even if this focuses mainly upon creating conditions for substantive agreement. Bridges suggests that the capacity for or the practice of civic freedom assumes commitment to a particular concept of the good and to membership in a particularistic community. Yet "it requires . . . at the same time, an affirmation of its revocability, an affirmation of the purely voluntary nature of that commitment."[81] To the extent that one's identity is defined through a particular life narrative, "a capacity for civic freedom consists of a capacity to incorporate into every narratively constructed identity or self a recognition and affirmation of its own narratively constructed status."[82] That is, individuals come to see that their particularistic or communitarian identities may be constitutive of their original identities, but in a provisional sense. Narrative imagination recognizes the possibility of commitment to different ideals from those to which one is committed, or of giving different narrative readings to the same series of life events. And in the context of narrative imagination, rationality is "the capacity to examine critically the means and ends involved in the pursuit of a particularistic concept of the good."[83] To achieve this understanding requires, however, the development of the capacity for reflective decision making, itself a particularistic virtue within the civic culture of liberalism. If we can hone this capacity, we may recognize that there is more than one way to be a Jew, an African-American, an American citizen, or a citizen of a liberal state. Although this does not require a universalist or essentialist stance, it does require an attitude in common shared by all liberal citizens.

Notes

1. Charles Taylor, *Multiculturalism and "The Politics of Recognition"* (Princeton, N.J.: Princeton University Press, 1992), 25.

2. Ibid., 32; emphasis in original.

3. Yael Tamir, *Liberal Nationalism* (Princeton, N.J.: Princeton University Press, 1993), 33.

4. Thomas Bridges, *The Culture of Citizenship: Inventing Postmodern Civil Culture* (Albany: State University of New York Press, 1994), 35. See also, 10, 86, 120.

5. Ibid., 39.

6. Ibid., 57; see 53–57.

7. William E. Connolly, *Identity/Difference: Democratic Negotiations of Political Paradox* (Ithaca, N.Y.: Cornell University Press, 1991), 93; see also 87.

8. Bridges, *Culture of Citizenship*, 156.

9. Ibid., 157.

10. Ibid., 202; see also 157, 165, 215, 234, 264.

11. Will Kymlicka, *Liberalism, Community and Culture* (Oxford: Clarendon Press, 1991), 192; see also 169–72.

12. Tamir, *Liberal Nationalism*, 7.

13. Ibid., 30.

14. Ibid., 32; see also 20–32; Taylor, *Multiculturalism*, 87.

15. Tamir, *Liberal Nationalism*, 68; see also 65–68.

16. Ibid., 70; see also 42–48.

17. Ibid., 74.

18. Ibid., 94; see also 63, 83–86, 96–102, 115.

19. J. Donald Moon, *Constructing Community: Moral Pluralism and Tragic Conflict* (Princeton, N.J.: Princeton University Press, 1993), 8; see also 8–9, 35, 45–46.

20. Bridges, *Culture of Citizenship*, 33.

21. Ibid., 115.

22. Ibid., 69.

23. Ibid., 82.

24. Jeff Spinner, *The Boundaries of Citizenship: Race, Ethnicity, and Nationality in the Liberal State* (Baltimore: Johns Hopkins University Press, 1994), 3.

25. Ibid., 47; see also 37–38, 45–48.

26. Ibid., 48; see also 185–86.

27. Moon, *Constructing Community*, 37–38.

28. Spinner, *Boundaries of Citizenship*, 59

29. Ibid., 114.

30. Ibid., 74; see also 167.

31. Ibid., 75.

32. Ibid., 80; see also 60–62, 171–75. On the state's purported neutrality, see ibid., 10, 79; Tamir, *Liberal Nationalism*, 141–43; Moon, *Constructing Community*, 11, 55–58; Taylor, *Multiculturalism*, 43–44.

33. Connolly, *Identity/Difference*, 161.

34. Spinner, *Boundaries of Citizenship*, 51; see also 25–26, 29–32, 49–53.

35. Ibid., 30.

36. Ibid., 125–26; see also Taylor, *Multiculturalism*, 80–81.

37. Spinner, *Boundaries of Citizenship*, 62.

38. Ibid., 173; see also Tamir, *Liberal Nationalism*, 53–56.

39. Spinner, *Boundaries of Citizenship*, 159; see also Tamir, *Liberal Nationalism*; 45; Taylor, *Multiculturalism*, 54–56.

40. Amelie Okensburg Rorty, "The Hidden Politics of Cultural Identification," *Political Theory* 22 (1994): 152–53.

41. Spinner, *Boundaries of Citizenship*, 184.

42. Ibid., 185; see also William A. Galston, *Liberal Purposes: Goods, Virtues, and Diversity in the Liberal State* (New York: Cambridge University Press, 1991), esp. 143–49.

43. Bernard Yack, "Reconciling Liberalism and Nationalism," *Political Theory* 23 (1995): 171–72.

44. Kymlicka, *Liberalism*, 127.

45. Ibid., 190; see also 185–93, 237–42.

46. Ibid., 168; emphasis in original.

47. Ibid., 167; see also 165–72, 59–61, 87–89.

48. Ibid., 191.

49. Chandran Kukathas, "Are There Any Cultural Rights?" *Political Theory* 20 (1992): 117–18.

50. Ibid., 127; emphasis in original.

51. Will Kymlicka, "The Rights of Minority Cultures: Reply to Kukathas," *Political Theory* 20 (1992): 142.

52. Chandran Kukathas, "Cultural Rights Again: A Rejoinder to Kymlicka," *Political Theory* 20 (1992): 680.

53. Moon, *Constructing Community*, 100; see also 42; Rorty, "Hidden Politics of Cultural Identification," 158–59.

54. Kymlicka, *Liberalism*, 186–87.

55. Moon, *Constructing Community*, 181.

56. Ibid., 188; see also 178–89; Spinner, *Boundaries of Citizenship*, 135–36.

57. Tamir, *Liberal Nationalism*, 48; see also 48–53; Rorty, "Hidden Politics of Cultural Identification," 154–56.

58. Tamir, *Liberal Nationalism*, 37; see also 7–8.

59. Ibid. 41–42; cf. Kymlicka, *Liberalism*, 189–90, 237–42.

60. Connolly, *Identity/Difference*, 176.

61. Spinner, *Boundaries of Citizenship*, 30.

62. Ibid., 96; see also 96–99.

63. Ibid., 97; see also 103–4.

64. Ibid., 135–36; see also 62, 66–73, 149; Tamir, *Liberal Nationalism*, 37, 48–53.

65. Spinner, *Boundaries of Citizenship*, 76; see also 183–88, esp. 186.

66. Moon, *Constructing Community*, 219.

67. Charles Larmore, *Patterns of Moral Complexity* (New York: Cambridge University Press, 1987), 60.

68. John Rawls, *Political Liberalism* (New York: Columbia University Press, 1993), 64, n. 19.

69. Tamir, *Liberal Nationalism*, 127; see also 124–30, 160–62.

70. Connolly, *Identity/Difference*, 88; see also 88–90.

71. Brian Walker, "John Rawls, Mikhail Bakhtin, and the Praxis of Toleration," *Political Theory* 23 (1995): 104–5; and James Bohman, "Public Reason and Cultural Pluralism: Political Liberalism and the Problem of Moral Conflict," *Political Theory* 23 (May 1995): 264.

72. Connolly, *Identity/Difference*, 64.

73. Ibid., 66; see also 65–66.

74. Walker, "John Rawls, Mikhail Bakhtin," 113.

75. Bridges, *Culture of Citizenship*, 165.

76. Walker, "John Rawls, Mikhail Bakhtin," 120.

77. Ibid., 121; also see Bohman, "Public Reason and Cultural Pluralism," 269–70.

78. Melissa S. Williams, "Justice Toward Groups: Political Not Juridical," *Political Theory* 23 (1995): 69; emphasis in original.

79. Walker, "John Rawls, Mikhail Bakhtin," 116; see also 117, 109.

80. Ibid., 118.

81. Bridges, *Culture of Citizenship*, 173.

82. Ibid., 181; see also 169–89.

83. Ibid., 188; see also 209.

Part III

Cultural, Ethnic, and Religious Rights

Introduction

Education, Religion, and Affirmative Action

Leslie Francis

A remarkable amount of recent writing in political theory has concerned the justification of various specific group rights. This part of the volume takes up three group rights that have drawn a great deal of attention: rights to affirmative action, rights to religious practice and the education of children, and rights to land. Among these particular rights, some, such as religious rights, are defended as central to community life and values. Others, such as rights to land, may be seen as important to community values but may also be given the more limited justification that they are instrumentally important to the ongoing viability of the group. Still others, and the example here is affirmative action, are supported as part of securing justice for groups that have labored under burdens of poverty or discrimination.

Will Kymlicka's writings provide a useful framework for organizing the discussion of particular group rights in this part of the volume, as indeed they have set the terms for much of the recent debate, including several of the chapters here.[1] Kymlicka's writing lies at a crossroads between liberal and communitarian views. His central tenet is the liberal value of individual choice: individuals, he argues, should be free to choose their own conceptions of the good life, to lead their lives in accord with their own beliefs about values, and to question and rethink their conceptions of the good. At the same time, Kymlicka holds, people are born into cultures and share deep cultural bonds. Access to their own culture—in both public and private spheres—is a critical feature of the good life for most people; cultures thus play crucial supporting roles in the realization of liberal values.

In Kymlicka's view, liberals should favor group rights that support individual choices but equally should disfavor group rights that impede individuals' abilities to affirm or reevaluate their conceptions of the good. Rights of the group against outsiders—what Kymlicka calls *external group rights*—frequently further the autonomy of group members and promote fairness among groups. Examples include rights of groups to use their own languages in public contexts, rights to educational subsidies, rights to the protection of homelands, including the right to deny outsiders the ability to purchase land from group members, and rights to political institutions such as the establishment of electoral districts that afford groups political representation, or the devolution of governmental responsibilities to the local group level. On the other hand, rights of the group against their own members, which Kymlicka calls *internal group rights*, are not justified if they conflict with the autonomy of group members. Examples would be groups forbidding members to leave the group, groups limiting the education of children to discourage them from leaving the group, groups imposing traditional gender roles (including bodily mutilation or arranged marriage), or groups requiring members to continue to engage in traditional religious practices. Kymlicka's view is that groups should be protected against external coercion, but that individuals should be protected against internal coercion; the coherence of this position both for liberals and for defenders of group rights is a central focus of this part.

Kymlicka draws a second, intersecting set of distinctions among the content of group rights: polyethnic rights, group representational rights, and self-government rights. Polyethnic rights are group-specific measures intended to help religious and ethnic groups enjoy their cultural practices; examples would include requiring employers to accommodate different principal days of worship or permitting education in different languages. Representation rights are rights to have representatives of the group in the larger political unit; legislative districts drawn on ethnic lines are a clear example. Self-government rights include the variety of forms of devolved political authority, such as local government or territorial authority. The rights of affirmative action and religious practice discussed by Nelson, Van Wyk, and Anderson are polyethnic rights; the rights of governance for indigenous groups discussed by Tsosie are self-government rights. Kymlicka contends that self-government rights can be justified only for national minorities, such as conquered peoples or the Native American populations in the United States and Canada discussed by Tsosie. When immigrants leave their home societies voluntarily, Kymlicka believes, they should not expect to re-create structures of self-government in new lands. Polyethnic rights, on the other hand, can be justified for ethnic groups as a way of welcoming immigrants to new lands and encouraging their success within the larger culture, as well as a way of enriching the larger culture which they join. On these grounds, Kymlicka supports such polyethnic rights as educating children in native languages and exempting certain cultural practices (Sikh turbans) from otherwise valid regulation (wearing motorcycle helmets).

Kymlicka's liberal defense of group rights has been attacked both by communitarians, who claim it does not fully understand the role and importance of groups, and by liberals, who claim that it is insufficiently supportive of autonomy. The contributions to this part reflect attacks from both of these directions. Communitarian critics argue that "internal" group rights are critical to the maintenance of the group and to the understanding of individuals as group members. A particularly good example is education of the young in the teachings of their faith, a policy defended by both Robert Van Wyk and Erik Anderson in their contributions. Kymlicka believes that education for autonomy is critical to the individual's ability to assess and reevaluate the good of group membership. Community supporters contend that creating the possibility for such reassessment both is unrealistic about group prospects for survival and fails to respect the importance to community members of sharing their values with their children. For different reasons, involving respect for indigenous groups, Tsosie also believes that Kymlicka's understanding of group needs is insufficient.

Liberal critics, on the other hand, argue that Kymlicka's defense of groups fails to protect the individual in critical ways. An example given in Edmund Abegg's chapter is the right of groups to exclude nonmembers from property ownership, a right that may also function to restrict the liberties of group members to make individually important choices about the disposition of their property. Other examples include group rights to insist on participation in practices such as arranged marriage or religious rituals, as a condition of continued membership in the group.

The contributions to this part take up some of the most controversial issues about the recognition of group rights and the protection of individual autonomy. They concern affirmative action, where the issue is compatibility between group rights and the individual rights of nongroup members; religion, where the issue is group practices that may coerce internally and restrict autonomy; and land, where the issue is both protecting the group against interlopers from without and restricting group members' rights to do what they see fit with economic values they possess or have produced. The chapters that follow are both enlightening about the particular issues they discuss and revealing about underlying trends, unsolved problems, and ignored aspects of the group rights debate.

With respect to affirmative action, Bill Nelson argues that its permissibility and its desirability are different questions. In Nelson's view, it is much harder to show that affirmative action is impermissible in a given context than to show that it is undesirable. Nelson's argument is that the permissibility, and in some cases the desirability, of affirmative action can be defended in terms of equality of opportunity, without recourse to group rights. Nelson suggests we understand equal opportunity as the idea that for each person there should be some available career—or, more broadly, some life—in which that person can flourish. (A stronger version of this approach would be that individuals should have at least some minimal range of choices among lives within which they can flourish. This alternative allows for more choice than Nelson's view but is also weaker than the very strong view Nelson criticizes, that equal opportunity demands that individuals should have access to the optimal range of lives in which they might flourish.) Nelson argues that affirmative action is permissible in terms of equal opportunity when it does not impose severe opportunity costs on others, and when the costs it does impose are fairly distributed. He argues that it is desirable when it is needed to assure equal opportunity for some who have been severely disadvantaged, particularly when the disadvantages suffered by some group members interact to hurt others as well. His example is a situation in which there are a few large employers and in which for some reason or other Blacks have not been successful in obtaining employment.

Nelson does not view his defense of affirmative action as relying particularly on group rights. It is indeed individualistic in the sense that its focus is opportunities for individuals. But it does look to interactive disadvantages among group members as a basis for defending affirmative action for individual group members. It is thus a nice example of how references to groups may be relevant even within a fundamentally individualistic framework.

Both Robert Van Wyk and Erik Anderson argue that liberal views do not adequately respect group religious rights. Both are, to a significant extent, on the side of respect for diverse religious communities. Van Wyk, who begins by outlining how liberal values of neutrality and autonomy may conflict with diversity, concludes with a positive case for what he calls the *diversity state*. The case is based on opportunity, political legitimacy, and political stability. Anderson probes the idea of respect for autonomy and argues that the perfectionist view of autonomy as central to the good life does not provide adequate support for religious diversity. Instead, Anderson holds, a better case for diversity is to be made in terms of the religious conscience, tempered by the insistence that at least some degrees of critical thinking skills are needed to ensure that religious commitments are authentic. Both Van Wyk and Anderson are troubled by examples of oppression in the name of religion, such as insistence on marriage within the faith—the internal group rights that Kymlicka regards as illiberal—and each ends up to some extent recognizing a limited set of group rights over individual autonomy. The difficulty for each is to provide a principled justification for the limits, against a background of overall support for group rights.

Van Wyk begins by showing that there are conflicts between the traditional liberal values of autonomy, diversity, and neutrality among competing conceptions of the good. Autonomy and diversity conflict because policies that further liberty of choice may undermine the continued vitality of religious groups; the perhaps clichéd example of this is the Old Order Amish refusal to continue public education for their children beyond the age of fourteen. The conflict between neutrality and autonomy arises if insistence that lives are inauthentic unless they result from autonomous choice itself assumes a conception of the good. The conflict between neutrality and diversity, which is Van Wyk's principal concern, is that neutrality in various guises may undermine diversity, because apparently neutral state policies, such as historic preservation regulations, may in fact severely disadvantage particular religious groups. Neutral policies may thus not be neutral at all. This conclusion should not be surprising; the point is familiar that neutrality can be consistent with much that is morally troubling. Van Wyk's perhaps more controversial claim is that neutrality is not necessary for the defense of public policies, either. Here, Van Wyk argues that efforts to insist on neutrality in public life—such as purging our politics of the use of religious reasons, or insisting on an overlapping consensus agreeable to a wide range of groups—both diminish the quality of public life and marginalize the importance of group voices.

As positive support for diversity, Van Wyk argues that it is valuable because tradition matters in human life (religious values, for example, are not chosen; they are part of identity), people have moral responsibilities to those within their communities that they cannot realize without respect for diversity (such as education of children in the faith), people would limit their consent based on deep convictions, and a society will be more stable if it recognizes deep convictions. The case Van Wyk makes for diversity is limited to traditional, flourishing groups. He is not arguing for the formation of new groups for diversity's sake, for the preservation of "museum" examples of groups that are dying out (such as the Shakers), or for the invention of new groups by individuals to suit their needs. Van Wyk offers, in sum, a conservative rather than a libertarian case for diversity.

In reply, a defender of autonomy might point out that tradition, depth of conviction, and stability are all compatible with a remarkable lack of respect for the individual, citing female genital mutilation as a case in point. Van Wyk does believe that there are limits to diversity, and genital mutilation is his example. But he does not elaborate a theoretical basis for these limits; what he says is that groups that violate "fundamental moral convictions" should not be supported on diversity grounds.

Erik Anderson's contribution to this volume is to offer just such a theoretical basis, within the context of an overall defense of group rights. While Van Wyk's defense of diversity rests largely on political grounds, Anderson's interest is the role of the religious conscience in individual lives. The religious conscience consists in the affirmation of religious beliefs as deeply meaningful. Both autonomy in a limited form and group membership are central to the religious conscience as Anderson understands it. For groups, religious commitments are inherited tradition; for individuals, they are authoritative horizons framed in childhood and constitutive of identity. Religious commitments are not like occupations, to be chosen, perhaps rechosen, possibly discarded. They are not simply different ways of life, to be taken on as preference directs. Thus Anderson rejects what he calls "liberal perfectionism," the view that assigns primary value to autonomy, in the sense of choosing among a wide variety of life options.[2] At the same time, he believes that a limited form of autonomy is critical to the exercise of the religious conscience. Individuals of religious conscience, Anderson contends, must be able to affirm the importance of the religious worldview in their lives. This means that they must be able to understand their view, that they affirm it as meaningful, and that this affirmation takes place against the possibility of alternatives. Education to the point of understanding what affirmation means and that choice is possible is thus important for the religious conscience.

Anderson thus contends that group rights should be protected, within the limits set by meaningful affirmation. On the side of protection, Anderson advances two fundamental limits on the state. First, the state must allow religious groups the liberty to instill their beliefs and practices in their children, to bring them up in the faith. Second, the state has no authority to make judgments about the truth, value, or meaningfulness of religious views; only group members themselves can make such judgments authoritatively. On the side of meaningful affirmation, Anderson holds that groups should not be able to prohibit their members from exit, apostasy, or heresy. Nor should they be permitted to limit the education of children to the extent that meaningful affirmation is no longer possible. Children should receive enough of a liberal education to develop the cognitive skills necessary to understand what choice means. It seems also to follow—although Anderson does not say this—that groups should not be able to impose practices on their children that foreclose the later possibility of meaningful affirmation. The refusal of lifesaving medical care for children would seem to be a clear example of an imposition that forecloses later affirmation; the imposition of major, life-altering practices such as female genital mutilation or arranged marriage at puberty are more problematic cases, about which more in a moment. Otherwise, groups should be able to impose internal restrictions on their members, including "dietary restrictions, ritual observances, modes of dress, social roles, attitudes towards science, medicine and the modern state, and educational norms that conflict with the beliefs and practices that dominate modern societies." Anderson's conclusion is that the limited autonomy required for the religious conscience allows the line to be drawn between permissible state intervention and the free exercise of religion.

In addition to education and religion, land has been another important focus of the group rights discussion. Rebecca Tsosie and Edmund Abegg take up the question of group rights to land. Tsosie's focus is identity and the recognition of the unique status of indigenous peoples in the United States. Like Kymlicka, she believes that self-government rights are historically justified and critical to group survival. But she goes beyond liberal support for self-government as a patronizing "special" right, a kind of separate-but-equal, to defend dialogic interchange between indigenous, Anglo, and other cultures. On Tsosie's view, recognition of indigenous identities requires active intervention to allow indigenous cultures to flourish, as well as respect for difference in the larger society. Moreover, it requires understanding of the multifaceted, relational nature of indigenous identities—as tribal, Indian, and American, perhaps among others. Tsosie thus rejects as inadequate the liberal basis of Kymlicka's defense of group rights in terms of individual choice. Far beyond the protection from external interference urged by Kymlicka, tribes must be supported in their development of their own conceptions of the good. Here Tsosie joins company with both Van Wyk and

Anderson. But she finds contemporary communitarian views misguided as well in their support for conventional, uniform community values, against which the concerns of indigenous peoples appear deficient or "special." She argues that tribes should be permitted to insist on internal rights such as preservation of traditional religious practices on reservation lands, and to employ tribal self-government in support of such cultural preservation. Moreover, tribes should be able to articulate their concerns on their own terms, instead of being forced into a universal framework, such as American constitutionalism, international human rights, or Euro-American court systems. It is for the tribe to decide whether participation in a spirit dance, or marriage within the tribe, is central to the tribe's survival as the kind of entity it wants to be. At this point, like Van Wyk and Anderson, Tsosie sides with the groups themselves to determine when cultural practices that involve intragroup coercion have gone too far.

Edmund Abegg explores justifications for separationist group land rights to secession, native reservations, and federations. In contrast to Tsosie's nationalism, Abegg's approach is individualistic. Abegg's starting point is the well-being of individuals. (Because he regards values as mere preferences, Abegg describes this as a preference; the significance of such claims about the status of values will be taken up at the end of this introduction.) Abegg is a libertarian, but interestingly enough he agrees with Kymlicka that recognition of some group-differentiated rights may support the well-being of individuals. Land is a primary example. Under certain circumstances, group secession might contribute to individual well-being, although there is a need to consider the problems of territorial inholders who disagree with the secession decision, as well as the impact of secession on the larger polity. Likewise, Abegg suggests with Kymlicka that group rights to reserved land may be critical to individual contexts of choice—despite their restrictions on the liberty of outsiders who might want to enter the reservation, or insiders who might want to sell off their holdings. Indeed, Abegg toys with the possibility that every citizen should have group membership that comes with an inalienable tract of land as a kind of economic safety net for everyone to rely on. Noting, however, that libertarians are unlikely to offer general support for limits on property rights to promote social welfare, Abegg suggests the possibility of an array of communities offering different levels of welfare support, among which individuals might choose their preferred pattern. This possibility might be realized by a federation granting land rights to the different groups making it up. As a problem for further exploration, Abegg notes the logistical difficulties of constant migration, including the possibility of serious mismatches between populations and territory. Abegg's contribution is perhaps the only example of a libertarian voicing support for group land rights.

The contributions to this part thus defend central examples of group rights—affirmative action, religious practice and education, and land claims—from a remarkable variety of perspectives: the sovereign claims of indigenous peoples, the importance to groups of their religion, liberal equality of opportunity, and libertarianism. They represent the richness of the case for particular group rights. But there is as well a darker side to the group rights debate, the problem of what Kymlicka calls *internal group rights* or *intragroup coercion*. In *On Liberty*, John Stuart Mill famously left this problem up to groups themselves, at least for their adult members who were free in the end to leave. However much society might disapprove of polygamy among the Mormons, Mill concluded, they ought to be left free to pursue their own conceptions of the good in their own way. Equally famously, he applied this conclusion only to adults in full possession of their capacities. Mill's discussion has left liberals ever since struggling with whether intervention in intragroup coercion can be theoretically justified, even when the intervention is directed to children. Particularly in bioethics, a field that grew with autonomy as a central value, philosophers have devoted significant critical attention to group practices that affect the likely future choices of their children, by affecting their health or physical integrity. Christian Scientists are criticized for refusing lifesaving medical care for their children who have not yet reached the age of competence to decline medical care on their own behalf. Groups that impose physically damaging rituals on their children, such as female genital mutilation, are also criticized for violating their children's right to choose whether to undergo such impositions in adulthood. Defenders of group rights sometimes reply that if these criticisms rely solely on the value of autonomy, they show a simplistic failure to appreciate the importance of these practices to the groups that engage in them, for enjoyment of the practices themselves, for group cohesion, and for long-term survival of the group. Yet it is very difficult to defend a theoretically grounded position about when interference with such practices can be justified that respects both the individuals and the groups to which they belong.

Although no chapter in this volume is directed exclusively to this darker side of the group rights debate, much is said by the contributors that is useful to it. In concluding the introduction to this part, I want both to underscore the importance of what is said here and to suggest some further approaches liberals might pursue with respect to this side of the group rights debate. Because arranged marriage has received very little philosophical attention, unlike the medical examples, it is the example of a potentially coercive group practice that I will use as my focus. Arranged marriage seems to me to be a particularly good illustration of the tensions at work here. On the one hand, marriage is a critical element in group family structure and quite likely crucial to group survival in the long term. On the other hand, marriage is a choice of deepest intimacy, typically regarded as a central individual right, along with procreation. What do the chapters here have to say about conflicts between group and individual rights in cases like arranged marriage? And what resources does liberalism, in the end, have to deal with such cases? Can liberalism avoid passing judgment on groups' conceptions of the good life, as Mill tried to do, and at the same time defend intervention when groups would significantly limit the life choices of their members, particularly their young? Or are the tensions here absolutely irreconcilable, and the choice either liberalism or a version of communitarianism?

To one extent or another, all of the contributors to this volume take positions that are relevant to this conflict in the group rights debate. Although group liberty and coercion is not Nelson's main focus, he conceives of equality of opportunity in a manner that is consistent with considerable group liberty. Equality of opportunity, for Nelson, is having a chance to live a life that is satisfying rather than having the opportunity to choose among a whole panoply of good lives. Group practices that allow for a satisfying life, even if they cut off other possibilities, as arranged marriage surely would do, would be consistent with equal opportunity in this sense. Because Abegg understands values as preferences, his view would support group practices that further individual choice of preference satisfaction but not group practices that interfere with preference satisfaction. Abegg does not comment on the upbringing of children, but it seems quite consistent for him to say that children should be raised to become capable of choices that maximize preference satisfaction. Arranged marriage, at least before the age of majority, arguably is inconsistent with this approach.

On the group side, Tsosie would favor group rights of native peoples to determine marital and family structure. Hers is an example of a position that is weighted toward groups, at least when they have the kind of national status that Native American tribes can claim. Van Wyk also would conclude that group rights prevail, although for reasons that have to do with the political value of group membership, with the limit that they are not inconsistent with fundamental human rights. It is unclear whether he would say that the free choice of a spouse is a basic human right, although some might argue that it is so. Anderson provides the most developed theory here. For Anderson, groups may limit the upbringing of children only to the extent consistent with the limited form of autonomy required for religious beliefs to be genuinely affirmed. I think it is likely that arranged marriage at a very early age would not be consistent with even the awareness of alternatives required for affirmation, although upbringing with the understanding that an arranged marriage is the eventual outcome most likely would be.

What further resources do liberals have for dealing with such conflicts? In recent discussions, liberals have adopted three kinds of approach. One is neutrality. Liberalism, it is said, should not pass judgment about individuals' conceptions of the good life. Perhaps they will judge wrongly—as Mill held—or perhaps they have no business making judgments about what makes life good for others. Charles Larmore has recently argued for neutrality at the level of the state, in the sense that the state should not favor one conception of the good life over others, but he has also pointed out that neutrality at this level does not entail neutrality about particular conceptions of the good.[3] Anderson, in this volume, likewise argues that respect for the religious conscience requires that states not favor one conception of the good over another. The disadvantage with this strategy is its instability. If judgments are made about individual good lives—and if the state is authorized to protect children—official neutrality would seem to have been undermined. Erik Anderson's chapter contains one of the most convincing answers to this dilemma: the state may intervene only to the extent needed to protect another liberal value, autonomy in a limited degree.

A second strategy is procedural. For procedural liberals, the state should not take a stand about conceptions of the good life within the constraints of willingness to live in civil society. The procedures here vary, from minimal tolerance of the viewpoints of others to willingness to play by the rules of a democratic polity. Rawls's idea of an overlapping consensus is an example of such procedural liberalism.[4]

A final strategy, which has been explored by several theorists with at least liberal sympathies, is to attack the problem of the good directly. William Galston, in *Liberal Purposes*, argued that neutrality is inconsistent with liberal inclusiveness about conceptions of the good, and that liberal-ism embodies a commitment to liberal goods and virtues.[5] More recently, George Sher has argued that the idea of neutrality is confused and has defended a conception of the good that he believes is consistent with liberalism.[6] Liberals have found conceptions of the good to be risky territory, but it may be a territory they would do well to explore if they are going to confront the difficult tensions between the community and the individual that are manifest in such examples as arranged marriage.

Notes

1. Will Kymlicka, *Multicultural Citizenship: A Liberal Theory of Minority Rights* (Oxford: Clarendon Press, 1995); Kymlicka, *Liberalism, Community and Culture* (Oxford: Clarendon Press, 1989). See also Ian Shapiro and Will Kymlicka, eds., *Nomos XXXIX: Ethnicity and Group Rights* (New York: New York University Press, 1997); Will Kymlicka, ed., *Rights of Minority Cultures* (Oxford: Oxford University Press, 1995).

2. Perfectionist liberals, Anderson argues, part company with neutralist liberals in the defense they offer for the diversity state. Perfectionists argue that diversity should be protected because autonomous choices should be protected. Neutralists argue that diversity should be protected because the state should not endorse judgments about the goodness of different forms of life. Where they disagree is over whether to tolerate practices that thwart autonomy. The neutrality thesis can be advanced at different levels. Charles Larmore, for example, argues that the state should be neutral among competing conceptions of the good, but that neutrality in the private sphere does not follow. *Patterns of Moral Complexity* (Cambridge: Cambridge University Press, 1987), esp. chap. 3. In addition, neutrality can be based on different views in moral epistemology, including a rejection of moral truth, skepticism about the possibility of moral knowledge, or a belief in fallibilism in ethics. There are also significantly different views about what it means to be neutral among competing conceptions of the good, and what a conception of the good is in any event. See George Sher, *Beyond Neutrality: Perfectionism and Politics* (Cambridge: Cambridge University Press, 1997), esp. chap. 2.

3. Larmore, *Patterns of Moral Complexity*, esp. chap. 3.

4. See John Rawls, *Political Liberalism* (New York: Columbia University Press, 1993).

5. William Galston, *Liberal Purposes* (Cambridge: Cambridge University Press, 1991).

6. Sher, *Beyond Neutrality*.

Chapter 11

Indigenous Groups and American Democracy: Substantive Approaches to Cultural Pluralism

Rebecca Tsosie

Indigenous peoples pose a significant challenge to liberal democracies, such as the United States, which are supposedly founded on principles of toleration for pluralism and equality of citizenship. Many contemporary political scholars have considered the issues of recognition that arise in multicultural societies and have queried whether basic liberal principles of equality of citizenship in fact protect the interests of racial and ethnic minorities.[1] Indigenous peoples are generally pointed to as an example of a group that requires "special rights" as a means of protection. Yet many citizens remain unconvinced that special rights are necessary for ethnic groups, given the fact that they already possess equal rights of citizenship under the Constitution. Multiculturalists, however, argue that the national constitution that serves majority citizens so well often fails to take account of the *differences* that exist among minorities and thus treats their interests as subordinate to the uniform goals that are defined by the dominant society.

This chapter discusses liberal and multicultural approaches to the "politics of recognition,"[2] focusing on the struggles of indigenous peoples for cultural survival and arguing that indigenous peoples have a unique status within American democracy.

The Importance of Indigenous Group Identity

Identity forms a starting point for the discussion of why cultural survival is so important to indigenous peoples and other minority cultural groups. What is indigenous group identity, and why does it matter in the politics of recognition? Tribal identity is both socially and politically constructed. Although Indian people view *tribal* sovereignty and rights to self-determination as critical means to preserving cultural identity, federal legislation often treats

215

tribes collectively as "Indians" entitled to special protections.[3] Indeed, the law has been a powerful external influence on American Indian political identity. Domestic law defined the groups entitled to establish a treaty and "trust" relationship with the United States, while contemporary international concepts of "indigenous rights" tend to "encourage the formation of coalition groups that cross tribal lines," thereby focusing "a sense of political identity beyond the individual's tribe."[4]

The status of Indian tribes is unique among ethnic or cultural minorities because of their separate governmental status within domestic and international law. The tribes are separate nations that were resident upon the soil when the Europeans landed, entered treaties with the European sovereigns, and continue to retain important aspects of their sovereignty. Today, the special "trust" status of the Indian tribes justifies federal legislation that enables them to be granted special rights (e.g., tax exemptions, health and education benefits, and freedom from state laws) and exempts them from the prevailing legal norm of racial equality.[5] Yet, despite their separate status, Indian people have been classified as American citizens since 1924, and thus they are participants in American democracy along with all other citizens.

The American Indian experience confirms Charles Taylor's belief that human identity is formed "dialogically," in response to our relations with others.[6] Thus, multicultural citizens often have "overlapping" group identities; for example, a Navajo person is simultaneously "Navajo," "American," and "Indian." This is what James Tully refers to as "the challenge of *intercultural citizenship*, the idea that citizens are in cultural relations that overlap, interact and are negotiated and reimagined."[7] Taylor asserts that identity is what gives impetus to the struggle for cultural recognition within pluralistic societies. Because identity can be "formed or malformed through the course of our contact with significant others," *withholding* recognition to certain groups can in fact constitute a form of oppression.[8] Thus, Anglo-American society has tended to ignore the authentic identities of African-Americans and Native Americans and instead visit upon them demeaning stereotypes of inferior, less civilized peoples.[9] These stereotypes have been destructive of group identity and have been an obstacle to the human flourishing and development of African-Americans and Native Americans. Group claims for recognition seek to overcome stereotypes and assert racial or cultural identity as different than that of the dominant society.

As Taylor points out, however, there is a certain tension between the liberal principle of equality of citizenship, which carries with it the norm of nondiscrimination, and the claims of cultural groups for recognition of their unique identities. Taylor notes that contemporary group assertions of cultural identity are premised on two rather different claims for recognition—the principle of equal dignity of all citizens and the recognition of cultural distinctiveness.[10] Thus, while the Constitution may protect the rights of Indians as American citizens, it may not protect their rights as tribal members. Indigenous identity may be suppressed within the dominant society's institutions, unless special protections are available.

Interculturalists[11] assert that citizens have various "constitutional identities" and that a just society would enable citizens to participate as they are already culturally constituted.[12] This could mean an expansion of current legal and political institutions, the creation of new institutions founded on a policy of inclusion, rather than exclusion or assimilation, or perhaps recognition of special group rights. The latter approach is one that liberal scholars such as Will Kymlicka have suggested as a solution to the problems caused by cultural pluralism.

Indeed, Adeno Addis asserts that the issue of "cultural rights" has become important because of the existence of *cultural domination*.[13] According to Addis, there have been three main political responses to minority groups: total negation, assimilation, and pluralism. To the extent that separate groups are perceived as undermining or "negating" the majority group or culture, they may be exterminated or removed. Historically, this occurred with American Indian people, who were subjected to a genocidal series of "Indian wars," as well as federal "removal" policies designed to uproot and destroy settled cultures, such as those of the Cherokee and Choctaw peoples, who possessed their own courts and systems of laws at a very early time.[14]

Addis defines *assimilation* as the desire to "mold, to the extent possible, the minority in the image of the dominant group, by requiring the minority to learn the language of the majority, to follow the cultural practices of the majority, and generally to adjust its social practices and rituals to conform to those of the majority."[15] Assimilation was the predominant federal Indian policy until the 1970s. In the late nineteenth century, the assimilation policy was responsible for forcible removal of Indian children to distant boarding schools, where native languages were forbidden, and for federal policies that criminalized practice of indigenous religions and cultural traditions and broke up collective tribal landholdings for individual ownership. In the 1950s, assimilation drove the federal "termination" legislation, designed to sever the trust relationship between tribes and the federal government, sell off communal landholdings, and reduce Indians to "equal citizenship." The assimilation policy was also responsible for the federal relocation policy of the 1950s and 1960s, which was designed to entice young Indians to relocate to urban centers and enter the mainstream workforce. Despite its destructive impact on Indian people, the assimilation policy remained unquestioned by the dominant society until the 1970s, when the federal government articulated the "self-determination" policy in response to a burgeoning Native American activism.

The third response, pluralism, is the subject of this chapter. Addis defines *pluralism* as the view that "differences are to be celebrated rather than feared," and that "development and democracy" need not be "incompatible with the acknowledgment and celebration of differences."[16] Yet substantive approaches to pluralism may be inconsistent with those ideals. For example, Addis points to the contemporary treatment of indigenous peoples in the United States and Canada as examples of "paternalistic pluralism," where the minority culture is protected from the dominant culture in the same way that one would protect a "vanishing species."[17] Indigenous peoples are not perceived as full partners in a dialogue but rather are seen as vulnerable people who must be protected from annihilation by the majority.

Addis compares "paternalistic pluralism" with "critical pluralism," asserting that only the latter does more than "protect" the minority.[18] Critical pluralism is committed to actively intervening to provide the resources that will enable the minority culture to flourish, and also to "developing institutional structures that will enable the majority to open itself up to the minority, to accept the minority as a dialogue partner."[19] According to Addis, "Critical pluralism will adhere simultaneously to the politics of difference and dialogue."[20] In other words, critical pluralism, like the interculturalist position that Tully speaks of, affirms the separate constitutional identities of multicultural citizens and encourages their equal participation in the process of political dialogue.

Indigenous claims for group recognition comprise two distinct assertions. On the one hand, indigenous groups are attempting to preserve their separate cultural identity. This struggle manifests itself in tribal efforts to preserve and maintain land bases, reinvigorate tribal languages and cultural institutions, and guard cultural resources against appropriation by outsiders. On the other hand, indigenous groups are attempting to gain recognition of their separate political identity and respect for tribal legal and political institutions. They resist the thought that they are merely "equal citizens" in American democracy. In some ways they are; but in other ways they are tribal citizens in a separate political society that must coexist with and within American democracy. This feature distinguishes indigenous peoples from other minority groups that may press for recognition of their different cultural identities, and may seek special rights to ensure equal political participation and representation but do not have a historical tradition of separate governmental status. "Political pluralism" is a reality for American Indians, despite the attempts of American courts and legislatures to undermine tribal sovereignty by, for example, removing criminal jurisdiction over non-Indians[21] and removing tribal zoning authority over certain lands within the reservation under non-Indian ownership.[22] The two claims are intimately connected, of course, and many Indian people feel that without adequate recognition of their separate political status, "cultural survival" is not a realistic possibility.[23]

Substantive Approaches to Cultural Pluralism

Several substantive approaches to cultural pluralism have been articulated, both within the liberal tradition and from alternative approaches, such as the "interculturalist" perspective.

Transcending Cultural Differences

Liberal, communitarian, and nationalist theorists have often argued that group claims for cultural recognition are incompatible with essential norms; for example, for liberals, the norms of cultural neutrality and equal citizenship; for nationalists, the norm of national integrity; and for communitarians, the value of a *shared* concept of community.[24] Thus, to the extent that groups cannot be reasonably integrated or assimilated, and cultural differences transcended, then the group should perhaps secede. John Rawls, for example, advocates a political conception of liberalism that can transcend individual cultural differences and give each citizen a common basis to engage in mutual democratic governance.[25] And Michael Walzer, writing from a communitarian perspective, has indicated that while cultural membership in a community is important in defining "shared meanings," we should not promote ethnic rights that will impede the final goal of "common citizenship."[26] Under both approaches, "common citizenship" is the ultimate goal of a stable and harmonious democracy composed of diverse cultures, religions, and ethnicities, although Rawls's approach is more consistent with mainstream liberal tradition.

Rawls's theory recognizes cultural diversity but seeks a "common ground" among citizens—the "political conception of justice"—that can overcome the fractious quarrels among citizens over whose comprehensive conception of the good shall prevail. How do racial and ethnic minorities fit into Rawls's theory? To the extent that these groups possess "reasonable" comprehensive conceptions of the good, they may participate in the constitutional democracy. Their claims for disadvantage and oppression will be dealt with at the political level according to basic principles of justice: the *equality principle*, which asserts that every citizen has an "equal claim to a fully adequate scheme of equal basic rights and liberties," and the *difference principle*, which specifies when social and economic inequalities are permissible—for example, when they would be to the "greatest benefit of the least advantaged members of society."[27] Members of racial and ethnic minorities are considered "free and equal citizens" who share a mutual confidence in the political conception of justice, which is composed of "certain fundamental ideas seen as implicit in the public political culture of a democratic society."[28]

Rawls's vision of modern constitutionalism represents a departure from that of earlier liberal philosophers who held a vision of society as founded upon the collective agreement of the people. For Rawls, the collective agreement is found only within the hypothetical structure used to generate the basic principles of justice. The "social contract," of course, is pure fiction for all the diverse peoples now encompassed within contemporary multicultural societies who had no voice and no role in the creation of the constitution or institutions of government that currently wield power over them. Nevertheless, contemporary theorists allege that this is a "just" system because culture is irrelevant. For example, under Rawls's theory, any social actors behind a veil of ignorance and with the purpose of reaching agreement on a uniform political association would have chosen the same set of shared principles of justice. For Rawls, "Society's main institutions, and their accepted forms of interpretation, are seen as a fund of implicitly shared ideas and principles."[29]

The communitarian version of this historical conception of justice also stresses the uniform agreement of social actors, although the emphasis shifts from individual actors to the community: "The people are seen as a community bound together by an implicit and substantive common good and a shared set of authoritative European institutions, manners and traditions of interpretation. Within the horizons of these institutions and traditions, they interpret and articulate the common good through public deliberation and give it expression in a constitution."[30]

These liberal and communitarian approaches to pluralism are problematic for indigenous peoples for several reasons. First, they are premised on concepts of equal citizenship and neutrality that may not allow for the coexistence of separate tribal governments which may or may not be founded on what Rawls would consider "reasonable conceptions of the good." To the extent that tribes retain normatively divergent conceptions of the good (and these are reflected in their political systems), the relationship between indigenous peoples and the United States may be more like that between foreign nations. In fact, indigenous peoples straddle a unique position within the global politics of cultural recognition, which contains aspects of both international and domestic multiculturalism.[31] Indigenous peoples are in many ways like international organizations, yet they are also domestic minority groups. Liberal principles of tolerance suggest that cultural diversity should be respected within both the international and the domestic sphere, although apparently for different reasons.[32]

Rawls's model of international pluralism may be more appropriate for indigenous groups than his model of domestic pluralism. In "The Law of Peoples," Rawls takes the somewhat controversial position[33] that a liberal law of peoples, justifying toleration, can be extended to certain "well-ordered hierarchical societies" provided that the society meets three essential requirements: (1) it respects the independence of other societies; (2) it imposes moral duties and obligations on everyone within its borders; and (3) it respects "basic human rights."[34] "Outlaw" regimes—those that disregard basic human rights—are disqualified from the reasonable community of nations and thus do not merit toleration. The best relationship that liberal and hierarchical societies could establish with such a nation would be a modus vivendi.[35] To the extent that Indian nations represent what Rawls considers hierarchical societies, they should enjoy respect (or at least toleration) from the majority society.[36]

Second, these traditional liberal and communitarian approaches to pluralism are premised on the idea that the claims and interests of all citizens can be adjudicated in a political structure that is composed of Western

European institutions and concepts. Tully, however, points out that the distinctive group claims of indigenous people may be lost when they are forced to be adjudicated according to the "common language of constitutionalism" and framed in terms of "popular sovereignty, people, self-government, citizen, agreement, rule of law, rights, equality, recognition and nation."[37] Thus, for example, Western nation-states have developed the criteria used to deny status to American Indian tribes as "peoples," thus failing to recognize their claims for "self-determination."

Finally, these approaches subordinate the importance to indigenous peoples of tribal citizenship, according to their own values and norms, in an effort to promote the paramount importance of "universal" or "common" citizenship. Philosopher Steven Rockefeller, for example, claims that "our universal identity as human beings is our primary identity and is more fundamental than any particular identity, whether it be a matter of citizenship, gender, race, or ethnic origin."[38] To the extent that political theory dismisses the unique claims of groups for cultural recognition and asserts that they should place primary value on their "universal" identity, it engages in the same "color-blind" ideology that has often disadvantaged cultural groups and fostered a norm based on European values. In short, these perspectives continue a European tradition of cultural dominance and represent an assimilationist approach to cultural pluralism.[39]

Reconciling Group Claims Within Liberalism

A second response has been to argue that many group claims can be encompassed within prevailing norms because "the recognition and protection of cultures is a necessary condition of some of the primary goods that liberals, nationalists and communitarians seek to realise."[40] Under this approach, the challenge is to come up with a theory of minority rights that will be normatively consistent with one of these major traditions. Will Kymlicka, for example, asserts that it is best to defend minority rights within the liberal tradition because nonliberal arguments are quite controversial, both legally and morally, and because, practically speaking, judges and policy makers have the power to determine indigenous rights, and they need to perceive these rights as being consistent with liberalism.[41]

Kymlicka acknowledges the problems that liberalism faces in trying to conceive of collective rights. As he points out, because the community, unlike the individual, is not a "self-originating source of valid claims," once "individuals have been treated as equals, with the respect and concern owed to them as moral beings, there is no further obligation to treat the communities to which they belong as equals."[42] However, Kymlicka reconciles minority rights with liberalism by treating cultural membership as "an important good" and by recognizing that members of minority cultural communities may face particular disadvantages with respect to the good of cultural membership that may "justify the provision of minority rights."[43]

Kymlicka theorizes that the cultural community provides a "context of choice" within which individuals can pursue their conceptions of the good life.[44] He claims that liberal values require both individual freedom of choice and a secure cultural context from which individuals can make their choices.[45] So, for example, because minority groups are vulnerable to the actions of the dominant society, an Indian tribe's claim for preservation of an ancestral site from development might not be respected without according the group some right to secure their "freedom of choice" to pursue indigenous religious traditions.[46]

Significantly, Kymlicka's theory would provide minority groups with sufficient rights to prevent forcible assimilation by *external* forces, but it would not quarrel with the idea that a minority group could *itself* change its culture to approximate the dominant society. Kymlicka asserts that "rather than subsidizing or privileging their choices, the special measures demanded by aboriginal people serve to correct an advantage that non-aboriginal people have before anyone makes their choices."[47] In fact, Kymlicka supports maximum autonomy of tribal members and asserts that his theory would not support actions of a tribal government attempting to bar outside religions from the reservation in order to protect an ancestral theocracy.[48] Kymlicka believes that it is important for tribal members to have the right to *choose* which conception of the good to adopt, whether ancestral or not.

Kymlicka's theory promises to reconcile indigenous rights with liberalism by demonstrating that without some concept of special rights, indigenous peoples will continue to suffer injustice at the hands of the dominant society. Kymlicka's theory, however, is only responsive to unfair treatment by the majority society that threatens to compromise the ability of tribal members to make individual life choices. In that sense, it is akin to the "paternalistic pluralism" that Addis speaks of, in that it seems not to take account of indigenous peoples as full partners in a political dialogue.

Kymlicka's theory does not include a coherent account of tribal sovereignty. Indeed, Kymlicka queries whether most indigenous people would even qualify as "sovereign or self-determining peoples under international law," asserting that most should use a "liberal defence of minority rights" instead.[49] He thus uses the "common language of constitutionalism," which stems from European tradition, to disenfranchise indigenous people of their separate political claims. Kymlicka's theory also fails to address the needs of indigenous people for *cultural survival*. As Charles Taylor notes, "Kymlicka's reasoning is valid (perhaps) for existing people who find themselves trapped within a culture under pressure, and can flourish within it or not at all. But it doesn't justify measures designed to ensure survival through indefinite future generations."[50]

Kymlicka's interpretation of liberalism "protects the right to a cultural context but not to a particular culture."[51] In comparison, Margalit and Halbertal advocates a "right to culture," which would grant cultural groups the right to practice and maintain their own unique traditions, regardless of whether these traditions conflict with liberal norms.[52] According to Margalit and Halbertal, the liberal state's duty of neutrality extends only to the dominant culture, which is capable of taking care of itself: "The state is obligated to abjure its neutrality . . . in order to make it possible for members of minority groups to retain their identity."[53] Under this view, the concept of culture is coextensive with a "comprehensive way of life," and the state has an affirmative duty to ensure that groups are able to flourish within their own particularist cultures so long as this would not unduly intrude upon the fundamental rights of others.

The Interculturalist Approach to Multicultural Constitutionalism

Although Margalit and Halbertal argue that a "right to culture" is not necessarily inconsistent with liberal norms, alternative schools of interpretation, such as postmodernism, cultural feminism, and interculturalism, argue that the diverse demands of groups for cultural recognition cannot receive justice under the "authoritarian" traditions because their demands are in fact a challenge to the European male hegemony of these three traditions and "their shared language of constitutional recognition."[54] Tully's interculturalist position, for example, affirms cultural diversity and challenges the norm of uniformity that is so much a part of the liberal commitment to a unitary legal and political order, pointing to a need for a "diverse" federation that recognizes and accommodates citizens in the ways that they are already culturally constituted."[55]

Under Tully's theory, multicultural constitutionalism is a "form of activity, an intercultural dialogue in which the culturally diverse sovereign citizens of contemporary societies negotiate agreements on their forms of association over time in accordance with the three conventions of mutual recognition, consent, and cultural continuity."[56] In this respect, Tully's theory is responsive to Addis's call for a "critical pluralism" that would recognize cultural groups as equal partners in a dialogue. Such a dialogue enables cultural groups to participate on their own terms instead of being forced to articulate their claims under the dominant society's institutions and conceptual framework.

Tully points out that modern constitutionalism developed around two main forms of recognition: the equality of independent, self-governing nation-states and the equality of citizens.[57] To the extent that cultural groups within a unified nation-state assert separate status and distinctiveness, they violate these forms of recognition. Thus, internationally, indigenous people have faced an uphill battle in gaining recognition as nations. However, internally, their claims to distinctive status within domestic society have faced the liberal roadblocks of equality and neutrality. Thus, Tully's interculturalist approach would presumably recognize indigenous people within the constitutional system as they are *actually situated*—as separate nations within another nation. This suggests that indigenous claims for sovereignty would be recognized; however, Tully cites some cases that raise questions about this.

Tully discusses how conflicting claims to cultural recognition involving indigenous groups have been adjudicated by courts concerned about applying rights in such a way as to not discriminate against citizens' "identity-related differences" that are "worthy of protection."[58] In a conflict between Indian and non-Indian fishing rights, for example, the court found that "fishing a specific body of coastal water is constitutive of the cultural identity of the Aboriginal Musqueam nation" in a way that is not for the non-Indian commercial fishers.[59] Thus, although the court concluded that both groups were limited by conservation goals, it found that their respective rights could be limited "differentially" to account for the distinctive meaning to the Indian tribe.[60]

In another case, a court adjudicated a claim by the Coast Salish nation that it had the collective right to force one of its members to participate in a spirit dance and to punish the member for a failure to do so.[61] In this case, the court found that the spirit dance and tribal action to force a member to participate were not central features of the Salish way of life. Therefore, the group claim "to involuntarily initiate participants into the Spirit Dance" could not overcome the individual members' rights to be protected from assault, battery, and false imprisonment.[62]

In both the Musqueam case and the Salish case, a Euro-American court system undertook the task of deciding what is a "central feature" of tribal life. In the Musqueam case, this inquiry appears essential to adjudicating the rights of Indian and non-Indian fishermen to a common resource in a way that serves the diverse interests of each group. Arguably, a fair allocation of the resource would be impossible without acknowledging the distinctive cultural value of the fish resource to the Native fisherman. This is an example of the use of cultural differences to achieve equity among diverse groups in a pluralistic society.

In comparison, the Salish case involves a purely internal tribal matter in which a Euro-American court attempts to adjudicate the respective rights of tribal members under tribal law according to European norms of appropriate conduct. It is unclear whether a Euro-American court system has the authority to determine what features of tribal life are "central" enough to justify specific tribal governmental policies toward tribal members. As the United States Supreme Court noted in *Santa Clara Pueblo v. Martinez*, issues of internal tribal life are beyond the competence of Euro-American court systems and are better left to the tribal courts to adjudicate.[63]

Tully appears to accept the legitimacy of each court's action, suggesting that the interculturalist theory supports tribal rights to engage in cultural practices when this is necessary to the continuity of tribal life and does not infringe on the individual rights of the members. Recognition of tribal sovereignty, therefore, is conditional rather than presumptive. In this sense, Tully's approach is similar to that of liberal theorists who are willing to tolerate cultural pluralism so long as it does not offend individual rights.[64] In fact, some Indian nations might query whether the interculturalist approach is in fact better than the recognition that they receive under the American constitutional system, which acknowledges their separate government status and treats them as exceptions to basic liberal guarantees of equality of citizenship.[65]

Indigenous Rights and Democracy: Some Concluding Thoughts

Can the American constitutional tradition encompass the claims of Indian nations for recognition of their separate cultural and political identity?

According to Addis's vision of critical pluralism, ethnic minorities must be provided with resources to enable them to affirm and nurture their cultures, and there must be institutional means that would enable the minority to engage the majority in a multicultural dialogue. Addis notes that the rights necessary to ensure cultural survival will vary from group to group, thus suggesting that indigenous claims for land and political sovereignty must be recognized, although other cultural groups may not be entitled to the same rights.[66]

Although indigenous nations share some commonality with international governments, American constitutional tradition *requires* American Indian tribes to assert their sovereignty as "domestic dependent nations," in other words, as separate governments within the domestic sphere.[67] Yet many contemporary scholars assert that international law is better able to provide indigenous peoples with the necessary recognition for their collective rights to cultural survival.[68] Indeed, indigenous peoples currently seek recognition of their status as "peoples" entitled to rights of self-determination under international law. As Robert Clinton notes, because indigenous peoples lack structural or political guarantees to enforce their group rights to land, culture, religion, and political autonomy, they require special legal protection.[69] Thus far, the domestic constitutional limits that protect states from overreaching federal power have not assisted tribes. And tribes remain vulnerable to the majority political process, as the recent Mount Graham controversy in Arizona illustrates.[70]

But what form should indigenous rights take, and are such rights consistent with the liberal principles that underlie American constitutional democracy? The strong concept of collective rights embodied in international law documents such as the Draft United Nations Declaration on the Rights of Indigenous Peoples[71] may indeed be more protective of indigenous cultural survival than domestic law and would also be consistent with modern human rights law, as well as certain other liberal conceptions of rights. For example, Kymlicka argues for "community-specific" rights as a way of protecting a minority group against unfair actions by the majority society and claims that these rights are consistent with liberalism because they are based on the primary good of cultural membership.[72] Margalit and Halbertal assert that because a "way of life" is an attribute of a group, "the right to maintain it seems prima facie available only to a collective and not to individuals."[73] And John Harbison, arguing for a collective right to territorial sovereignty for Native Americans, claims that while tribal sovereignty may threaten the liberal commitment to equality of citizenship, it is compatible with a version of liberalism dedicated to the flourishing of cultures.[74]

It is not clear that indigenous rights to cultural survival fit into American constitutional democracy as it presently exists.[75] America's conception of democracy may need to be retooled to encompass indigenous claims for self-determination. This is not to suggest that all minority cultural groups are entitled to rights of self-government and self-determination.[76] Indigenous groups are clearly a special case because of their unique historical and legal status. Building on this status, Robert Williams has advocated a return to principles of treaty constitutionalism, which recognized the mutually co-existing sovereignty of the Indian nations and the European nations, to govern domestic constitutional interactions.[77] Tully agrees, finding the basis for a new multicultural constitutionalism in these Indian treaties, which were based on principles of mutual recognition, cultural continuity, and consent.

American democracy cannot ignore the impacts of colonialism on indigenous peoples, nor can it deny recognition to indigenous claims for political autonomy and cultural survival. Perhaps the government does not have an obligation to ensure cultural survival for every group.[78] However, indigenous peoples are not in the same constitutional position as other cultural groups. They are separate nations that entered into a treaty relationship with the United States and continue to reside on ancestral lands. American democracy should recognize this unique status instead of maintaining "a comprehensive, monolithic conception of shared identity and citizenship."[79] Indigenous group survival depends on the recognition of difference.

Notes

Portions of this chapter have been excerpted from a longer paper that raises similar issues. See Rebecca Tsosie, "American Indians and the Politics of Recognition: Soifer on Law, Pluralism, and Group Identity." I want to express my appreciation to the participants at the Lexington AMINTAPHIL conference for a spirited and valuable discussion of the ideas in this chapter. I also want to thank my colleagues Jeffrie Murphy and Joan McGregor for their helpful comments on earlier versions of this chapter.

1. See, e.g., James Tully, *Strange Multiplicity: Constitutionalism in an Age of Diversity* (Cambridge: Cambridge University Press, 1995); Charles Taylor, *Multiculturalism and "The Politics of Recognition"* (Princeton, N.J.: Princeton University Press, 1992); Robert Justin Lipkin, "Liberalism and the Possibility of Multicultural Constitutionalism: The

Distinction Between Deliberative and Dedicated Cultures," *University of Richmond Law Review* 29 (1995): 1263–325.

2. Building on Taylor's work and the accompanying commentary, I use the phrase "the politics of recognition" to refer to the ongoing process of how democratic social institutions recognize the distinct cultural identities of the diverse constituent groups of a pluralistic society. See Taylor, *Multiculturalism*. My emphasis in this chapter is on legal and political structures, although the inquiry is much broader and extends to educational and social institutions, as well.

3. See, e.g., the Indian Child Welfare Act, 25 U.S.C. §§ 1901–63; the Native American Graves Protection and Repatriation Act, 25 U.S.C. §§ 3001–13; the Indian Self-Determination and Education Assistance Act, 25 U.S.C. §§ 450a–450n.

4. Carole Goldberg-Ambrose, "Of Native Americans and Tribal Members: The Impact of Law on Indian Group Life," *Law and Society Review* 28 (1994): 1124.

5. See, e.g., *Morton v. Mancari*, 417 U.S. 535 (1974) (upholding employment preference for Native Americans in the Bureau of Indian Affairs against an equal protection challenge based on the "political" rather than "racial" status of Indian groups).

6. Taylor, *Multiculturalism*, 7.

7. Tully, *Strange Multiplicity*, 54.

8. Taylor, *Multiculturalism*, 36.

9. Native Americans have also been the subject of stereotypes built upon the idea of the "noble savage." While non-Indians sometimes perceive these stereotypes to be flattering rather than demeaning, the stereotypes have also been destructive of authentic indigenous identity because they tend to lock contemporary groups into the restraints of a mythic past.

10. Taylor, *Multiculturalism*, 40.

11. I am building on Tully's use of the term *interculturalist* to describe an alternative and potentially more inclusive constitutional structure. See Tully, *Strange Multiplicity*, 2. The interculturalist position builds on postmodern theory and multiculturalism yet is a more specific application of these ideas to the issues of cultural recognition in a democratic society.

12. Tully, *Strange Multiplicity*, 55.

13. Adeno Addis, "Individualism, Communitarianism, and the Rights of Ethnic Minorities," *Notre Dame Law Review* 67 (1991): 619.

14. For historical background on the different eras of Indian policy, including removal, assimilation, termination, and self-determination, see Vine Deloria Jr. and Clifford M. Lytle, *American Indians, American Justice* (Austin: University of Texas Press, 1983).

15. Addis, "Individualism, Communitarianism, and the Rights of Ethnic Minorities," 619–20.

16. Ibid., 620.

17. Ibid.

18. Ibid., 621.

19. Ibid.

20. Ibid.

21. *Oliphant v. Suquamish Tribe*, 435 U.S. 191 (1978).

22. *Brendale v. Confederated Tribes and Bands of Yakima*, 492 U.S. 408 (1989).

23. Douglas Sanders, for example, notes that cultural minorities seek group survival, not merely the equal rights of members to equality and participation within the larger society, and mentions that rights to self-government are seen as a way to protect this interest. Douglas Sanders, "Collective Rights," *Human Rights Quarterly* 13 (1991): 370.

24. Tully, *Strange Multiplicity*, 44.

25. John Rawls, *Political Liberalism* (New York: Columbia University Press, 1983).

26. Will Kymlicka, *Liberalism, Community and Culture* (Oxford: Clarendon Press, 1989), 221–28 (discussing Michael Walzer's *Spheres of Justice*).

27. Rawls, *Political Liberalism*, 5–6.

28. Ibid., 13.

29. Ibid., 14.

30. Tully, *Strange Multiplicity*, 64.

31. As Robert Lipkin has noted, multicultural problems arise in both international and domestic spheres. Robert Justin Lipkin, "In Defense of Outlaws: Liberalism and the Role of Reasonableness, Public Reason and Tolerance in Multicultural Constitutionalism," *DePaul Law Review* 45 (1996): 264. Problems of international multiculturalism include how nations deal with one another, how separate peoples within one nation deal with one another, and whether Western nations can establish a cultural hegemony over international law through liberal doctrines. Problems of domestic multiculturalism include how minority cultures should be treated within a liberal democracy, and whether liberal constitutionalism can embrace and respect minority cultural rights.

32. The subject of liberal toleration for diverse cultures is itself the subject of a lively debate, of course, although one that is outside the scope of this chapter. See, for example, Chandran Kukathas, "Cultural Toleration," in *Ethnicity and Group Rights*, ed. Ian Shapiro and Will Kymlicka (New York: New York University Press, 1997), 69–104; and Michael Walzer's response to Kukathas in the same volume at 105–11. Addis argues for a more comprehensive understanding of toleration, which he terms *pluralistic solidarity.* Ibid., 130–33.

33. Rawls's theory of a liberal law of peoples has been criticized by scholars both within and outside of the liberal tradition. Lipkin criticizes Rawls's approach as imposing a Western liberal conception of the good on vastly different nations, and thus engaging in a sort of cultural hegemony, echoing Tully's interculturalist critique. Lipkin, "In Defense of Outlaws," 275–79. On the other hand, Fernando Teson criticizes Rawls as being "too forgiving of serious forms of oppression in the name of liberal tolerance," affirming a universalist conception of liberal toleration premised on respect for human rights. Fernando R. Teson, "The Rawlsian Theory of International Law," *Ethics and International Affairs* 9 (1995): 79–99.

34. John Rawls, "The Law of Peoples," in *On Human Rights: The Oxford Amnesty Lectures—1993*, ed. Stephen Shute and Susan Hurley (New York: Basic Books, 1993), 60–63.

35. Ibid., 73

36. I will not discuss the valid issue, which Lipkin raises, of whether Rawls's theory would in fact extend only to liberal societies, or whether it would truly encompass non-liberal societies that do not violate fundamental human rights. See Lipkin, "In Defense of Outlaws."

37. Tully, *Strange Multiplicity*, 36.

38. Quoted in Taylor, *Multiculturalism*, 88.

39. See e.g., Addis, "Individualism, Communitarianism, and the Rights of Ethnic Minorities," 647 (commenting that "communitarianism does not offer much hope to minorities. It is assimilationist in its nationalist dimension, and exclusionist in its localist version").

40. Tully, *Strange Multiplicity*, 44.

41. Kymlicka, *Liberalism, Community and Culture*, 153–54.

42. Ibid., 140.

43. Ibid., 162.

44. Ibid., 172.

45. Ibid., 169.

46. Ibid., 187.

47. Ibid., 189.

48. Ibid., 195.

49. Ibid., 158–61 n. 4.

50. Taylor, *Multiculturalism*, 40–41 n. 16.

51. See Avishai Margalit and Moshe Halbertal, "Liberalism and the Right to Culture," *Social Research* 61 (1994): 504.

52. Ibid., 491.

53. Ibid., 492.

54. Tully, *Strange Multiplicity*, 135.

55. Ibid., 55.

56. Ibid., 30.

57. Ibid., 15.

58. Ibid., 172.

59. Ibid.

60. Ibid.

61. Ibid.

62. Ibid.

63. *Santa Clara Pueblo v. Martinez*, 436 U.S. 49, 54 (1978) (quoting *Martinez*, 402 F. Supp. at 18–19). In the *Martinez* case, Justice Marshall affirmed the district court's holding that the equal protection guarantee of the Indian Civil Right Act should not be

construed to require a federal court to determine which "traditional values will promote cultural survival and therefore should be preserved and which of them are inimical to cultural survival and should therefore be abrogated." Id. Such a determination "should be made by the people of Santa Clara, not only because they can best decide what values are important, but also because they must live with the decision every day." Ibid.

64. In fact, Tully quite clearly states that interculturalism does not violate liberal norms. He claims that if a liberal constitution is to provide the basis for its central values of freedom and autonomy, it must protect the cultures of its members and inspire the public attitude of mutual respect for cultural diversity that individual self-respect requires. According to Tully, "The primary good of self-respect requires that popular sovereignty is conceived as an intercultural dialogue." Tully, Strange Multiplicity, 190. Furthermore, he asserts that there is no inconsistency with the neutrality principle: "If a contemporary constitution is to be culturally neutral, it should not promote one culture at the expense of others, but mutually recognise and accommodate the cultures of all the citizens in an agreeable manner." Ibid., 191.

65. Congressional power over Indian tribes is viewed as a limit on tribal power to infringe fundamental rights. For example, the Indian Civil Rights Act imposed statutory guarantees similar to those of the Bill of Rights as a limitation upon the actions of tribal governments and judicial institutions. 25 U.S.C. §§ 1301–3.

66. Addis, "Individualism, Communitarianism, and the Rights of Ethnic Minorities," 661–62 (noting that the resources necessary to enable one culture to survive will not necessarily be the same as those that enable another culture to survive).

67. The Constitution gives Congress the exclusive right to regulate commerce with the Indian tribes, which has been interpreted as giving Congress "plenary" authority to deal with the tribes in its capacity as trustee. See Worcester v. Georgia, 31 U.S. (6 Pet.) 515 (1832) (holding that Congress has exclusive right to regulate commerce with the tribes); Nell Jessup Newton, "Federal Power over Indians: Its Sources, Scope, and Limitations," University of Pennsylvania Law Review 132 (1984): 195 (discussing plenary power doctrine).

68. See, e.g., Robert A. Williams Jr., "Encounters on the Frontiers of International Human Rights Law: Redefining the Terms of Indigenous Peoples' Survival in the World," Duke Law Journal (1990): 667 (advocating "international legal recognition of indigenous peoples' collective rights to exist as culturally autonomous peoples, to continue in the peaceful possession of their traditionally occupied territories, and to exercise greater self-determining autonomy over their ways of life"); S. James Anaya, Indigenous Peoples in International Law (New York: Oxford University Press, 1996), 4 (the "central contention" of Anaya's book "is that international law, although once an instrument of colonialism, has developed and continues to develop, however grudgingly or imperfectly, to support indigenous peoples' demands").

69. Robert N. Clinton, "The Rights of Indigenous Peoples as Collective Group Rights," Arizona Law Review 32 (1990): 746.

70. A group of Apache Indians is protesting the University of Arizona's decision to site a huge telescope project on Mount Graham, which is a sacred site to many bands of Apaches. See *Apache Survival Coalition v. United States*, 21 F.3d 895 (1994). However, lobbyists for the University of Arizona were successful in securing an exemption from the federal environmental statutes—which also trigger an inquiry into the "human" costs of the project—so the project could move forward quickly. See Arizona-Idaho Conservation Act of 1988, Title VI, P.L. 100-696, 102 Stat. 4597 (1988). The Mount Graham controversy represents a case where majoritarian politics have displaced the very federal statutes designed to ensure environmental equity. This case, unfortunately, is representative of how indigenous claims for preservation of sacred sites have been treated in the dominant society's courts and legislatures. See Richard Herz, "Legal Protection for Indigenous Cultures: Sacred Sites and Communal Rights," *Virginia Law Review* 79 (1993): 691–716.

71. See Anaya, *Indigenous Peoples in International Law*, 207–16.

72. Will Kymlicka, "Individual and Community Rights," in *Group Rights*, ed. Judith Baker (Toronto: University of Toronto Press, 1994), 17–33; Kymlicka, *Liberalism, Community and Culture*, 169.

73. Margalit and Halbertal, "Liberalism and the Right to Culture," 499.

74. John Harbison, "The Broken Promise Land: An Essay on Native American Tribal Sovereignty over Reservation Resources," *Stanford Environmental Law Journal* 14 (1995): 370.

75. Indeed, some scholars have queried whether "rights talk" is even appropriate to secure the interests of minority groups or women. See, e.g., Sherene Razack, "Collective Rights and Women: 'The Cold Game of Equality Staring,'" in Baker, *Group Rights*, 66–78. I tend to agree with Robert Williams, however, that many of the interests of indigenous groups in cultural survival are best articulated within the contemporary rubric of rights. See Williams, "Encounters on the Frontiers of International Human Rights Law," 701 (arguing that the discourse of human rights, for example, has "enabled indigenous peoples to understand and express their oppression in terms that are meaningful to them and their oppressors"). This is not to minimize the significant disagreement over whether groups can even have rights, or what moral theories would support the exercise of such rights. I acknowledge the complexity of that debate but do not explore it in this chapter.

76. See Leslie Green, "Internal Minorities and Their Rights," in Baker, *Group Rights*, 105 (discussing the argument that "rights inflation" would occur to the extent that rights of self-government are accorded to all minorities).

77. Robert A. Williams Jr., *Linking Arms Together: American Indian Treaty Visions of Law and Peace, 1600–1800* (New York: Oxford University Press, 1997).

78. I acknowledge the debate, for example, over whether the government has the obligation to ensure cultural survival for groups that voluntarily immigrated to the United States seeking the same status and rights as other citizens. As Anaya observes,

the assimilation of immigrant groups into the dominant culture is arguably not "cultural discrimination" to the extent that these groups are reasonably held to have consented to subordinate their own unique cultural expressions to those of the majority society. See S. James Anaya, "On Justifying Special Ethnic Group Rights: Comments on Pogge," in Shapiro and Kymlicka, *Ethnicity and Group Rights*, 228.

79. See Wayne J. Norman, "Towards a Philosophy of Federalism," in Baker, *Group Rights*, 88 (arguing that "the most suitable basis for a just and stable federal union will thus be some form of overlapping consensus that demands more of federal partners and their citizens than a modus vivendi, but less than a comprehensive, monolithic conception of shared identity and citizenship").

Chapter 12

Group Land Rights

Edmund Abegg

What justification can be presented for the moral right of groups of individuals to hold land? Several group rights to land may be distinguished: the right to use or traverse land in certain ways, the right of ownership, and the right to govern. My concern is with the rights in liberal polities either to govern or to hold nonalienable land rather than with the usual rights of partners or corporations to own land. By *nonalienable land* I mean land that is not permitted to be further divided or sold in the routine ways common to liberal polities. I shall consider three types of proposals for land rights: secession, native (and other) reservations, and federations. Most of these group rights lead to a greater or lesser separation of groups, and it is important to recognize that unity, especially more and more unity, is not always an appropriate goal.

I need to make some preliminary remarks on the nature of moral values in order to set the framework for this chapter. In my view, values are simply preferences that have themselves undergone a social construction that cannot confer on them an ultimate authority over other preferences. One of my basic preferences requires that I try to maximize concern for the well-being of each individual and thus minimize the scope of aggregative utilitarian decision making. This reference to well-being represents, of course, one direction that concern can take. Libertarians tend to hold that their concern for strangers (as opposed to friends or family) is limited to a requirement not to interfere with them in certain ways. Many vectors of concern and unconcern are psychologically possible. How an orientation plays out in each context depends on other operating assumptions and preferences. A developed construction, then, presents rules or goals that indicate the scope and strength of any concern for the individual. At one extreme, such a construct may reveal such a dilution of a fundamental concern for the individual that critics may correctly conclude that it has been abandoned. At the other extreme, critics may correctly conclude that any aggregate policy making has been simply excluded. The meaning and weight, then, of this basic value will emerge in its development and application. Humans have a tendency, of course, to deceive themselves and others, to give lip service to one value while living another, and to be guided by the motto *Decit non facit*, "Let's say it but not do it." With this worry in mind, I want to insist that any concern for each individual be quite evident in the policy outcomes.

Group Rights

In the liberal polity or state, one that grants legal rights to individuals, often based on moral rights, citizens are allowed to choose their own plans of life and to implement them. The freedom and the autonomy of individuals are emphasized. These rights are against other individuals, private groups, and government; and they are to be limited, at least directly, only by government, and only then in the name of the preservation or enhancement of these very same individual rights.

Thus in the relevant moral-political sense, liberalism opposes holism or corporatism and emphasizes the individual rather than the group. An extreme holism that denies the reality of individual humans in any strong sense is simply false from this point of view. The language of individual rights is useful to express this concern for the individual.

Liberals can, however, also readily construct and use a concept of group rights and may use this concept where and to the degree that aggregate considerations are useful and appropriate. We commonly speak of group rights in federal polities. For example, in the United States, states have rights to have two senators each and to tax state residents, and in all liberal polities legislatures have the right to pass laws. These rights are legal ones, but we also often claim group moral rights, such as the rights of churches or other voluntary groups, or even the primal right of a group to become a polity. This use of group rights is based primarily on moral considerations and not on ontological doctrine.[1]

Will Kymlicka points out that the most crucial issue for liberalism is not group rights as opposed to individual rights but rather the status of "group-differentiated rights," rights that one group has and another does not.[2] Are such rights always unfair to other groups that do not have them? Kymlicka argues that they are fair when the group awarded the right is in appropriate different circumstances than the other groups. He thus is in a position to avoid particularism and to justify such differentiations on the basis of an equal concern for the well-being of all individuals.[3]

Thus group rights are part of every liberal political culture and are not at all mysterious. But the liberal would hope to minimize group rights and to justify them on the basis of their contribution to the well-being of individuals. What are to be avoided are rights of groups, whether governmental or private, to well-being regardless of or in opposition to the well-being of individuals. Kymlicka refers to these latter as rights to impose "internal restrictions" in a polity, to control citizens for the sake of the polity, in contrast to group-differentiated rights, which impose "external restrictions," that is, controls on members of other groups.[4]

Suppose that in the context of a liberal polity we seek to support the well-being of each individual citizen. We may help them in many ways: health care, food, housing, tools, land, education, or jobs. One way to institutionalize such help is to establish individual rights or entitlements to goods. But another way, either in addition or alternatively, is to grant rights to some of these goods to groups. In some cases, such group rights would be fashioned so that the group would then distribute the good to individuals. In the United States, the use of federal block grants to states for welfare programs could be construed in this manner (under the law, each state has a right to this grant). But in other cases, the good may be regarded as a public or collective good to be held in common by the members of the receiving group. Among the goods listed here, the most likely candidate for such a collective good is land. I am ready, then, to consider the group rights to land noted at the outset.

Secession

The right to secede is based on the right of a group to govern its land. The act of secession becomes possible for a group when it resides in a territory that is part of a larger polity. What are the justifications that may be offered for such an act? Liberals argue that such a justification must be based on the well-being of individuals. However, while different liberal theorists offer varying arguments that make secession more or less morally acceptable, no one argues that the group right of secession is a moral absolute.

Harry Beran argues that secession is often justified morally. Liberals hold that "individual freedom is a basic value" that follows from the individual right of "personal self-determination." The relation between the citizen and the liberal polity is voluntary.[5] What further follows is not simply the individual right of emigration but also the right of "territorially concentrated groups" to secede rather than to conduct a mass emigration (38). But the prima facie right to secede is, of course, defeasible and is finally justified only if it is "morally and practically possible" (41). Some of the conditions that would tend to make secession impermissible are the immoral and oppressive nature of the seceding group, the location of the seceding territory away from borders so that an enclave would result, and the essential importance of the territory to the larger polity due to its relative wealth or richness of economic or cultural resources. But these latter conditions, that is, apart from the immorality, are not "insuperable barriers to secession." Compromises and compensation may justify the secession (41–42).

For Beran, since political ties are to be voluntary, the justification for secession is relatively easy. He adopts a version of the consent theory of political obligation that regards consent as the acceptance of membership in a polity, an acceptance that is a kind of promise to follow the rules of that polity until such time as the citizen resigns the membership (28–31). Further, if the polity is indeed consistently liberal, it will allow secession, which will then be amicable. Beran concludes that there is no danger of destructive "Balkanization" through "recursive" secessions (41).

Christopher Wellman argues for a group right of secession through a consideration of the issue of the legitimacy of the polity. The consent theory of legitimacy has been the "most popular," since it "reconciles nicely the liberal conceptions of the person and the state."[6] If a person consents to an intrusion by the state, autonomy has been preserved. Wellman, like Beran, limits the consent, model to views that claim the need for actual consent since hypothetical consent reduces to a teleological theory of legitimacy. But Wellman, in a *reductio* aimed at Beran's theory, argues that if individual consent is required for political legitimacy, then "each individual has a full right to political self-determination, which includes the right to secede from any political union to which she has not consented" (154). Voting is no cure for the radical implications of the consent model, since the individual voter in the typical case does not have the choice whether there shall be a vote. Unless each "voter is given an option of being exempt from the political imposition (i.e., allowed to secede), she cannot be bound by the outcome of an election in which she voted" (154). The consent model, then, regards all current polities to be illegitimate. In fact, current polities do not rely on the consent theory, and most liberal theorists reject the consent requirement (155). Wellman thus turns to examine the second model.

According to the teleological model, a polity is justified in exerting coercive force within its territory if it performs its function well. Consent is not required. As long as the polity maintains internal peace and avoids committing injustices, it is legitimate. Wellman notes that this model allows a justification for secession not permitted under the consent model, namely, efficiency. We should conclude that "any competitor better able to perform the very same function would thereby extinguish or outweigh the existing state's claim" (158). Political self-determination becomes a right under this model in that any group with its territory may secede if it can perform the function of government more efficiently. Transition costs must be counted, but they do not preclude secession (158–59). The telic model, however, is rejected by Wellman because it justifies violent annexations in some cases (159–60). I might note that all the difficulties that afflict utilitarianism apply to this telic model.

Thus Wellman argues for a hybrid model that includes the best aspects of these two theories. First, consent (a deontic, emergent value) is a necessary condition for justified secession. The consent to the secession is a group right that can be exercised by the group occupying territory. No consent is required from the former whole polity (morally, the former polity ought not to oppose the secession). The other condition, with the two being sufficient, is that the secession not be "excessively harmful" (a telic value) (161–64). This second condition serves to limit and trump the first. The moral principle underlying this condition is that "states may permissibly restrict excessively harmful political liberty" (162). To avoid the harm arising from incompetent or unjust government in the new polity, secessionist groups may be required to qualify, to be in effect licensed like drivers of cars. Another harm that would disallow secession is that the remainder of the former whole polity would be left unable to function. Wellman finds this theory justified because it "thoroughly coheres with our considered judgments" about secession and annexation (162, 164).[7]

Allen Buchanan does not attempt to derive from the basic values of liberalism a prima facie right to secede, as does Beran, but on the contrary argues that the right to secede is only "conclusory," a final practical decision based on balancing many factors in the particular case.[8] He rejects a pure right of self-determination but accepts the moral right to react to injustices which the larger polity allows to continue, including both violations of civil rights and the exploitation of one group to benefit others, a "dis-criminatory redistribution" (74, 152). Like Beran, he includes among the conditions that block a right of secession the immorality of the group that would secede (153).

In his later essay, Buchanan more strongly emphasizes the importance of compatibility with current international law for any proposal that pre-tends to practicality. He calls his theory of secession a *remedial right only* theory and concludes that it fits with current institutions of international law much better than *primary right theories*, which advocate a general right to secede, even from "perfectly just states." Beran and Wellman, who pro-pose primary right theories, fail to recognize the morally legitimate princi-ple of the territorial integrity of states and the perverse incentives and unintended consequences of its rejection. Especially, polities will have a motivation to avoid federalism or granting local autonomy, since this may establish the conditions that justify secession and the disruption of delib-erative democracy under the constant threat of secession by minorities (46–49). Buchanan calls his own proposal "ideal theory," but he argues that proposals like those of Beran and Wellman are "so 'ideal' that they fail to engage the very problems that lead us to seek institutional reform in the first place" (61). I agree with Buchanan that the rather perfunctory refer-ences by Beran and Wellman to bad consequences and practicality are inad-equate and that any proposal that might be currently considered for adoption will need to cohere with progressive international law, but I would also argue that more utopian ideals do have an important place in the spec-trum of moral and political thought.

The full evaluation of these theories of the group right of secession is beyond the scope of this chapter, but I need to make some comments rel-evant to my theme of the well-being of individuals. First, all three liberal theorists agree that the right of any polity to govern its territory is contin-gent and that a polity may be morally required to surrender the land occu-pied by a seceding group. Second, all agree that the group right to secede is a qualified right, that it must be justified by reference to conditions pres-ent in the particular case, conditions that have to do with morality and well-being.

From the point of view of a concern for each individual, however, there are some differences, perhaps mostly in emphasis, among these liberal the-orists. Beran, with his insistence on a strong right of individual choice, always allows the individual to resign and leave a polity, and he further suggests that alienated individuals might be given "dissenters' territories" or, even if native-born, be allowed to remain as resident aliens.[10] They could also be compensated if in some cases they need to emigrate in connection with a secession (42). Buchanan spends less time on the well-being of the alienated individual, but in remarks he shows sympathy for "individual independents" and suggests that those stranded by a secession ought to be given compensation, the right to emigrate, or dual citizenship.[11] Wellman's shorter work allows him little time for the individual outsider, but he might well agree with ideas of emigration and compensation in some cases. He does require that the boundaries be drawn so that the seceding territory would "include as many secessionists and as few unionists as possible." But having some misfits is "unavoidable given the contiguity and size constraints of political viability."[12]

Native Reservations

I now turn to another candidate for a group right to land: the right of each native group to own in common the territory in which it lives, under special laws that prohibit the division or sale of the land.

Kymlicka argues from within the individualist liberal tradition that minority cultures occurring in a distinct territory have a strong value for the individuals who bear them, and that for the sake of these individuals in appropriate cases we ought to prevent the destruction of cultures by outsiders who move in or buy native land. Cultural membership is a primary good that provides a context of choice and the ability to choose, that is, to be a functional individual. The destruction of the culture can be a "devastating problem" that will disable its individual bearers.[13] Kymlicka's solution is to impose on both natives and outsiders some moderate restrictions that do violate traditional liberal individual rights. These impositions would include, typically, limits on mobility rights, especially the right to enter the native land, and a ban on the sale of the collective native land. Again, the underlying moral premise is a concern for individuals who become dysfunctional. This premise and facts of the particular case provide the justification for these group-differentiated rights.[14]

Kymlicka considers the narrow case of native cultures in specific territories. We could generalize his solution by adopting the thesis that calls for every citizen to be a member of a group of persons who occupy a nonalienable tract of land. Members of this group need not live on the land, but if they want or need to do so, they have this right and also the right to receive sustenance from the land in exchange for their fair contribution of labor. This mode of life would be close in many ways to the situation of the average factory worker (other than new immigrants) in the United States in the late nineteenth century, when almost everyone had parents, grandparents, or an uncle who lived on a farm that could be expected to stay in the family indefinitely.

The main justification for this proposal is the one given by Kymlicka, that without this help many individuals will crash and become dysfunctional. For those, especially, at the economic bottom rung, the loss of a job may lead to homelessness and hunger, a crash just as serious as natives might endure with the loss of their culture. In this case we could even say that in a sense the jobless person has lost her or his culture.[15] Kymlicka considers this case of losing a job in the context of a counterargument that concludes that we can deal with the loss of a native culture through subsidized instruction of the natives in the language and history of the larger culture, just as we can offer job retraining to workers. He replies that giving up one's culture is not something we have a right to ask people to do, even if some people do it voluntarily.[16] My claim is that one way to provide support for the jobless worker, in an ongoing and preemptive way, is through group rights to land. Of course, if all workers can be smoothly helped to new jobs (or supported if disabled), then there would be less need for this proposed land right.

Federation

A federation grants group rights to the states or provinces that constitute it. The degree of autonomy granted the provinces may vary enormously, from what amounts to a mere facade or show disguising strong central authority to an extremely minimal central government. If the provincial autonomy is extensive and if the provinces themselves have enough homogeneity so that each one represents important values or cultural traits not shared by the others, ordinarily no need for secession or for native homelands would arise. Kymlicka presents the example of the Ottoman Empire, a successful but not liberal federation that, for hundreds of years before World War I, was a "federation of theocracies," with Muslim, Jewish, Greek Orthodox, and Armenian Orthodox communities functioning with significant autonomy.[17] Kymlicka argues that the world needs "multination states" (federations, we may say), each one of which can find some unity as it affirms its differences. He cites Switzerland as a successful example but worries about the many failures (187, 192).[18]

We need to consider the types of federation that liberals might design to cope with our world today. Perhaps different language or cultural groups might form the basis for distinctive provinces. Otherwise, if we are simply dealing with the issue of the utility of different levels of government, crucial issues of differences among people are not addressed. As an ideal example of a federation that might be formed to deal with important moral differences, I shall present here briefly a proposal for a federation based on opposing moral views concerning welfare programs, cooperation, and competition.

I have defined liberalism simply in terms of individual freedom, but in so doing I have glossed over a major moral conflict between advocates of a more libertarian polity and of a more cooperative "welfare-state" polity. The theorists I have considered often seem either to assume a more "welfare-state" stance or to slide over the problem. Libertarians, as such, are not likely to support any proposals that include granting anyone land or restricting the sale of land. Perhaps only secession, among the group rights I have considered, would be accepted by them. Thus it is appropriate to consider efforts to resolve this conflict, especially if, as seems likely, there are good reasons to reject John Rawls's claim that we can reach an "overlapping consensus" on a single polity.[19]

Given moral pluralism but some agreement on trying to end the suffering of each individual (this goal is rejected by libertarians, but see later), we might get agreement on establishing a federal array of states, each with a different economic-political ideology. Citizens of the larger region will then migrate to the polity of their choice. The consent model is thus implemented in a way that minimizes coercion. Individual autonomy is enhanced. Political stability is promoted. Of course, some compromises and even coercion may be necessary, since practically we cannot have in every case just the polity that someone chooses. But this array model is far superior to others in this regard. There will be many fewer morally and ideologically homeless persons. Political philosophy has assumed that a successful theory will propose a single unified polity (namely, the best one). But if pluralism is our condition, then having plural polities is not a sign of failure, especially provided that the plurality is organized into a federal array of minimally cooperating states. The use of planning, then, can avoid the need for secession, or reduce it greatly.

A very limited federal government will provide joint defense, a court to adjudicate claims of one array state against another, and an administration to provide the benefits of coordination. But this government will not be burdensome to the individual array states and their citizens.

The difficulties with this proposal arise when we begin to consider the federal array's career. If we allow citizens to change their minds and migrate again to their new choice, we may find that the territory once adequate for a polity is now too small. Will the polity losing population be required to yield territory? Or can the gaining polity modify its policies to accommodate the influx? What if all the weak and ill migrate to a welfare state, overburdening it? Should even a libertarian polity be required to donate to care for these citizens of the welfare polity? Perhaps the array idea may prove so useful to the libertarians that they might be willing to contribute (not for the sake of the suffering people, but in their own self-interest).

The issue of migration cannot be addressed fully here, but some remarks may be helpful. Some might object that migration should never be a solution to political problems, but surely this a priori decree is not plausible. Migrations have been implemented by treaty and have often occurred spontaneously. Kymlicka reports that the "late twentieth century has been described as 'the age of migration.' Massive numbers of people are moving across borders, making virtually every country more polyethnic in composition."[20] Presumably migration might be used as well to help gain moral and ideological compatibility.

The array proposal and its implementation would be the work of a continuing construction, one that would require cooperation and agreement among those willing to participate. But the array requires fewer shared values than other proposals, such as that of Rawls, who calls for a single polity with extensive cooperative and welfare programs. Nevertheless, the array proposal is part of ideal theory, and the world seems far from ready to consider such ideals. The current global economy makes it difficult for polities—whether federations, their provinces, or centralized states—to exercise economic control and independence. We may get the impression that the world is hurtling onward, with little human control, so that we can only hope that the results are good (or at least I can hope that I am lucky or good enough to be a winner). But, perhaps, when this phase has played itself out, a time of opportunity may emerge.

The array model values, however, may be applied in some contexts although no array exists. The array values may serve to help justify secession in a wide range of cases, particularly those that deal with sharp differences of political morality. Similarly, array values will support native reservations and several types of federations. And even beyond these issues, array values include the moral principle that significantly large minority groups have rights not only to a place at the negotiating table but also to some concessions. The principle, in a sense, would be one of proportional accommodation, an analogue of the principle of proportional representation. In political decision making, we ought not simply seek to gain a majority victory but also to find places for diverse values. In Rawlsian terms, we ought to seek a consensus rather than a modus vivendi. Possibly, just a hint of these values of accommodation may be guiding current policy in the United States of allowing states to structure programs based on their local situation (but, of course, there are other values at work that may mask exploitation, etc.).

Conclusion

Could a spirit of accommodation go so far as to grant to groups the right to land on which to construct or preserve their own way of life, as in different ways and degrees would be required by proposals for the right of secession, native and other reservations, and certain kinds of federations such as the array model? The problem, of course, is that there is no empty land, no *locus vacuis*, so that we face such practical issues as the need for compensation for those surrendering their land. But consider what often happens in human societies: citizens of like mind migrate, often gradually, to certain territories. For example, believers in a certain type of survivalist libertarianism have tended to migrate to Idaho. Some cults have moved into localities and attempted to gain majority control of local governing bodies. To the extent that such efforts succeed, the holders of such ideologies find themselves living in a morally congenial community. Even if the land owned by like-minded citizens looks more like a gerrymandered or even somewhat scattered congressional district, the nearness of compatible fellow citizens may be quite valuable. The problem, of course, is that the original residents may come to feel like outsiders who would have to move to find compatible neighbors. Yet, perhaps, on balance finding ways to encourage such tendencies is what is most beneficial and practical (but not if any group's ideology is too immoral and illiberal).

One basic issue is how we deal with moral diversity, with others who do not share some of our important values. Typically, we judge some to be beyond what is tolerable and thus to be subject to some kind of avoidance, containment, or attack. We are willing in varying degrees to deal with the others, to whom we grant a more ample respect. In these negotiations, we are guided by our basic values, and if a strong concern for individuals' well-being is prominent among these values, we may find along the way that various strategies of separation, including secession, native reservations, and federation may be useful and appropriate. Given our current context of moral pluralism, no overriding moral need arises in every case for universal individual rights as opposed to group-differentiated rights or for unitary polities as opposed to federations. Strategies of cooperative separation are crucial and need to be fully explored.

Most of us operate with two opposing principles: first, that we ought to help people, acting on a concern for the well-being even of the citizen stranger; second, that individuals ought to be responsible for bringing about their own well-being, making do with what fortune has given them and what their own efforts provide. We need, then, to strike a balance between the two, but many of us will find that equilibrium at quite different points. The relevance of group land rights arises with the moral pluralism that is thus generated. If we then attend to the concurrent issues of language and traditional culture, we see how complex the issues become. The construction of group rights to land in the form of rights to secession, nonalienable reservations, and autonomy in federations may be useful as we deal with many problems of human frustration and suffering.

Notes

1. Allen Buchanan, *Secession* (Boulder, Colo.: Westview Press, 1991), 709; Will Kymlicka, *Multicultural Citizenship: A Liberal Theory of Minority Rights* (Oxford: Clarendon Press, 1995), chap. 3; see also 68, 137; cf. Harry Beran, *The Consent Theory of Political Obligation* (London: Croom Helm, 1987), 38.

2. Kymlicka, *Multicultural Citizenship*, 46–47.

3. Will Kymlicka, *Liberalism, Community and Culture* (Oxford: Clarendon Press, 1989), 150–52.

4. Kymlicka, *Multicultural Citizenship*, chap. 3.

5. Beran, *The Consent Theory of Political Obligation*, 37.

6. Christopher H. Wellman, "A Defense of Secession and Political Self-Determination," *Philosophy and Public Affairs* 24 (1995): 149.

7. If we go back to our basic relevant value, to the worry about the human suffering of each individual, it might seem that we could go either toward invisible-hand solu-

tions to problems, supported by general predictions of favorable outcomes, or toward direct social planning carried out by the people collectively, that is, by government. But relying mainly on invisible-hand mechanisms is ruled out because it abandons this concern for individuals in favor of an aggregating morality. Wellman seems to emphasize invisible-hand strategies, those that rely on the competitive market mechanism to provide efficient government, with the threat of secession as the spur (171).

8. Buchanan, *Secession*, chaps. 2, 5, esp. 151–52.

9. Allen Buchanan, "Theories of Secession," *Philosophy and Public Affairs* 26 (1997): 40.

10. Beran, *The Consent Theory of Political Obligation*, 32, 59, 153.

11. Buchanan, *Secession*, 13–14, 159.

12. Wellman, "A Defense of Secession," 163 n. 25.

13. Kymlicka, *Liberalism, Community and Culture*, 151.

14. Ibid., 145–56, 166–69, 177–78, 253–58; Kymlicka, *Multicultural Citizenship*, 43–46.

15. I grant that this is a bit vague. In one sense, the person has not lost "cultural membership," and the cultural loss has been only partial. But one's job is an important part of one's culture, and the loss of the job can lead to the loss of more of one's culture and to a serious crash.

16. Kymlicka, *Multicultural Citizenship*, 84–86.

17. Ibid., 156–58.

18. By the way, Kymlicka supports under appropriate conditions not only federations and reservations but also secession (*Multicultural Cititzenship*, 186).

19. John Rawls, *Political Liberalism* (New York: Columbia University Press, 1993), see lecture IV.

20. Kymlicka, *Multicultural Citizenship*, 193.

Chapter 13

In Defense of the Diversity State

Robert N. Van Wyk

Three ideals associated with liberal thinkers are autonomy, neutrality, and diversity. There are, however, conflicts between these ideals. Making the furtherance of autonomy a state goal would be a violation of neutrality. Some authors are concerned with the state's furtherance of liberal ideas and have no sympathy for the idea of state neutrality.[1] Neutrality-oriented liberals, such as Charles Larmore, attack autonomy-centered liberalism on the grounds that it makes "liberalism yet another controversial and partisan vision of the good life" and so incapable of solving the problem of finding "some way of living together that avoids the rule of force."[2] The third idea is diversity. Respecting diversity would seem to involve respecting the rights of groups, and individuals as members of groups, to fulfill their obligations as they see them as much as possible without the interference of the state. It might also involve valuing the practice of groups contributing their distinctive perspectives in the public arena. It is one purpose of this chapter to point out that there are also conflicts between diversity and both of these other liberal ideas. Liberal practice and liberal theory, at least of the American variety, do not seem to be very sympathetic to diversity and the rights of groups. A second purpose of this chapter is to defend a view of the state that puts a higher value on respect for diversity with a particular emphasis on religious diversity, since that is the area where diversity is most likely a matter of deep conviction.

Liberalism, Groups, and Diversity

Respect for diversity would seem to involve respect for the rights of groups and individuals as groups members, but this is something with which liberalism seems to have difficulty. This difficulty is seen in cases where group rights conflict with the rights of individuals seen as autonomous individuals and, second, where these rights conflict with government policies that can be supported on the basis of appeals to neutrality or autonomy.[3] The conflict between respect for diversity and the furtherance of autonomy can be seen in the way some liberals have argued that *Wisconsin v. Yoder* was decided wrongly when it permitted educational exceptions for Amish children because it compromised a child's autonomy or "right to an open future." The conflict between diversity and neutrality can be seen in the controversy over the Religious Freedom Restoration Act and the issues it addressed. This act was a reaction to Justice Scalia's opinion in *Employment Division v. Smith* (1990) that no unconstitutional violation of religious freedom occurs so long as the burden on the exercise of one's religion occurs because of a law or policy that meets the criterion of neutrality of intent. This act, recently overturned by the Supreme Court, could be seen as sympathetic to diversity.

A number of authors have commented on this situation. Frederick Gedicks writes that "American liberalism, with its uncompromising focus on state and individual, often overlooks institutions, like religious groups, that are neither governmental nor individualistic."[4] Vernon Van Dyke, with reference to Rawls's *A Theory of Justice*, writes that "somehow the social contract theory in its dominant form neglects the obvious."[5] Mary Ann Glendon writes:

> The vocabulary and conceptual apparatus of modern law and politics is primarily geared to the relations among individuals, the state, and the market. Legal theory lacks adequate terms and concepts for grappling with the 'thousand different types' of social groups that provide the immediate context for most people's lives and that flourish within and among the megastructures of the state and the market.[6]

The phenomenon pointed to by Gedicks, Van Dyke, and Glendon is often manifested in the way that church and state issues are seen and dealt with. Dean Kelley, an authority on church and state issues, notes that

> the civil libertarian's solicitude for religious liberty is made uneasy if two or more persons gather together to seek to exercise their religious liberty in *concert*, and if they do so as a *church*, the civil libertarian becomes positively apprehensive and his/her solicitude for the "free exercise of religion" tends to be replaced by intense anxieties about "establishment." Thus the *collective* free exercise of religion by believers joined together in organizations has enjoyed a somewhat more limited recognition in American church-state law and a distinctly suspicious reception in less reflective circles.[7]

The Conflict Between Autonomy and Diversity

Many American liberals see autonomy as the fundamental political value, and, of course, autonomy is valued as something possessed by individuals. The emphasis on autonomy, however, is not something that has deep roots in the American tradition. The American Founding Fathers did not seem to be concerned with it.[8] Michael Sandel notes that neither such words as *autonomy* and *choice* nor the concepts they refer to play any role in the fifteen arguments for the separation of church and state in Madison's "Memorial and Remonstrance."[9] The desire of some liberals to regard a child's "right to an open future" as a right to be protected by the state would seem to be a major threat to the freedom of groups to live their own lives and to the freedom of families to raise their own children.[10] The glorification of autonomy can be seen in public education, for example, in sex education textbooks that preach the message that parents are treating teenagers unjustly if they do not provide them privacy so that they can make and carry out their sexual decisions.[11] A common view is that "teachers, parents, and churches do not have the right to tell a youngster what to choose," since "students have to decide for themselves what is right."[12] William Galston would seem to be correct when he writes that "in the guise of protecting the capacity for diversity, the autonomy principle in fact represents a kind of uniformity that exerts pressure on ways of life that do not embrace autonomy."[13] If a central concern of classic liberalism is, as William Sullivan puts it, "to enhance for individuals the plasticity of life, especially in regard to the constraints of social institutions and cultural norms,"[14] the conflict with the freedom of families and groups to produce a next generation that shares their values and commitments would seem to be obvious.[15] This concern would seem to be in conflict with any commitment to diversity and also with the original intent of the free exercise clause of the First Amendment of the U.S. Constitution.[16]

The Conflict Between Neutrality and Respect for Diversity

As has been noted, an alternative version of liberalism is one that centers on the idea of the "neutrality" of the state. There are powerful objections against any approach that aims at neutrality of results,[17] so neutralist-oriented liberalism usually talks about justification and intent.[18] Expanding on a quote from Joseph Raz, the neutralist position seems to be the following: "No political action may be undertaken or justified on the ground that it promotes (or inhibits) an ideal of the good nor on the ground that it enables individuals to pursue (or inhibits individuals from pursuing) an ideal of the good."[19] Such neutrality is intended to provide the foundation for a modus vivendi.[20] But neutrality, so understood, is in tension with the traditional liberal concern with rights. As George Sher writes, "Because naturalism prohibits only acts performed for certain reasons while legal rights prohibit certain acts in themselves, the two notions are logically at cross purposes."[21] This can be seen in the case of the free exercise clause of the First Amendment. Attempts by political theorists, and now by the courts, to subsume the religion clauses of the First Amendment under a principle of neutrality as a sufficient condition for legitimacy end up emasculating the free exercise clause and threatening the vital interests of religious people or religious groups.[22] Critics of Justice Scalia's opinion in *Employment Division v. Smith* (1990), claim—in my opinion, correctly—that it leaves the state free to run roughshod over the rights of religious groups as long as its action is not intended to hurt those groups, that is, as long as the state's action does not violate neutrality of intent. One reason for supporting the idea of state neutrality is for the sake of a modus vivendi. But whether individuals or groups see something as a modus vivendi to which they have a reason to subscribe depends on the actual consequences for those individuals or groups, intended or unintended, not just on intentions and justifications. So whether contemporary liberalism emphasizes neutrality or whether it emphasizes autonomy, it does not seem to be very sympathetic to diversity and the rights of groups.[23]

Political Liberalism, Public Reason, and the Overlapping Consensus

I have noted problems for the rights of groups and individuals when "neutrality" is taken as a sufficient condition for the legitimacy of state action. There may also be problems when neutrality is treated as a necessary condition for the legitimacy of state action. If government policy is produced by a democratic process, then the requirement that the state be neutral in some sense would seem to imply that in some sense individual citizens should observe some sort of standards of neutrality when they vote and when they discuss issues of public policy. This point of view would impose on individual citizens restrictions regarding what sort of reasons they may use for deciding how to vote or what policies to support, or what sort of reasons they may appeal to in public discussion. Proposals concerning such a restriction vary widely with respect to why such restrictions should be accepted, to what sort of reasons are restricted, to whether they apply to some arenas of discussion but not to others, to whether they apply to all public issues or only to some, and, if the latter, which ones, to whether there are exceptions for issues that cannot be decided by nonexcluded reasons, and so on.[24] One question that concerns me in this chapter is whether such restrictions should be seen as something that protects diversity and pluralism, or something that threatens diversity and pluralism. A complete answer may require the sorting out of the variations and distinctions mentioned earlier, which cannot be done here. Perhaps, however, something of an answer can be given.

John Rawls, one defender of such restrictions, offers a version of "political liberalism" that is designed to take the fact of pluralism seriously. One can take pluralism seriously for one or both of two reasons: (1) in order to protect against its dangers, perhaps by neutralizing its effects, or (2) in order to promote its flourishing. Rawls seems more interested in protecting against its dangers by neutralizing its effects. According to Rawls, in some contexts and with respect to some issues (constitutional essentials and matters of basic justice), citizens should vote and argue on the basis of a balance of public values they "sincerely think can be seen to be reasonable by others" and not on the basis of "comprehensive religious and philosophical doctrines."[25] Presumably to violate these restrictions is to violate a civic duty. For Rawls, the commitment to public reason is part of an overlapping consensus that gets unanimous support from holders of various "reasonable" comprehensive theories. The overlapping consensus is justified by making possible the existence over time of a stable and just society in the context of pluralism.[26]

One might be concerned about protecting pluralism and protecting against pluralism at the same time if one sees the situation as still being that of Locke's day in which the principal threat to the freedom of groups is the desire of other groups to coercively impose their will on others. Jeremy Waldron notes that Rawls writes "as if each comment that is made in public debate is nothing more than a proposal to use public power to forcibly impose something on everyone else."[27] Is this the appropriate way of seeing things today? Those who fear the religious right and/or are primarily concerned with such issues as gay rights do see it that way, and so see public reason restrictions as a protection of pluralism and diversity and the observance of such restrictions as a way of showing respect for individuals and groups.[28] For them we are in the same situation as Locke was. But others point out that the situation may be quite different. First, in some cases religious groups may appeal to a doctrine "as one contribution among others in a debate on how political power is to be used," as with the Catholic bishops' pastoral letter on the American economy, regarded by many as a valuable contribution.[29] So Maimon Schwarzschild seems to be arguing for pluralism against such restrictions when he writes:

> A liberal society ought to embrace as many of the world's contradictory goods as it can possibly carry. And religious values are surely among these goods. Today's religious groups, at least those with a calling to social action, offer views which are in some measure a counterweight to the values of secular modernity. The presence of such counterweights strengthens pluralism, and hence stands to strengthen liberal society itself.[30]

Second, in other cases religious groups are not concerned with imposing anything on anybody, but just with being left alone and protected from state coercion and interference.[31] In the eyes of many people, the primary issue today is not protecting some groups from the will of other groups but "the conflict between religions collectively on the one hand and insensitive government regulation on the other."[32] Those who focus on this issue are quick to see a conflict between contemporary liberal theory and diversity. Critics see such quests for consensus as tending to produce "a debilitating uniformity of thought,"[33] which threatens to reduce public debate to "bland appeals to harmless nostrums that are accepted without question on all sides."[34]

Samuel Scheffler notes that when Rawls gives a model case of overlapping consensus, all three views that are described "appear to be drawn from the same relatively narrow portion of the broad spectrum of evaluative conviction."[35] Is everyone else relegated to second-class citizenship? What happens to groups, and members of groups, whose comprehensive doctrines or religious beliefs do not lead to a wholehearted endorsement of liberal political principles? They would seem to be labeled as unreasonable (or heretical).[36] It would seem that toleration only necessarily applies to subscribers to reasonable pluralism.[37] So while some would defend public reason restrictions as a matter of respect for persons, others oppose them on the grounds that they show a lack of sensitivity toward and respect for groups and members of groups who are told to keep their opinions to themselves, if indeed they are entitled to have such opinions at all. Bruce Brower writes: "Respecting others . . . requires that we recognize the depth of their concerns. If we acknowledge other's considerations only insofar as they accord with public reason, then, even if we hold that the desire for public reasons should regulate the ideal person, we fail to respect nonideal persons."[38]

Stephen Macedo writes that "liberalism requires not merely an overlapping consensus but a consensus that practically *overrides* all competing values."[39] Herein lies the problem. No theist, and perhaps no parent, can say that political values should always override competing values. Even if, as is likely, one's comprehensive view is a basis for subscribing to an overlapping consensus up to a certain point, this must always be with some qualification. It is not clear why political values and duties should take precedence over others even when we are talking about secular ideals.[40] The problem is even greater when religious commitments are involved. Sandel and Garvey both point to the fact that religious people usually do not see themselves as choosing their beliefs but as being bound by obligations they did not choose,[41] and cannot bargain away, even for the sake of political stability.[42] McConnell points out that for the Founders, "Conflicts arising from religious convictions were conceived not as a clash between the judgment of the individual and the state, but as a conflict between earthly and spiritual sovereigns."[43] If Madison's views are in fact a key to the proper understanding of the free exercise clause of the First Amendment to the U.S. Constitution, then what Madison denies, and what the First Amendment denies, is precisely the priority of the political. Madison wrote that

> a person's duty towards the Creator . . . is precedent, both in order of time and in degree of obligation to the claims of Civil Society. Before any man can be considered as a member of Civil Society [or a subscriber to the overlapping consensus], he must be considered as a subject of the Governor of the Universe. . . . [E]very man who becomes a member of any particular Civil Society [must] do it with a saving of his allegiance to the Universal Sovereign.[44]

Perhaps a strong defense of religious freedom and a pro-accommodationist understanding of the First Amendment can be defended by arguments that meet the criteria of public reason, perhaps arguments about the value of religion.[45] But the religious believer's support of the Madisonian view is not and cannot be contingent upon the success of such arguments. So there is at least one issue of basic justice that the believer must take a position on whether it can be defended by nontheological reasons.

The Diversity State

The Nature of the Diversity State

William Galston defends what he calls the *diversity state*, which is an out-growth of what he calls the *reformation project*, which he contrasts to the *enlightenment project*. Autonomy-oriented liberalism is historically related to the enlightenment project.[46] The diversity state is historically related to the most satisfactory of the ways of dealing with the results of the reformation, that of "accepting and managing diversity through mutual toleration."[47] Part of the basic structures of the Diversity State is oriented to promoting pluralism and includes cultural (as well as religious) disestablishment, a strong system of tolerance, and civic education promoting tolerance. Part of the basic structure defends the rights of individuals by prohibiting coerced entrance into groups and by prohibiting the prevention of exit from groups. Part of the basic structure is oriented toward preserving the unity of the diversity state by defending "principles, institutions, and practices that constitute the core requirement of shared citizenship."[48] Specific policies exhibited by the diversity state should include "wide parental rights, limited only by compelling state interests, a non-autonomy-based education, supplemented by private education whose center bounds are defined by the basic structure, wide rights of group association; and an accomodationist, pro-exemption understanding of free religious exercise."[49]

Defending the Diversity State

Why should we accept the ideal of the diversity state? Part of an answer is found in the failure of those who defend the autonomy-furthering state to give good reasons for taking autonomy as the highest good.[50] A positive defense is given by Galston, who writes that the reformation project, which takes deep diversity as its point of departure, offers the best hope for maximizing opportunities for individuals and groups to lead lives as they see fit."[51] He then asks: "But why should we take diversity so seriously?"[52] His answers include (1) that diversity is an inescapable fact of modern life and (2) that it has instrumental value. But perhaps additional arguments in favor of the diversity state can be given, some of which appeal to rights of groups and individuals as members of groups. Below I claim (1) that group rights have a place in our legal tradition, (2) that there are good reasons for ascribing rights to groups and for treating these rights as often overriding individual rights and government policy, and (3) that the diversity state provides better answers to the questions of legitimacy and stability than does a system based on the idea of ideally rational people consenting to a set of principles.

Groups and Rights

Vernon Van Dyke gives many examples of the recognition of the rights of groups in the laws and policies of many countries.[53] In the United States the courts have not always failed to take into account the rights or freedom of groups. Garvey points out that in church property disputes state courts in the United States have *sometimes* appealed to a rule of deference, which Garvey defends, by which the courts defer to the highest decision-making body of a religious group, rather than to a rule of neutral principles. In these cases group freedom prevailed over individual freedom.[54]

What is the foundation for regarding groups as having rights?[55] While some would ground all rights in autonomy, and thus regard rights as inapplicable to groups, there is in fact no reason to believe that all rights must be derived from one source or even that a single right may not "find a foundation in several reasons."[56] The sources of justification for rights that seem most applicable to group rights are instrumental justifications,[57] and those that would derive rights from duties or responsibilities.[58]

An instrumentalist argument for group rights and for their often taking priority over individual rights can refer to the value of mediating structures, a value that seems undeniable. Peter Jones points out that "sometimes what matters most to people are traditions, practices and institutions that they enjoy, and can enjoy, only as members of collective entities,"[59] and that legal supervision of groups within society will often do more harm than good.[60]

A second argument for group rights is one that is based on responsibilities. David Norton, advocating an Aristotelian approach to ethics, writes that "rights are entitlements by the individual to what he or she needs and can utilize in living the life that he or she is responsible for living" or needs "to recognize and undertake his or her" moral responsibilities.[61] If groups and individuals with roles within groups (e.g., parents) and governing bodies (e.g., synods) can have moral responsibilities, then groups, as well as individuals, can have rights.

Some rights and duties that compete with political duties might derive from consent or competing social contracts.[62] But there might also be pre-existing duties not based on consent or contract. The most obvious candidates are religious duties and natural duties with respect to the family. I have already quoted Madison with respect to religious duties. With respect to duties within the family, Jacob Joshua Ross writes:

> I posit therefore a primary right of parental-ownership (partly bodily, partly spiritual and throughout genetic) as the fundamental principle of an improved conception of parental authority.
>
> If asked where those moral rights and duties come from, we may answer, choosing the terminology of the natural law tradition, that they issue from the divine will and are discoverable by reason. Or we may prefer a more secular way of putting the matter and say that they come from the conventional rules involved in the practices that human society has accepted. What we must not say, it seems to me, is that society has simply invented such rules; they are as much recognized by society as invented by society.[63]

While some would disagree with either or both of these claims, they must be taken seriously, first because they are at least plausible and second because they are accepted by many people (perhaps the vast majority) who are part of the political order.

A Pluralist Political Philosophy

Members of families and religious groups might have good reason to see themselves as encumbered selves who have duties, and thus also rights, prior to their political membership and which they would not want to be compromised by political considerations. Does the political system have good reason to see things in the same way? One can argue that these rights and duties should be recognized by the state because they are philosophically justifiable in themselves. One can also argue that recognizing such rights serves the purposes of the political order better than, or at least as well as, some other approach. Those advocating other approaches, for example, Rawls and Nagel, seem to be concerned about legitimacy and stability.

Legitimacy

According to Jeremy Waldron, a basic idea that most liberals share is that "the social order must be one that can be justified to the people who have to live under it"[64] and that an arrangement or institution is illegitimate if it "has not secured, or perhaps could not secure, the consent of the people."[65] Which people? Whose consent is to be sought? For Nagel and Rawls it would be the hypothetical consent and consensus of fully rational people.[66] But there are reasons to reject this point of view. First, by this standard it is quite possible to conclude that there are no legitimate governments. Second, suppose there are other good reasons to choose a government even though it fails to meet this particular test. Might not such a government still have all the justification it needs?[67] Suppose we modify Nagel's position by focusing on institutions more than on principles, and by asking about what real people could reasonably accept rather than what ideally rational people could reasonably reject. Nicholas Rescher puts the difference between the two approaches very clearly: "Consensus-seeking societies will aim to *maximize* the number of people who approve of what is being done; acquiescence-seeking societies seek to *minimize* the number of people who disapprove very strongly of what is being done."[68] The points of view dealt with in this chapter, including those that deal with the views of ideally rational people, all approach the matter from the top down. According to Gary Leedes, "Rawls presumes to decide, *qua* philosopher king, that social unity is more compelling than a person's religion even though the social unity he has in mind alienates many religious persons from their traditions and gods."[69] But minimizing the number of people who disapprove and so withhold consent entails not looking at the matter as a philosopher-king. This can be seen particularly clearly in a country, such as the United States, that has a written and ratified constitution. As Laurence Tribe writes:

> If one believes, as the Framers believed, that legitimate power is delegated *to* the state by individuals and groups, and that certain groups under our constitutional scheme have never relinquished their private authority and autonomy as centers of deeply shared experience and faith, then religious institutions emerge not as repositories of unaccountable, delegated state power, but as irreducible components of our social order, secure against all but the most limited and most compellingly justified forms of government intervention.[70]

One could say the same things about families. The Bill of Rights was included in the Constitution for the sake of gaining consent or acquiescence from those fearful of autocratic government, including those who shared the beliefs of Madison and Ross. The means of achieving that goal was to exclude certain things from the arena of government decisions (or top-down thinking) about what proper political theory requires of public policy (even if that theory is the latest version of philosophical liberalism). I can consent to the diversity state because, while the system will require that I make compromises with respect to my interests, it will not readily interfere with my fulfilling what I regard as my sacred obligations or compromise my identity.

Stability

The other concern of many writers is stability. For Rawls the consensus on basic principles found in the overlapping consensus and the adherence to public reason serves the purpose of stability. However, Joseph Raz, Nicholas Rescher, George Klosko, and John Haldane, among others, have all argued that stability does not depend to any significant extent on agreement on principles.[71] So Joseph Raz claims that it is doubtful "whether Rawls has identified the concerns which should dominate political philosophy today."[72] John Haldane points to the British system, which has "no coherent set of organizing principles" and which is "a *modus vivendi* writ large," *and* which nevertheless "seems no less stable than an overlapping consensus."[73] Since dissatisfaction and alienation are felt by real people, not by ideal or perfectly rational people, it would seem that a system that aims at minimizing the dissatisfaction of real people will be more stable than one that aims at a rational consensus of ideal people. Historically, civil strife came to an end with the "tacit recognition that secular government had no jurisdiction over religious conscience."[74] Rescher claims that

> what matters for the smooth functioning of a social order is not that the individuals or groups that represent conflicting positions should think alike [or talk alike] but simply that they acquiesce in certain shared ways of conducting society's affairs.[75]
>
> What is needed for co-operation is not consensus but something quite different—*a convergence of interests.* And it is a fortunate fact of communal life that people's interests can coincide without any significant degree of agreement between them.[76]

Groups with strong commitments to various ways of life can have a convergence of interests in support of the diversity state. They are also likely to reach a consensus on principles in the sense that, insofar as government is structured on principles, all of those principles may have the support of a majority of people even if none of them is supported by every person. This is of course a quest for a modus vivendi, but what is wrong with that? It certainly seems much friendlier to pluralism and the acceptance of group differences. "Consensuality looks to uniformity of thought, pluralism to reciprocally fruitful harmonization of discordant elements."[77] Why should not this approach be productive of stability? Rescher writes: "No system will be viable in the long term if the acquiescence it elicits is too often and too deeply reluctant. The rational person's acquiescence is, after all, based on a cost-benefit calculation that weighs the costs of opposition against the cost of 'going along.' . . . [S]ensible people are distinctly unlikely to acquiesce in arrangements that are oppressive to them."[78] It would seem that the diversity state serves the interests both of legitimacy and of stability while protecting diversity and pluralism and reflecting the spirit of the free exercise clause of the First Amendment, "the most philosophically interesting and distinctive feature of the American Constitution."[79]

Postscript on Limits

Diversity is not here being treated as something valuable in itself. What is required is that the diversity of conviction and the rights of groups that already exist in a society be respected, not that new groups be invited in or invented just for the sake of furthering diversity, or that groups that are almost extinct (e.g., the Shakers) get special support just to preserve diversity, or that deference be shown to the wishes of individuals (e.g., prisoners) who, apart from any existing religious tradition, invent new religious requirements in order to avoid legal requirements (e.g., prison rules). What is being called for is respect for the diverse practices of groups, including families, that are matters of deep conviction. There are obviously limits to such diversity when the practices of some groups (e.g., female genital mutilation) are seen (in this case, rightly so) as intolerable by the vast majority of citizens belonging to various groups. It would be an infringement on the deepest convictions of most Americans, for example, to stand idly by while a child died because of a religion-based refusal by his or her parents to get medical attention for a curable life-threatening disease. It would not be such an infringement on anyone's convictions to let a Jewish psychologist wear a yarmulke in an army hospital, or to have the government refrain from plowing logging roads through Native American sacred territory, or to allow Sikhs to wear turbans instead of hard hats at construction sites, or to allow Native Americans to use peyote in worship, or to do most of the other things that have been at issue in free exercise cases that have come before American courts. There are historical considerations as well. Catholic, Protestant, Jewish, Islamic, Native American, and other practices are matters of tradition that antedate particular laws and regulations that may affect them and, indeed, in the United States, antedate the ratification of the Constitution. Those who participated in its ratification presupposed that they were not doing anything that would conflict with their sacred obligations and, as a matter of impartiality, the sacred obligations of others who may not then have been included insofar as these do not violate fundamental moral considerations.

Notes

1. See Brian Barry, "How Not to Defend Liberalism," in *Liberalism and the Good*, ed. R. Bruce Douglas, Gerald M. Mara, and Henry S. Richardson (New York: Routledge, 1990), 44–58.

2. Charles Larmore, "Political Liberalism," *Political Theory* 18 (1990): 357.

3. An example of the first sort of conflict can be found in how the courts deal with church property disputes. Another place where this difficulty can be seen is in the fact that American law and liberal theory give little recognition of the idea of libel applying to groups or communities. See Michael Sandel, *Democracy's Discontent* (Cambridge Mass.: Harvard University Press, 1996), 82–83.

4. Frederick Mark Gedicks, "Toward a Constitutional Jurisprudence of Religious Group Rights," *Wisconsin Law Review* 1989 (1989): 100.

5. Vernon Van Dyke, "Justice as Fairness: For Groups?" *American Political Science Review* 69 (1975): 614.

6. Mary Ann Glendon, "Individualism and Communitarianism in Contemporary Legal Systems: Tensions and Accommodations," *Brigham Young University Law Review* 1993 (1993): 394.

7. Dean Kelley, *The Law of Church and State in America* (Westport, Conn.: Greenwood, 1998), 9.

8. John H. Garvey, "Free Exercise and the Values of Religious Liberty," *Connecticut Law Review* 18 (1986): 790.

9. Michael J. Sandel, "Freedom of Conscience or Freedom of Choice?" in *Articles of Faith, Articles of Peace*, ed. James Davidson Hunter and Os Giness (Washington, D.C.: Brookings Institution, 1990), 87, 88.

10. The phrase in quotes comes from Jules Feinberg, "The Child's Right to an Open Future," in *Whose Child?* ed. William Aiken and Hugh LaFollette (Totowa, N.J.: Littlefield Adams, 1980), 124, 126. The conflict between the furtherance of autonomy and respect for group rights is seen also in the *Mozert v. Hawkins* case. See the chapter by Erik Anderson in this volume.

11. These ideas are expressed by Ruth Bell and associates, *Changing Bodies, Changing Lives*, rev. ed. (New York: Random House, 1981), 109.

12. William K. Kilpatrick, *Why Johnny Can't Tell Right from Wrong* (New York: Simon

and Schuster, 1992), 53. A similar critique is given by Dana Mack in "What the Sex Educators Teach," *Commentary* 96, no. 2 (1994): 33–38.

13. William Galston, "Two Concepts of Liberalism," *Ethics* 105 (1995): 523.

14. William Sullivan, "Bringing the Good Back In," in *Liberalism and the Good*, ed. Bruce Douglas, Gerald M. Mara, and Henry S. Richardson (London: Routledge, 1988), 148.

15. This conflict is explored much more thoroughly in the chapter by Erik Anderson in this volume.

16. Michael W. McConnell, "The Origins and Historical Understanding of the Free Exercise of Religion," *Harvard Law Review* 103 (1990): 1513.

17. Joseph Raz, *The Morality of Freedom* (New York: Oxford University Press, 1987), 112–24.

18. See Charles Larmore, *Patterns of Moral Complexity* (New York: Cambridge University Press, 1987), 44. See also John Locke, *Letter on Toleration* (1689) (Indianapolis: Hackett, 1983), 41–42.

19. Raz, *Morality of Freedom*, 114.

20. See Larmore, *Patterns of Moral Complexity*, 43, 47, 73–77. See also Robert Nozick, *Anarchy, State and Utopia* (New York: Basic Books, 1974), 33, 272–73.

21. George Sher, *Beyond Neutrality: Perfectionism and Politics* (New York: Cambridge University Press, 1997), 113.

22. See the following: Gail Merel, "The Protection of Individual Choice: A Consistent Understanding of Religion Under the First Amendment," *University of Chicago Law Review* 45 (1978): 808; Jessie H. Chopper, "The Religion Clauses of the First Amendment: Reconciling the Conflict," *University of Pittsburgh Law Review* 41 (1980): 608; and Douglas Laycock, "Summary and Synthesis: The Crisis in Religious Liberty," *George Washington Law Review* 60 (1992): 841–56.

23. Another area in which there is a conflict between the rights of groups and the appeal to neutral principles is in dealing with church property disputes. John Garvey argues that in its application to settling church property disputes, "the rule of neutral principles is perfectly consistent with individual freedom" (and thus also with the liberal ideal of autonomy), but it "often frustrates the goal of group freedom" and so comes into conflict with ideas of group rights. If so, "neutral principles" may not be justified on the grounds of providing the foundation for a modus vivendi that includes people who strongly identify with a group. John H. Garvey, "Churches and the Free Exercise of Religion," *Notre Dame Journal of Law, Ethics and Public Policy* 4 (1990): 585.

24. See the following: Bruce Ackerman, *Social Justice and the Liberal State* (New Haven, Conn.: Yale University Press, 1980); Robert Audi, "The Place of Religious Argument in a Free and Democratic Society," *San Diego Law Review* 30 (1993): 677–702; Audi, "Religion and the Ethics of Political Participation," *Ethics* 100 (1990): 386–97; Robert Audi and Nicholas Wolterstorff, *Religion in the Public Square* (Boulder, Colo.: Rowman and Littlefield, 1997); Gordon Graham, "Religion and Politics," *Phi-*

losophy 58 (1983): 203–13; Kent Greenawalt, *Private Consciences and Public Reasons* (New York: Oxford University Press, 1995); Greenawalt, *Religious Convictions and Political Choice* (New York: Oxford University Press, 1980); Thomas Nagel, *Equality and Partiality* (New York: Oxford University Press, 1991); John Rawls, *Political Liberalism* (New York: Columbia University Press, 1993); and Paul J. Weithman, ed., *Religion and Contemporary Liberalism* (Notre Dame, Ind.: University of Notre Dame Press, 1997).

25. Rawls, *Political Liberalism*, 225.

26. Ibid., xviii.

27. Jeremy Waldron, "Religious Contributions in Public Deliberation," *San Diego Law Review* 30 (1993): 841. Leif Wenar notes that public reason restrictions are derived from restrictions that should be put on acts of coercion. Leif Wenar, comments on Robert Van Wyk, "Public Reason and Private Values" (paper presented at the Central Division APA meetings, Chicago, 1996). Since for Rawls these restrictions apply to acts of voting, making campaign speeches, debating on the floor of Congress, and so on, all of these activities would seem to be regarded (implausibly) as acts of coercion (ibid., 5). "The paradox of public reason may be that Rawls's public reason—which is after all supposed to be free, Kantian public reason—ends up being constrained by a demand concerning the legitimacy of coercion" (ibid., 7).

28. There is no doubt that there are religiously based arguments that are a threat to diversity and pluralism, such as ones that deny the equal humanity of all citizens. There is no doubt that people have moral duties not to set forth such arguments. See Martha Nussbaum, "Religion and Women's Human Rights," in *Religion and Contemporary Liberalism*, ed. Paul J. Weithman (Notre Dame, Ind.: University of Notre Dame Press, 1997), 121–35. But it is the content of the position being promoted, not its religious source, that is the decisive factor. There is no doubt that there are various reasons, moral and otherwise, for refraining from using certain kinds of religious arguments in certain circumstances. But these considerations do not add up to some sort of general deontological prohibition of appeals to religious foundations.

29. Waldron, "Religious Contributions in Public Deliberation." The quote is from page 841.

30. Maimon Schwarzschild, "Religion and Public Debate in a Liberal Society: Always Oil and Water or Sometimes More Like Rum and Coca-Cola," *San Diego Law Review* 30 (1993): 915.

31. Galston, "Two Concepts of Liberalism," 520–21.

32. Douglas Laycock, "Free Exercise and the Religious Freedom Restoration Act," *Fordham Law Review* 52 (1995): 885.

33. Nicholas Rescher, *Pluralism* (New York: Oxford University Press, 1993), 162.

34. Waldron, "Religious Contributions in Public Deliberation," 842.

35. Samuel Scheffler, "The Appeal of Political Liberalism," *Ethics* 105 (1994): 9. The reference to Rawls is to *Political Liberalism*, 145.

36. Some critics of Rawls see the issue this way: ad hominem arguments are given to

delegitimate the views and votes of nonconformists who refuse to be silenced. Richard Stith, "Why the Taint to Religion?" *Brigham Young University Law Review* 1993 (1993): 472. See also Frederick Marx Gedicks, "The Religious, the Secular, and the Antithetical," *Capital University Law Review* 20 (1991): 434; and Gary C. Leedes, "Rawls's Excessively Secular Political Conception," *University of Richmond Law Review* 27 (1993): 1098–100. Frederick Gedicks also writes: "Public secularization, then, is oppressive to the believer. It requires that she divide and compartmentalize her life at the same time that her religious experiences testify that life is an indivisible and unified whole. . . . Compartmentalization essentially asks the religious believer to approach her life as if she were not herself." Gedicks, "The Religious, the Secular, and the Antithetical," 434.

37. Galston, "Two Concepts of Liberalism," 518.

38. Bruce W. Brower, "The Limits of Public Reason," *Journal of Philosophy* 91 (1994): 15. See also Leedes, "Rawls's Excessively Secular Political Conception," 1098–100.

39. Stephen Macedo, "The Politics of Justification," *Political Theory* 18 (1990): 285.

40. John J. Haldane, "Identity, Community and the Limits of Multiculture," *Public Affairs Quarterly* 7 (1993): 209; Joseph Raz, "Facing Diversity: The Case of Epistemic Abstinence," *Philosophy and Public Affairs* 19 (1990): 24; Berys Gaut, "Rawls and the Claims of Liberal Legitimacy," unpublished manuscript; Elizabeth Wolgast, "The Demands of Public Reason," *Columbia Law Review* 94 (1994): 1941; Leif Wenar, "*Political Liberalism:* An Internal Critique," *Ethics* 106 (1995) 94. If the priority of the political is being defended on the basis of some metaphysical assumption "then Rawls' position fails its own neutrality test" (Haldane, "Identity, Community and the Limits of Multiculture," 209). Various authors claim that Rawls does appeal to a partially comprehensive doctrine" (Wenar, "*Political Liberalism:* An Internal Critique," 33; Gaut, "Rawls and the Claims of Liberal Legitimacy," 14). Rawls denies a metaphysical assumption and points to the word *normally* that occurs in a number of statements such as "political values *normally* outweigh . . . other values" (Rawls, *Political Liberalism,* 145) and explicitly adds the words "though not always" (Rawls, "The Idea of Public Reason: Further Considerations" [unpublished manuscript, 1994], 21). But it is not clear that this ends up making any practical difference for his position on issues that religious people are concerned about, such as free exercise issues.

41. Sandel, "Freedom of Conscience or Freedom of Choice?" 75–92; John H. Garvey, "Free Exercise and the Values of Religious Liberty," *Connecticut Law Review* 18 (1986): 791–92.

42. Sandel points out the failure of the modern secular courts to take this seriously. The Supreme Court's decision in *Thorton v. Caldor, Inc.* (1985) objected to Sabbath observers having an advantage over others in *selecting* the preferred day to take off ("Freedom of Conscience or Freedom of Choice," 90), and in *Goldman,* Justice Rehnquist never acknowledged that this case involved a religious duty.

43. McConnell, "The Origins and Historical Understanding of the Free Exercise of Religion," 1496.

44. James Madison, "Memorial and Remonstrance" (1785), in Edwin S. Gaustad, *Neither King Nor Prelate: Religion and the New Nation, 1776–1826* (1987; Grand Rapids, Mich.: Eerdmans, 1993), Appendix A, 142.

45. See chapter by Eric Anderson in this volume.

46. Galston, "Two Concepts of Liberalism," 525.

47. Ibid., 526.

48. Ibid., 528.

49. Ibid., 529.

50. See chapter by Erik Anderson in this volume.

51. Galston, "Two Concepts of Liberalism," 527.

52. Ibid., 537.

53. Van Dyke, "Justice as Fairness," 612–13.

54. Garvey, "Churches and the Free Exercise of Religion," 567, 585.

55. Garvey writes that the courts have done little "to explain *how* a church group [for example] can have its own free exercise right, separate and distinct from the rights of its members" (ibid., 580).

56. Peter Jones, *Rights* (London: Macmillan, 1994), 118.

57. Ibid., p. 67, 138.

58. See David Norton, *Democracy and Moral Development: A Politics of Virtue* (Berkeley: University of California Press, 1991), 118–20.

59. Jones, *Rights*, 187.

60. See Garvey, "Churches and the Free Exercise of Religion," 567, 587.

61. Norton, *Democracy and Moral Development*, 121, 110.

62. See Walzer, *Obligations*.

63. Jacob Joshua Ross, *The Virtues of the Family* (New York: Free Press, 1994), 156–57.

64. Jeremy Waldron, "Theoretical Foundations of Liberalism," *Philosophical Quarterly* 37 (1987): 146.

65. Ibid., 140.

66. Nagel, *Equality and Partiality*, 8. See Thomas Hill, "Reflections on Rawls" (paper presented at the Pacific Division APA meeting in Los Angeles, California, 1994), citing Rawls, *Political Liberalism*, 137.

67. Joseph Raz, "Facing Diversity: The Case of Epistemic Abstinence," *Philosophy and Public Affairs* 19 (1990): 3–46.

68. Rescher, *Pluralism*, 189.

69. Leedes, "Rawls's Excessively Secular Political Conception," 1124.

70. Laurence Tribe, "Church and State in the Constitution," in *Government Intervention in Religious Affairs*, ed. Dean M. Kelley (New York: Pilgrim Press, 1982), 31–40.

71. Raz, "Facing Diversity," 33–31; Rescher, *Pluralism*, chap. 9; George Klosko, "Rawls's Argument from Political Stability," *Columbia Law Review* 94 (1994): 1895–97; and John Haldane, "The Individual, the State, and the Common Good," *Social Philosophy and Policy* 13 (1996): 77–78.

72. Raz, "Facing Diversity," 31. Raz argues that "affective and symbolic elements may well be the crucial cement of society" (30).

73. Haldane, "The Individual, the State, and the Common Good," 78.

74. Gedicks, "The Religious, the Secular, and the Antithetical," 119.

75. Rescher, *Pluralism*, 167.

76. Ibid., 180.

77. Ibid., 187.

78. Ibid., 172–73. Frederick Gedicks writes: "Governments that do not respect culture are eventually forced into oppression to avoid their overthrow. If the large number of Americans committed to religious belief and experience come to believe, as many of them already do, that the political system does not respect their way of life to the same extent it respects secular lifestyles, then they themselves will tend not to respect that system or the government and laws that it generates" Gedicks, "Some Political Implications of Religious Belief," *Notre Dame Journal of Law, Ethics and Public Policy* 4 (1990): 438.

79. McConnell, "The Origins and Historical Understanding of the Free Exercise of Religion," 1513.

Chapter 14

Group Rights, Autonomy, and
the Free Exercise of Religion

Erik A. Anderson

A central aspiration of liberalism is to create a society that provides ample "social space" for a wide array of religious and cultural groups. Liberal theories of toleration define the contours of this social space, including its boundaries. Toleration is the practice of allowing an individual or a group to hold beliefs and to engage in practices that others find false, offensive, or morally objectionable, because interference with these beliefs and practices would sacrifice some value of overriding importance. In the case of one dominant strand of liberal theory, which I will call *autonomy-centered liberalism*, that overriding value is individual autonomy. Proponents of this view hold that we must tolerate morally objectionable "conceptions of the good" for the sake of respecting the autonomy of those who choose them.

Will Kymlicka has recently defended the autonomy-centered conception of liberalism. His position is noteworthy for two reasons. First, he reaffirms the central role of the value of individual autonomy, in opposition to recent arguments that individual autonomy is too contentious and sectarian an ideal to play a foundational role in liberal political morality. Second, his appeal to autonomy is unique in that it forms part of a larger argument to the effect that in some cases the granting of group rights is justified. In this chapter I examine Kymlicka's defense of the value of autonomy and explain its connection with toleration and group rights. I argue that we can construct a viable model of religious group rights using elements of Kymlicka's account. I then consider the claim advanced by a number of communitarian philosophers that basing religious toleration on individual autonomy is hostile to the claims of religious groups. I argue to the contrary that the exercise of autonomy is an essential component of the deep communal attachments that communitarians defend.

I

Kymlicka locates the heart of liberal political morality in the claim that individuals have an essential interest in becoming autonomous. His argument in support of autonomy relies on its instrumental value in enabling individuals to lead good lives. He begins with the claim that we have an essential interest in "leading a good life," where a good life is one that is lived in accordance with true beliefs about what kinds of projects, activities, and commitments are of value (Kymlicka 1989, 10). In pursuing this interest, however, it is important for us to realize that what we believe to be of value at any given time might turn out to be mistaken. We may realize later that what we had previously taken to be of value was not valuable at all. Because of our interest in leading a good life, and the ever-present possibility that our current views of what constitutes a good life might turn out to be wrong, we have a subsidiary interest in developing and exercising our ability to subject our beliefs about value to critical scrutiny and to revise them if necessary. Our ability to reason critically about the value of our projects and attachments is thus instrumentally valuable as the best means available for ensuring that these beliefs are not mistaken. The abilities to formulate, revise, and consciously to live in accordance with our beliefs about value constitute our capacity for autonomy.

Kymlicka stresses that a number of conditions must be met if we are to realize our capacity for autonomy. These conditions are met in part by such familiar features of liberal democracies as the protection of basic liberties and the provision of free public education. Less familiar among these conditions, however, is what we might call a *cultural requirement*. Kymlicka claims that in order for us to make intelligent judgments about the value of various ways of life, we must first have access to a cultural context that provides us with a range of meaningful options from which to choose. Cultural communities form the "context of choice" within which individuals decide what kind of life they want to lead. As Kymlicka puts it, "It's only through having a rich and secure cultural structure that people can become aware, in a vivid way, of the options available to them, and intelligently examine their value." A cultural community supplies the "roles," "models," and "cultural narratives" from which individuals select their conception of the good life (Kymlicka 1989, 165). The lack of such a context of choice deprives individuals of valuable options from which to choose, thus thwarting the realization of their autonomy.

The importance of cultural contexts of choice for the realization and exercise of autonomy grounds Kymlicka's argument for one kind of group rights. He argues that in some cases, group rights should be granted to members of minority cultures to protect them from being involuntarily assimilated by the dominant cultures of Western democracies. The rights of Native American tribes to restrict the freedom of non-Indians to own property, vote, and reside on Indian reservations, in order to protect the tribes from being overrun and dispersed by non-Indians, provide an example. These rights are wielded by members of a minority group against the larger society for the sake of preserving the existence and integrity of the cultural structure of the group. Kymlicka refers to rights that protect minority cultural groups from "the economic and political decisions of the larger society" as *external protections* (Kymlicka 1995, 35).

We might wonder, however, whether religious "forms of life" are among the cultural structures that warrant the protection of group rights? The impression one initially gets from Kymlicka's writings is that they are not. He gives extended consideration to religious toleration in his discussion of a second kind of group rights, which he calls *internal restrictions* (Kymlicka 1995, 35). This second model holds that religious groups have the right to preserve their traditional beliefs and practices by enacting "internal restrictions" against their own members in order to suppress dissent and restrict unorthodox behavior.[1] This kind of group rights is objectionable because while it may ensure the continued survival of the group, it does not provide any rationale for protecting the rights of individuals *within* a religious community. Kymlicka concludes that a plausible doctrine of religious toleration must include as one of its primary components a respect for individual autonomy. It is only on the assumption that individual autonomy is worthy of protection that we are forced to look beyond group rights to the right of individuals to criticize and reject traditional practices.

The question remains, however, whether group rights have *any* role to play in securing religious liberty. I believe that they do and that Kymlicka provides us with a cogent justification for this role. In addition to the general distinction between external protections and internal restrictions, he distinguishes a number of more specific kinds of group rights. Among these are the right of national minorities to a measure of self-government and the right of persistent minorities to adequate political representation. For my purposes, however, the most significant of these rights are what Kymlicka calls *polyethnic rights*, which are rights granted to members of ethnic minorities in order to provide external protections for particular religious and cultural practices. Kymlicka writes that polyethnic rights are "group-specific measures . . . intended to help ethnic and religious minorities express their cultural particularity and pride without it hampering their success in the economic and political institutions of the dominant society" (Kymlicka 1995, 31). Specific examples of such measures include laws that exempt Jews and Muslims from Sunday closing legislation and laws that exempt Sikhs and Orthodox Jews from police and military dress codes.

Polyethnic rights are designed to enable members of minority ethnic groups to have equal access to various institutions without having to sacrifice their cultural identity. Kymlicka's examples are significant, however, because the kinds of cultural practices that he cites as needing protection are practices that stem from people's religious identity. Indeed, he specifically singles out the "religious practices" of "religious minorities" as needing the protection of polyethnic rights. Polyethnic rights thus appear to be a form of group rights that has a role to play in protecting religious liberty. This appearance is strengthened when we recognize that many of the claims Kymlicka makes on behalf of respecting people's polyethnic rights are identical to claims made on behalf of religious groups in the United States under the free exercise clause of the First Amendment.

On what is known as the "pro-exemptions" reading, the free exercise clause protects minority religious groups from legislation that appears to be religiously neutral but actually incorporates hidden biases based on "majoritarian presuppositions, ignorance, and indifference" (McConnell 1990, 1418).[2] Such legislation often has the effect of substantially burdening the religious freedom of minority religious groups. These burdens can be alleviated by reading the free exercise clause to require the granting of exemptions from generally applicable laws for the sake of a religious group's right to free exercise, provided that compelling reasons do not speak against granting the exemption.

The convergence between polyethnic rights and the right to the free exercise of religion suggests that while there are some polyethnic rights that protect nonreligious aspects of people's cultural identities, those that do concern religious practices can be subsumed under the existing right to the free exercise of religion, interpreted along the lines of the pro-exemptions reading.[3] This possibility raises two questions, however. First, why should we interpret the right to the free exercise of religion along the lines of the pro-exemptions reading? And second, even if we do interpret it that way, in what sense can the right to the free exercise of religion be considered a group right?

The argument for interpreting the right to free exercise along the lines of the pro-exemptions reading is based on considerations of fairness and equality. The members of dominant religious groups—those with the most political power—enjoy access to economic, educational, and political institutions on terms that do not require them to alter or sacrifice their religious practices. These groups are able to influence the legislative process so as to ensure that laws do not unduly burden the free exercise of their religion. Indeed, claims for religious exemptions from members of mainstream religious groups rarely reach the Supreme Court. As Michael McConnell puts it, "One rarely sees laws that force mainstream Protestants to violate their consciences" (McConnell 1990, 1419–20). However, even laws passed for purely secular or religiously neutral purposes can inadvertently burden the practices of minority religious groups. These are groups that do not have the political power to influence the shape of legislation to their advantage. Thus, for example, the use of sacramental wine by Christians was spared the strictures of Prohibition by statute (Sullivan 1992, 216), while the use of peyote in religious rituals by members of the Native American Church has been declared illegal in some states. The pro-exemptions doctrine would alleviate these inequalities in people's ability to exercise their religion by requiring judicially enforced exemptions in cases where the burden on a group's religious practices is not warranted by a compelling state interest.

The argument based on equalizing—within limits—the ability of majority and minority religious groups to exercise their religion justifies the pro-exemptions reading of the free exercise clause. Now to address the second question posed earlier. In what sense can the right to the free exercise of religion be seen as a group right?

Before answering this question, some clarifications are in order. First, it is commonly supposed that group rights are possessed by corporate entities as opposed to individuals (Kymlicka 1995, 45). This view, however, is mistaken. While it is true that group rights are sometimes exercised by corporate entities, it is equally possible for them to be exercised by individuals. Kymlicka provides some useful examples illustrating this point. In Canada, the group right of the Quebecois to preserve their culture is exercised by a corporate entity, the Province of Quebec. On the other hand, the group right of francophones to have their language needs accommodated in schools and courts throughout Canada is a group right that is exercised by individuals. What distinguishes these as cases involving group rights is not the nature of the entity that exercises the right but the fact that the right is allotted on the basis of group membership. Group rights protect interests that individuals possess *as* members of groups. They are thus more accurately referred to as group-differentiated rights. The important question to ask, therefore, is not whether group rights are exercised by corporate entities or by individuals but why such rights are accorded to the members of some groups and not to others (Kymlicka 1995, 45, 46).

A second clarification involves the nature of rights claims in general. The autonomy-based conception of liberalism that I am developing denies rights a foundational role in political theory. Rights are not morally primitive; rather, rights promote and protect interests of individuals that are considered to be morally basic or primitive. The interest that lies at the heart of autonomy-based liberalism is the interest individuals have in directing their lives in accordance with their own rationally held beliefs about what is ultimately worthy of pursuit. This interest generates a set of core rights that are necessary to promote its realization, such as the rights to freedom of conscience and freedom of association, along with a set of derivative rights that provide more detailed specifications of these core rights.

In my view, the right to the free exercise of religion derives from the more basic right to the liberty of conscience, which protects an individual's ability to pursue, revise, or reject her own conception of the good. There is a sense in which the explicit reference to religious freedom in the U.S. Constitution reflects nothing more than a historical accident, since few would now deny—as some did during the founding era—that the liberty to pursue both religious and secular conceptions of the good is equally worthy of protection. One might thus be tempted to argue that we should simply read "the free exercise of religion" to refer to the liberty of conscience in general. I think such a move is mistaken if it implies that there are no salient differences between religious and secular conceptions of the good. The right to the free exercise of religion protects individuals' interest in pursuing *religious* conceptions of the good. While this right derives from the right to liberty of conscience in general, it is not reducible to the latter because it incorporates the idea that religious beliefs and practices have distinctive characteristics that call for distinctive protections.

I want to single out three features that distinguish religious from secular conceptions of the good.[4] The first feature is that religious conceptions of the good typically include some reference to a "transcendent" or "extrahuman" source of value, order, and meaning (Greene 1993, 1617). For religious believers, this transcendent authority guides their endeavors toward what is truly of value, supplies norms that transcend the prerogatives of individual choice, and gives each member of the group a sense of fulfillment that stems from living in the light of a higher truth. Secular conceptions of the good, in contrast, tend to locate the source of normative authority exclusively within the realm of human reason and experience.

The second feature is that religious belief is typically situated in the context of religious groups into which individuals are socialized as children. John Locke's influential description of churches as "voluntary societies" is misleading if taken as a description of the way most people actually acquire their religious beliefs (Locke 1983, 28). Instead of deliberately choosing a particular set of religious beliefs from among a variety of options, most individuals are socialized into religious groups in much the same way that they are socialized into cultures. Indeed, the line between religion and ethnicity is often hard to draw, as is evidenced by Kymlicka's repeated conflation of the two. Psychologists Benjamin Beit-Hallahmi and Michael Argyle point out that children tend first to develop identities as members of a religious group, and only later to accept the beliefs that are supposed to accompany that identity (Beit-Hallahmi and Argyle 1997, 25-26). They state that "continuity in religious identity between generations is the rule rather than the exception," and that in most cases religious identity is "ascribed, not chosen" (112, 25). Furthermore, while conversion to other religions is always a possibility, in the majority of cases conversion is simply "a reaffirmation of the tradition in which the person has been raised" (114). The ascriptive character of religion contrasts with secular conceptions of the good which tend not to be so deeply implicated in the development of individual identity and can with more plausibility be seen as the product of deliberate choice.

The third feature refers to the fact that the cognitive components of religious conceptions of the good are typically embedded in rituals and practices in a way that makes it difficult to draw a clear line separating belief from practice. We might say that religious beliefs and practices *interpenetrate* each other: religious practices enact, express, and reinforce religious beliefs; religious beliefs direct and fortify religious practices. As a result of the interpenetration of religious belief and practice, protecting an individual's ability to pursue a religion involves protecting her ability to engage in the practices and rituals that play an essential role in forming, expressing, and justifying her religious beliefs. Protecting the religious conscience thus requires protecting practices and rituals that, from an external perspective, appear to be only tangentially related to claims of conscience.

The fact that many religions require their members to perform rituals, to abide by religious prescriptions, to cultivate certain virtues, to wear symbolic dress, to observe religious holidays, and so on, multiplies the opportunities for conflict that exist between the consciences of religious believers and laws—even those enacted with the most innocent of intentions. There is an asymmetry between religious and secular conceptions of the good in this respect, for while it is not impossible to imagine secular conceptions that required their members to engage in elaborate ritual observances, it is not a general fact about our social world that they do. It is much less likely, therefore, that laws will inadvertently burden the conscience of adherents of secular conceptions of the good.

Taken together, these three features give us a general picture of religious conceptions of the good as typically inhering in the practices of groups, being deeply implicated in the self-identity of religious individuals, comprising both belief and practice, and being informed by a vision of extra-human authority. The argument for holding the right to the free exercise of religion to be a group right rests on these distinctive features of religion in combination with the claim that religious free exercise is derivative of the general liberty of conscience.

The right to religious free exercise protects individuals' interest in being able to pursue religious conceptions of the good. The right is "group-differentiated" in that it protects forms of behavior that people engage in as members of religious groups. These forms of behavior include rituals and practices that are essential elements of religious belief and that would not be recognized as deserving protection if the individuals involved were not members of a religious group. Moreover, the right also protects the ascriptive character of religion by protecting the ability of religious group members to transmit their religious identity and beliefs to their children. In some cases, providing this protection involves granting exemptions from generally applicable laws to religious individuals under the free exercise clause. Since there is a wide range of difference among the practices of religious groups, the specific protections and exemptions afforded to religious individuals will vary depending on the group to which they belong.

In a sense, the right to the free exercise of religion protects an interest that is shared by all religious individuals, much in the same way that for

Kymlicka the right to a secure cultural context protects an interest that all individuals possess. However, protecting this interest requires treating the members of different religious groups differently. Members of mainstream religions find that their beliefs and practices mesh comfortably with the institutions and policies of a liberal society, in part because they have the political power to ensure that this is the case, and in part because majority assumptions about what constitutes accommodating religious belief and practice take mainstream religions as their model. The members of majority religions typically find that their right to the free exercise of religion is amply respected and requires no special protections. The same is not true of the members of minority religions. The right to the free exercise of religion requires that this inequality be righted, at least in some cases, by the provision of accommodations and exemptions for the practices of minority religious groups.[5]

II

The last question I want to consider concerns the relationship between the right to the free exercise of religion and the promotion of individual autonomy. I have defended the right to the free exercise of religion as a group right on the basis of Kymlicka's autonomy-centered liberalism. But what, it may be asked, is the relationship between a group's right to the free exercise of religion and the exercise of individual autonomy? The impression one gets from the writings of Kymlicka and other liberal philosophers is that the relationship is one of mutual antagonism. Kymlicka suggests that the typical group rights claim on the part of a religious community is an attempt to impose internal restrictions on its members—either through overt coercion or through educational practices that discourage individual autonomy. The focus of attention is typically on the need to protect an individual's right to revise or reject her religious conception of the good. The right to the free exercise of religion is thus conceived primarily as a right that an individual wields *against* her religious community.

This focus on the oppressive potential of religion has led communitarian philosophers to reject the value of individual autonomy. In response to Kymlicka, Moshe Halbertal argues that individuals often come to their conceptions of the good by other routes than the exercise of autonomy. Many people acquire their conceptions of the good through being brought up in a religious tradition, or, like the apostle Paul, they find their lives suddenly and dramatically altered by an experience of conversion (Halbertal 1996, 108–13). Religious toleration is not to be valued because it protects the individual's ability to rationally choose a conception of the good. Rather, religious toleration protects an individual's ability to remain loyal to the conception that she grows into as part of a religious community.

In a similar vein, Michael Sandel has argued that autonomy-based liberalism reduces religions to mere "lifestyles" to be chosen by an independent and uncommitted self. As a result, liberalism misses "the role that religion plays in the lives of those for whom the observance of religious duties is a constitutive end, essential to their good and indispensable to their identity" (Sandel 1990, 88–89). Both Halbertal and Sandel see religious toleration as concerned primarily with protecting the rights of religious groups from the interference of the state and society at large, rather than protecting individual members from the religious group itself.

The opposition between liberals and communitarians on this topic suggests that there is an antagonism between the right to the free exercise of religion as it applies to the individual ability to criticize or reject an inherited religious perspective and the same right as it applies to a religious group's ability to preserve and transmit its religious traditions. I do not want to deny that these two aspects of religious free exercise may come into conflict. However, I want to suggest that there is no essential antagonism between them that should lead communitarian philosophers to reject the value of individual autonomy. Providing a precise characterization of autonomy is beyond the scope of this chapter, but I want to mention some features of an adequate conception of autonomy that dispel the idea of an essential antagonism between religious groups and individual autonomy.

The most important point is that the opposition between "encumbered selves" and autonomous selves that communitarians criticize does not exist. One will assume that the autonomous self is necessarily unencumbered by deep communal attachments only if one believes that becoming autonomous requires transcending one's socialization. This view of autonomy presupposes that we each possess a ready-made self just waiting to be unearthed from beneath layers of socialization. As communitarians rightly point out, a person who did manage to become a "socialization-transcending agent" (Meyers 1989, 42) would find himself looking indifferently upon a series of "lifestyles" from which to choose. Having been "emptied" of all deep value commitments and identity constituents, he would have no criteria to govern his choice. The freedom of such a self would be entirely empty, since the values that guide an individual's judgment of what kind of life is worth living stem—at least initially—from the communities into which he has been socialized.

However, the idea of a socialization-transcending agent is not essential to the idea of personal autonomy. Diana Meyers has argued that we should replace the ontological conception of autonomy, according to which the goal is to emancipate the self from socialization, with a procedural account, which stresses that autonomy is achieved through the exercise of a set of skills or virtues that enable a person to take over the identity and values bequeathed to her by her family and community (Meyers 1989, 45). The autonomous person engages in a process of self-discovery, in which she acquires knowledge of her desires, values, and commitments; self-definition, in which she applies critical rationality to these constituents of her self in order to distill from them a coherent ideal of how to live; and self-direction, in which she tries to express this ideal in her life (Meyers 1989, pt. II). These three aspects of autonomy interact with each other and form part of an ongoing process. The self revealed to the agent through self-discovery changes over time, as one's choice of how to live reinforces some aspects of the self and discourages others. Insights prompted by the changing nature of the self provide new material for critical reflection and may lead to changes in one's personal ideal. And the consequences of attempting to realize an ideal of how to live may lead one to revise one's conception of the self or one's beliefs about what is truly valuable. Throughout this process, certain values and commitments are accepted as authoritatively binding, although not beyond all possibility of reassessment.

The procedural conception of autonomy is compatible with the existence of religious commitments that, as Sandel puts it, are "essential to [people's] good and indispensable to their identity" (Sandel 1990, 89). The procedural conception of autonomy does not envision people as choosing their religious beliefs, values, and identity from a detached point of view. It does, however, require that these be endorsed by the agent in the light of critical reflection and experience. One consequence of the separation of church and state is that the state has no authority to make judgments about the truth, value, or meaningfulness of religious doctrines. Therefore, the only test of whether a particular religious group provides a meaningful religious vision for its members is whether the members themselves think so. The beliefs and practices of a religious group cannot be said to embody the conscience of its members unless each member is able to endorse the group's commitments as her own.

In order for a religion to be willingly endorsed, each member of the group must be allowed to develop the ability to understand the religious doctrines and practices of the group, to reflectively evaluate them, and to be aware that there are alternatives. The cognitive skills necessary for a person to understand and examine the beliefs and practices of her religious group are those involved in the exercise of autonomy. If constitutive religious commitments are to matter deeply to a person and to be an essential part of her identity, then those commitments must be the object of conscious reflection. She will want to understand the beliefs and practices of her religious community, to grasp the justifications and explanations offered for these beliefs and practices, and to deliberately and willingly express them in her life. Even a convert like Paul will need to engage in critical reflection in order to understand the source and nature of the transformation he has undergone and to radically revise his goals, as Paul did, to reflect his newly acquired beliefs and values. Rather than being incompatible with deep religious commitments, the exercise of autonomy seems to be a necessary condition for saying that these commitments are genuinely constitutive of a person's identity, instead of the product of mere habit.

It is clear that fidelity to a religious community is compatible with the development of autonomy. Liberals such as Kymlicka, with their emphasis on the potentially oppressive nature of religion, do not give this point adequate emphasis.[6] The protections afforded to religious individuals and to religious groups by the right to the free exercise of religion harmonize in those cases where religious commitment goes hand in hand with individual autonomy. In cases of apparent conflict, it seems to me that the burden of proof is on people outside the religious community to show that the practices of the religious group are truly incompatible with autonomy. As we have seen, there is no reason to think that deep religious commitments and individual autonomy are necessarily opposed, as communitarians claim. Indeed, there is good reason to think that authentic religious commitment presupposes the exercise of individual autonomy.

Notes

This chapter has benefited greatly from the questions, comments, and criticism of Diana Meyers, Garry Brodsky, Kathleen Moore, John Troyer, Robert Van Wyk, Larry May,

Nicholas Wolterstorff, Robert Audi, James Sennett, and audiences at conferences for the Society of Christian Philosophers, the North American Society for Social Philosophy, and AMINTAPHIL.

1. Kymlicka cites as a historical example of this kind of group rights the millet system of the Ottoman Empire (Kymlicka 1996, 83ff.). For nearly five hundred years, the Ottoman Turks sanctioned the existence of self-governing Jewish and Christian communities, or "millets," within the larger Muslim empire. The Muslim majority agreed to coexist with the members of minority religions, who were given group rights in order to protect themselves from both external persecution and internal dissent. Internally, each millet was essentially a theocracy, with substantial restrictions on the rights of individuals to question official religious doctrine.

2. The meaning of this clause is subject to two competing readings (McConnell 1990, 1416–20). In the text, I consider only the pro-exemptions reading. On the alternative "no exemptions" reading, the free exercise clause simply prevents government from passing laws that single out a particular religious group, or religious belief in general, for discriminatory treatment. As Michael W. McConnell explains it, this understanding of free exercise would prevent religious groups from being able to challenge "facially neutral legislation, no matter what effect it may have on their ability or freedom to practice their religious faith" (McConnell 1990, 1418–19). The no-exemptions reading seemed to gain the upper hand in the Supreme Court's free exercise jurisprudence in *Employment Division, Department of Human Resources of Oregon v. Smith*, 494 U.S. 872 (1990). My argument in favor of the pro-exemptions reading is thus an argument that the Court's current interpretation of the free exercise clause is incorrect.

3. Kymlicka might resist this suggestion on the grounds that polyethnic rights are "special" rights granted to the members of recent immigrant groups, while the right to the free exercise of religion is one of the standing rights of citizenship (see Kymlicka 1995, 206 n. 19). However, the distinction between a special right and a standing right does not hold in this case. First, as Kymlicka notes, the protections afforded by polyethnic rights are not "temporary measures," since "the cultural differences they protect are not something we seek to eliminate" (Kymlicka 1995, 31). This means that an immigrant group whose religious practices were once deemed to warrant the protection of polyethnic rights would not lose that protection if its members became assimilated into the dominant culture in all nonreligious respects. The group would have a standing right to have its religious practices protected, regardless of whether its members were recent immigrants. If we recognize further that the granting of legal immunities and exemptions for religious groups dates back to the colonial period in America (see generally McConnell 1990), and that with the exception of Native Americans we are all immigrants or the descendants of immigrants, there is no reason to distinguish between a "special" right that protects the religious practices of immigrants and a standing right that, in the correct circumstances, can be invoked to protect the practices of any religious group.

4. I do not claim this list of features to be exhaustive or to characterize uncontroversially every social phenomenon that might possibly be called "religion." Trying to define religion may be an impossible task. Fortunately, where political questions are at issue, it suffices to provide a characterization that picks out paradigmatic instances of religion. This characterization can then be applied to disputed instances to see whether they are similar enough in the relevant respects also to be considered "religious" (cf. Greene 1993, 1618).

5. It might be objected that the right to the free exercise of religion as I have developed it requires the state to ensure that its policies have no adverse effects on any religious groups. This would be to insist that the state should aim to achieve substantive neutrality toward all religious groups, by canceling out any negative effects liberal institutions and policies have on their religious practices. Substantive neutrality has rightly been criticized as neither possible nor desirable (see, for example, Rawls 1993, 193). My argument does not entail that religious groups have a right to substantive neutrality on the part of the state. For example, nothing I have said entails that the practices of deeply illiberal religious groups ought to be accommodated. Such groups do not have the right to have the "negative" effects of liberal policies on their practices "canceled out." My argument does entail, however, that those religious groups whose practices are consistent with the values and institutions of a liberal regime, but which face difficult choices between adhering to their religious practice and participation in liberal institutions, have a right to be accommodated in the absence of some compelling reason to the contrary.

6. As Shelley Burtt has recently complained, many liberal philosophers seem to assume that religious parents are "irredeemably hostile to the development of their children's critical rationality" and that "to reason from the basis of God's word as reflected in Scripture is somehow to abandon the exercise of critical rationality" (Burtt 1996, 416). However, there is no incompatibility between a commitment to reason on the basis of God's word and the exercise of autonomy. To do so autonomously is to do so with an understanding of the nature of this commitment and the justifications offered for it by one's religious community, and to have the liberty to reject this commitment should one no longer find these justifications persuasive.

Chapter 15

One Cheer for Affirmative Action

William Nelson

Defenders of affirmative action occupy a stronger position than opponents. At least this seems to be so if defenders mean to argue for the permissibility of affirmative action and opponents mean to argue for its impermissibility. The opponent of affirmative action must construct and argue for the principle that affirmative action is supposed to violate, and it is hard to find plausible principles that are not far too strong.[1]

It is another question whether affirmative action is actually desirable, much less required. I believe that this must depend mainly on the costs and benefits of the particular program under consideration and on how these costs and benefits are distributed. For example, it may depend on whether the program is public or private and on whether a public program consists of mandates or incentives, for different kinds of programs may have different consequences.[2]

Space limitations prevent a full discussion of all the issues. I will concentrate on affirmative action in the job market rather than in education. I hope, in the course of discussion, to isolate some of the factors that bear on issues of permissibility and desirability and to bring out some of their consequences for specific cases. Although I will argue that affirmative action is generally permissible and that it is desirable in some cases, my argument will not make recourse to ideas of group rights. Affirmative action can be defended independent of these.

I will divide my discussion into two parts: in the first, I address the issue of permissibility; in the second I discuss some of the factors that bear on the desirability or undesirability of some otherwise permissible practices.

I

At a minimum, I suppose, affirmative action requires that we advertise jobs widely and take applicants seriously, even when they are members of

281

minority groups or groups underrepresented in the workforce. That such a practice is at least permissible is unlikely to be questioned. That it is required, in general, seems to me less obvious. Consider the following practice I learned about from a student from a small community in north Texas whose father worked in manufacturing. It was the policy of his father's employer to provide summer work for employees' sons and daughters who were going to college. Now, I assume that these summer jobs could have been advertised more widely and that applicants more qualified than the vacationing students might have been found. Nevertheless, I am not inclined, without further information, to conclude that the policy of the factory was wrong. It does involve preferential treatment for one group—the children of employees—but the motives of the program seem to me benign, and the consequences need not be particularly bad.

I suspect there are small, closed job markets like this all over the economy: family businesses hiring mostly within the family, close-knit immigrant groups hiring from within their own community, and so on.[3] If affirmative action includes a requirement that all jobs be openly offered to everyone, then requiring affirmative action would mean prohibiting all of these closed markets.

It is true that, when those now holding jobs have acquired them in arbitrary or unfair ways, practices like those I have described serve to perpetuate this unfairness. And in some situations, as I will later claim, this is closely related to an argument for the desirability of positive preferences for minorities. Still, it is also true that closed markets can serve an important function within their communities. They are probably one of the mechanisms by which some relatively disadvantaged persons manage to make their way eventually into the economic mainstream. It is not obvious that we do well, on the whole, if we break them up, and so I doubt that even the relatively minimal form of affirmative action mentioned so far represents a general requirement.

More controversial is the kind of affirmative action that actually gives some preference to minority applicants. Call this the *policy of preference*. Such policies probably never involve hiring or admitting applicants solely on the basis of race or minority group status. There are usually independent eligibility standards or qualifications that must be satisfied before someone is even considered for a position. But many people seem to think it wrong to give any preference at all to members of disadvantaged groups, even if decisions are based largely on other considerations. If that is so, then many policies that go under the name *affirmative action* are wrong. But what are the arguments for this conclusion?

Objections might fall into either of two categories. On the one hand, there might be a principle mandating some goal or social condition with which the policy of preference is incompatible. On the other hand, a policy of preference might be held to violate the rights of individual applicants for jobs or other positions. I begin with the second: Does a policy of preference violate the rights of any applicants?

One might think those making hiring or admissions decisions have a right to choose whomever they want, as they seem to be doing in the "closed markets" mentioned earlier.[4] Of course, in many public institutions, either universities or agencies, there may be statutory requirements such as the requirement that any graduate of a public high school with a certain grade point average must automatically be admitted to state universities. Or, again, there may be a requirement that hiring decisions in public agencies be based solely on standardized test scores. Rules like these do create rights—as do long-standing, public rules giving preferential treatment to veterans in the civil service.[5] But since the rights are created by statute, they can also be changed by statute. In particular, if a community chooses to pursue a goal of racial diversity or racial equality by instituting racial preferences, it then creates a new and different system of rights. Under such rules, the policy of preference does not violate applicants' rights.[6]

Desert

The interesting question is not whether rights to jobs can be created by institutional enactment, conventional understanding, or explicit pronouncement, but whether a policy of preference violates some basic, preinstitutional right. What could be the basis of such a right? A natural thought is that people with certain qualifications or achievements might deserve a job or admission to a school and that those who deserve it are entitled to it. This is a bit too crude, for a variety of reasons. First, someone who is superbly qualified may not apply, even though she might be most deserving. Surely that person does not have a right to the job that precludes hiring the best-qualified applicant. Second, and more interesting, many people may be well qualified and so be equally deserving, though there is only one position. We turn down deserving applicants all the time in college admissions and in hiring, and, at least when the other applicants also deserve the position, we certainly do not violate the rights of those who are turned down.

Let me elaborate on this second point. As Joel Feinberg argued years ago, the concept of desert is multifaceted. To put the point as he does, when we deserve something, we deserve it in one or another mode—for example, as a prize, a reward, a grade, a punishment, or a compensation for some misfortune. A concrete thing, like a job or a promotion, might be deserved in more than one mode by the same person, and certainly in different ways by different persons. Feinberg illustrates his point with an imaginary story about a competition for an honorific post at a college. His point is that considerations of desert fail to settle the question of who should get the post, since several members of the faculty deserve in different ways: one as a reward for his hard work on behalf of the college, another as a sort of prize, an expression of admiration for his scholarly achievements, and yet another as compensation for unusual burdens that have been imposed on him over the years.

There are many ways of being deserving, Feinberg reminds us, and that should lead us at least to take with a grain of salt claims of unique entitlement based on any particular form of desert. Moreover, even when a person does clearly deserve something—a reward or a prize, for example—there is the further question of whether that means she is entitled to a particular, concrete thing, such as a job or a certain salary. The concrete thing may or may not be the best, or only, token of the deserved mode of treatment. Is school admission like a prize to be awarded to the person who has done the best so far? Or should it be awarded to those who most love learning,[7] or perhaps to those who will benefit from it most? One could accept the latter, without denying that the person who has done the best in the past deserves recognition for his or her accomplishments.

Desert is an important moral concept. It reflects basic human attitudes that we are properly reluctant to give up. But if I am right, the concept of desert is far too multifaceted and the facts of life too complicated to generate anything like a unique answer to questions about how particular goods should be distributed at particular times. Too many people deserve too many things. The claim that someone is uniquely entitled to something because of desert should generally be viewed with suspicion.

Equal Opportunity

Even if considerations of desert do not mean that the talented have rights violated by the policy of preference, it does not follow that there are no such rights. While those who object to preferences sometimes use the language of desert, I suspect that, if asked to justify their claim that a more talented person should get the position, they might go on to say that it is unfair to give preference to someone else. And if asked to explain this, they would likely say something to the effect that everyone should compete for positions on an equal basis. The policy of preference, sometimes defended as an advance toward equal opportunity, can also be criticized as inconsistent with this ideal. Perhaps it is thought that everyone, in virtue of this ideal, has a right to equal consideration; or perhaps equal opportunity is thought to be a goal toward which we ought to advance, and the policy of preference is thought to impede our advance.

The issue here is just what a reasonable and defensible conception of equal opportunity actually does or does not permit. It is an elusive ideal. Rawls makes "fair equality of opportunity" one of his fundamental principles of justice, yet he tells us almost nothing about what it specifically requires. Of the eighty-seven sections of A Theory of Justice, only one, "Fair Equality of Opportunity and Pure Procedural Justice," has "equality of opportunity" in its title, and that section is devoted almost entirely to pure procedural justice. Among the authors who have offered a clear account of what equal opportunity might require, many are critics. They offer definitions of equal opportunity only to ridicule the ideal so defined.[8]

The right conclusion, surely, is that we have to rethink what the ideal is about. This is not the place for a detailed discussion of equal opportunity.[9] But I suggest that the beginning of wisdom in this matter is to step away from a narrow focus on the competition for specific goods—jobs, college admissions, and so on—and also to avoid a literal emphasis on equality. It is less important that opportunities[10] be *equal* than that everyone have *some*—that they be universal. And it is not important that each have an opportunity for every type of job or position (the *same* opportunities) but, rather, that each have *some* opportunities that are valuable for that person. As I have put it elsewhere, what is important is that all of us have opportunities to lead lives that are good for us. In much the same spirit, Thomas Hill has more recently expressed the idea of fair opportunity as the ideal that each have an opportunity to develop and exercise his or her talents and abilities.[11]

This ideal obviously implies a variety of social and educational policies (access to medical care, nutrition, and decent schools, for example); and these are policies of the sort that Rawls associates with fair equality of opportunity as opposed to what he calls mere "formal" equality of opportunity. It is less obvious, though, what it requires in the market for jobs and in college admissions. With regard to the issue of affirmative action, the important question is whether it rules out any kind of group preference. I believe the answer is no. In the abstract, at least, it neither rules out nor requires group preference. That some colleges admit only women, for example, hardly means that men are unable to develop their own abilities and exercise them in good and satisfying lives. There are plenty of colleges and universities that admit men. The point of equal opportunity is not that every person have every opportunity but only that, for each person, there be some available career—more broadly, some life—in which that person can flourish. That means that the hiring practices described earlier—for example, summer jobs for children of employees—are not necessarily ruled out by equal opportunity; and neither is the policy of preference necessarily ruled out. When "discriminatory" practices are small in scale, random or haphazard, and canceled out by discrimination in the other direction elsewhere, they are compatible with equal opportunity on this model.

The policies of preference associated with affirmative action certainly can lead to some redistribution, at least among marginal candidates, of college admissions and of jobs. Leaving aside the question of whether this is wise or desirable, it is not inconsistent with the ideal of equal opportunity as I have described it here. For that ideal does not, for example, conceive jobs and other positions as prizes to be awarded on the basis of meritocratic competition. It does not guarantee people a right to be evaluated for positions in any particular way, much less a right to get any particular job.

I have heard it said that the idea of equal opportunity is essentially connected with the existence of significant social or economic inequalities. Perhaps the thought is this: equal opportunity only makes sense against a background in which there are certain positions that carry with them great wealth, high incomes, or high social status. These advantages, by their nature, cannot be available to all. Policies of equal opportunity then seem desirable because they represent a fair way to ration these scarce goods— and they make success all the sweeter because those who do succeed are assured that they "really deserve" what they get. This conceives equal opportunity as a meritocratic competition for scarce rewards, and it is meant to contrast with, for example, a system in which access is hereditary or depends on connections and patronage.

But great inequalities are no part of the rationale for equal opportunity as I conceive it. More, where there are great inequalities, the defender of an unqualified meritocratic competition for positions owes us an argument for why this method of distribution is the unique best one. It is not obvious that it is.[12] But, in any case, the thought that life is a competition for a small number of desirable positions is, in fact, inimical to the conception of universal opportunity I mean to defend. Far from undermining the rationale for equal opportunity, as I conceive it, greater equality would arguably contribute to it.

II

I have focused so far on whether there is reason to think the policy of preference impermissible. I now turn to whether there is any positive argument in favor of this policy. Is it desirable, as well as being merely permissible? For example, does the ideal of equal opportunity require a policy of preference? It obviously does not if equal opportunity is identified with meritocratic competition. But does the idea of universal opportunity make a policy of preferential treatment desirable? It seems to me that it can. There is a chain of supermarkets where I live that appears to have the policy—I do not *know* that it does—of trying to hire mildly retarded persons to bag groceries. If it is true that retarded persons would not be hired without a policy of preference, that their lives are much improved by having jobs, and that this policy does not deprive the high school kids who might otherwise be hired of decent lives, then the policy is highly desirable from the perspective of universal opportunity. It is not that no one loses under this policy. There is a marginal redistribution of jobs and of income relative to a more "competitive" method of distributing jobs. But there is arguably a net gain in welfare, and there is likely an increase in the extent of well-being—in the number of persons who have good and satisfying lives.

Is there any analogous argument in support of preferences for racial or cultural minorities? I doubt that it will be easy to find cases in which a large number of jobs could be offered preferentially to large racial minorities, in which this would substantially improve their lives, and in which it would not simultaneously make the lives of others substantially worse. The case of preferences for the mentally retarded was easier, since jobs that might be valuable for them are of marginal importance in the lives of others. In the case of minority preference, however, the jobs and other advantages in dispute play a significant role in anyone's life. Where these positions are also scarce relative to demand, it would take a stronger argument to show that any redistribution of opportunities is required.

Where the number of qualified minority candidates is small, and many institutions attempt to practice a policy of preference, the result can be a perverse bidding war in which every institution tries to hire candidates that, necessarily, only a few institutions will get—and get at a very high price. Perhaps this has happened in some academic disciplines. It is hard to make a principled case that this practice is desirable, much less required by the ideal of equal opportunity.

But now suppose that there is a metropolitan area with one or two major employers. Suppose further that there are many qualified workers of all races in the community, but that employment in the large manufacturing plants is largely white and that unemployment and poverty are high in the African-American community. Perhaps the plants have not practiced overt discrimination for a long time, but turnover in the workforce is relatively slow, and the paper qualifications of white applicants, together with character references from present employers, continue to give them a slight edge in measures that bear some statistical relationship to good job performance. Meanwhile, moving to another community is not a promising strategy for members of the minority community, because similar conditions prevail elsewhere. Without a policy of preference for minorities, we can expect high unemployment in the minority community to persist for a long time.

My guts tell me that this is just the kind of situation in which a policy of preference is desirable, perhaps required. By hypothesis, there are plenty of qualified minority applicants who actually need jobs and who suffer if they do not get them. A policy of preference is anything but a symbolic gesture. Whatever dynamic led to the unequal treatment of the two communities needs to be changed, and those who have been excluded should be moved to the head of the queue.

But it is actually unclear what the argument for this conclusion is—how one responds to white job candidates who would lose out as a result of minority preference. Surely, it would be better to create new job opportunities, rather than just redistributing the few that there are. But suppose we cannot. Against someone who thinks hiring should be strictly meritocratic and who concedes that the minority workers are just as qualified as the whites, there is a kind of ad hominem argument that there has been an injustice here and that compensation is required.

But suppose we reject, as I have, a general meritocratic principle. This gives me an advantage, in that I can argue for the permissibility of a policy of preference for minorities even if, on average, minority qualifications might be a bit lower or training costs a bit higher.[13] But it prevents my making a straightforward argument for preference based on the need for reparations. Of course those who are newly hired benefit; but others lose.

I should emphasize that the issue here is not whether it would be *permissible* for a firm to give preference to those from the minority community. I argued against a general requirement that hiring be based solely on qualifications and that there never be any favoritism toward groups or individuals. It might be permissible, for example, for the firm to offer summer jobs to the children of employees without open competition. It would be equally permissible for the firm to offer summer internships to members of the minority community, perhaps to be followed by full-time jobs if they do well.

What I claim is that hiring practices are wrong if they are widely followed, if the result of their being followed is that groups of persons are systematically deprived of opportunities wherever they turn, and if they could be changed without serious adverse consequences. This is especially bad if it happens that those who are excluded are members of an interdependent group so that everyone is dragged down together. This is exactly the sort of situation that the ideal of universal opportunity is meant to rule out. But, while there is an injustice here, it is a result of a pattern of acts each of which is unjust partly because it occurs against the background of a more general pattern of acts.

Something ought to be done to improve both the present and the future prospects of those who have been systematically denied opportunities. But since the denial of opportunities has been general, it also seems plausible that the burdens of compensation should be shared widely.[14] One can imagine a number of policies that might help. Companies, perhaps with subsidies from tax revenues, could underwrite training programs for prospective employees and early retirement options for current employees. They could refrain from using tests or hiring criteria that lead to statistical discrimination, they could relax seniority rules governing promotions for newly hired employees, and minorities could receive some preference at the initial hiring stage.

It is not unreasonable to think that the benefits of such programs will extend to more people than just those who are hired and their immediate families: employees become role models for others in their community, and they provide vivid testimony that opportunities are now available. Insofar as future hiring decisions can depend on connections,[15] a whole community can be disadvantaged when it is not represented in the workforce.

If a policy of preference is desirable or even required, as opposed to being merely permissible, it is because it extends opportunities to those who have few and does so at a cost to others that is not excessive and is fairly distributed. We should not minimize or ignore the genuine costs to others, and we should be aware of the sometimes speculative character of some of the alleged benefits of practices. (Are role models really that effective?) But then again, we must also not forget that those who are already privileged are unlikely to underestimate the costs of preferences to them. A reasonable humility both about how much good we can do and about how well we estimate costs seems justified.

I have focused so far, in this section, on issues about jobs; and I have been concerned with reasons why it might be desirable that firms undertake to give some preference to minority applicants. I have said little about governmental policies or programs, partly because it is arguably better that preferential policies be conceived and carried out in a decentralized way. For one thing, the desirability of some type of policy may very much depend on particular circumstances; and, as these circumstances change, individual firms can respond flexibly. Legal mandates run the risk of inflexibility; they create entitlements that are not easily withdrawn even if they are no longer warranted; and these entitlements become valuable political prizes sought after by every group.[16]

While individual firms have the advantage of greater flexibility and some immunity to political pressure, it cannot be assumed in general that they will always exercise their power in the best way either. We certainly have reason, as a society, to try to break the cycle of poverty in minority communities and probably also reason to bring it about that those in positions of power are more representative of the population as a whole. Where it is likely that private firms will not take the initiative in hiring minorities— and when they may even be following, for example, practices of statistical discrimination that work against minorities—then there is some reason for public action. There are advantages, moreover, to explicitly imposing numerical quotas on firms rather than attempting detailed oversight of their hiring practices. This amounts to a kind of strict liability for results as opposed to a form of liability that depends on intentions and motives, and it is justified partly by the same argument that justifies strict liability elsewhere: the difficulty of establishing intent. But it has advantages both for those enforcing the policy and for those subject to it. It reduces the cost of investigation and enforcement; it simplifies record keeping; and it legitimizes (by requiring) a policy that firms might want to pursue, for simplicity's sake, as a rough-and-ready way of trying to eliminate discrimination.

As I have presented this rationale for enforcing quotas, its underlying goal is eliminating discrimination, but this is again not a rationale that is really available to me. I have not in fact defended a principle that prohibits discrimination, at least when it is haphazard rather than pervasive. Discrimination in the job market against African-Americans, however, does not have this benign character. Nor do I believe that this discrimination has ceased to be a factor in perpetuating inequalities. This is an empirical judgment. If it is correct, then eliminating discrimination would itself help to improve the lives of those now trapped in poverty. And if the argument of the preceding paragraph is correct, then the most effective and least costly way to eliminate this discrimination might involve the legal imposition of quotas. Indeed, well-meaning business persons, suspicious perhaps of their own motives,[17] might welcome legally imposed quotas in the same spirit in which it is sometimes rational to precommit to something that we know to be good for us but that we fear we will not do when the chips are down.[18]

Morality and Politics

After the regents of the University of California had voted to eliminate affirmative action, it was pointed out in state newspapers that a number of the same regents had, in the past, sought special consideration in the admissions process for their own friends and relatives. When questioned, one of the regents replied that there was no inconsistency in her position: the preferences she had sought were not based on race.

This might be thought a ludicrous reply. Who would ever have thought that the only injustices are racial injustices—that there are not also injustices of wealth, class, and family? And isn't all this about injustice, after all? I suspect for many people the answer is no. The principle that we not discriminate on the basis of race or sex is as fundamental a principle as most people subscribe to in this area. It plays the role, in ordinary thought, of a moral principle, as it also underwrites effective political arguments and as it seems to be treated as a fundamental principle in constitutional law. The idea of looking for an even deeper or more abstract principle of justice does not, in practice, occur to anyone.

Moral philosophers make careers out of arguing that the absolute principles of man-on-the-street morality are not absolute at all and maybe have little to do with morality. Philosophers see their job as that of uncovering the more basic, underlying principles or goals of morality; and that, of course, is what I tried to do earlier in discussing equal opportunity. But the fact is that most ordinary people do not get the message. And in this case, it does not help at all that the simple principle prohibiting racial preference currently works to the advantage of white males who suddenly find themselves losing the special privileges they so long enjoyed.[19] It also does not help that there seems to be no correspondingly simple principle that can be invoked in making a positive case for the kind of affirmative action that involves a policy of preference.[20]

What I said at the beginning of this section might suggest that I think the dispositive principles are not (just) about race or sex but are more general principles ruling out all preferences not based on pure "merit." But that actually seems to me wrong. The idea is not to create a world in which we all operate like robots, guided solely by "objective" test scores and educational credentials.[21] Skills and trainability will naturally be the biggest factors determining who is hired; but I have given examples of other preferences, like family connections, that surely continue to affect hiring decisions.[22] These, of course, tend to benefit the advantaged. Rather than trying to eliminate them entirely, though, we might adopt policies that, in time, will extend the range of these advantages to communities that are now without decent opportunities. This is not the least of the reasons supporting affirmative action.

Notes

I wish to thank Larry Alexander, Joseph Ellin, and David Phillips for helpful discussion and for comments on earlier drafts.

1. Judith Thomson focuses on permissibility in "Preferential Hiring," *Philosophy and Public Affairs* 4 (1973): 364–84. I take the Court's position in *Bakke* to reflect the difficulty of specifying a plausible principle that would completely rule out consideration of race. (Subsequent decisions have taken a different tack.)

2. I do not offer, at this point, a definition of affirmative action, for various programs can go under this name, and it seems likely that programs of different types will be desirable in different circumstances.

3. See Michael Walzer's discussion of the Sunset Scavenger Company in San Francisco, *Spheres of Justice* (New York: Basic Books, 1983), 179.

4. Cf. Thomson, "Preferential Hiring." Perhaps there is a kind of fiduciary obligation to act in ways consistent with a reasonable understanding of the interests of stock-

holders or of other students in a school. But this is not an obligation owed to applicants, nor is it an obligation to act in their interests.

5. Ibid., 379–80.

6. We also create rights if, in advertising a position, we specify that certain criteria will be used.

7. Walzer, in *Spheres of Justice*, tells the story of Hillel on the roof in this connection.

8. For example, Michael Levin suggests in "Equality of Opportunity," *Philosophical Quarterly* 31 (1981): 110–25, that equal opportunity might require that for any job and any two candidates, each should have literally the same chance of getting the job. This ideal could be realized if we distributed all positions by lot; but most of us, including Levin, see this as a reductio of equal opportunity so conceived. Similarly, Robert Nozick, following Kurt Vonnegut, suggests that equal opportunity might require that talented applicants be forced to perform under disadvantageous conditions so that the less talented could compete on a literally equal basis. *Anarchy, State and Utopia* (New York: Basic Books, 1974), 217.

9. See William Nelson, "Equal Opportunity," *Social Theory and Practice* 10 (1984): 157–84.

10. Following James Lloyd-Thomas, "Competitive Equality of Opportunity," *Mind* 86 (1977): 388–404, I construe an opportunity not as a mere chance but as the actual ability to do something. This means opportunities do not come in degrees, and so, for another reason, the term *equal* can be misleading.

11. Thomas Hill, "The Message of Affirmative Action," *Social Philosophy and Policy* 8 (1991), reprinted in Joel Feinberg and Hyman Gross, *Philosophy of Law*, 5th ed. (Belmont, Calif.: Wadsworth, 1995), 447.

12. Michael Young, *The Rise of the Meritocracy* (Baltimore: Penguin, 1961). One question Young raises is whether it isn't especially bad to create a system that enhances the self-satisfaction of the successful and reinforces the disappointment of those who fail. Thomas Nagel, in "Equal Treatment and Compensatory Discrimination," *Philosophy and Public Affairs* 2 (1973): 348–63, also calls into question the idea of distributing, on meritocratic grounds, income and social prestige. He apparently does think, though, that certain jobs or college admissions would ideally, *themselves*, be distributed on the basis of some kind of desert.

13. It has long been suspected that racial disparities in employment are partly explained not by racism defined in some narrow way but by "statistical discrimination"—by the not necessarily unreasonable belief that members of certain groups are, on average, less likely to be effective workers. The trouble is that the effects of statistical discrimination on individuals and on groups are just as devastating as those of any other kind of discrimination.

14. It is regrettable, but understandable, that some nonminorities who strongly advocate preferences for minorities already have secure positions that they are not about to give up. Ideally, these persons ought to share the burden of correcting for injustice.

15. Recall the practice, described earlier, of hiring the college student children of current workers for summer jobs. I argued that this is not necessarily wrong; but it is also obvious that it is the kind of practice that perpetuates the advantages of those who are already doing well at the expense of those who never had a chance.

16. I owe some of the thoughts in this paragraph to conversations with Larry Alexander.

17. In these matters, who among us can be anything but suspicious of our own motives?

18. Andrew Hacker, "Good-Bye to Affirmative Action?" *New York Review of Books*, July 11, 1996, 21, 24.

19. At the same time, if I have to choose which principles will prevail in political debate, I can imagine worse ones.

20. This is the kind of gap I think Hill is trying to fill in "The Message of Affirmative Action."

21. Cf. Young, *The Rise of the Meritocracy*.

22. It is a commonplace that university admissions depend on all kinds of factors other than grades and test scores. In this area it is especially silly to single out affirmative action preferences for criticism to the exclusion of others.

CONTRIBUTORS

Edmund Abegg, Edinboro University of Pennsylvania

Erik A. Anderson, University of Connecticut, Storrs

Ann E. Cudd, University of Kansas

Leslie Francis, University of Utah

Emily R. Gill, Bradley University

Carol C. Gould, Stevens Institute of Technology

Christopher Gray, Concordia University, Montreal

Steven Lee, Hobart and William Smith Colleges

Rex Martin, University of Kansas (emeritus)

Larry May, Washington University, St. Louis

Joan L. McGregor, Arizona State University

William Nelson, University of Houston

George Rainbolt, Georgia State University

Thomas W. Simon, Illinois State University, Normal

Christine Sistare, Center for Ethics, Muhlenberg College

Patricia Smith, Baruch College, CUNY

Rebecca Tsosie, Arizona State University Law School

Robert N. Van Wyk, University of Pittsburgh, Johnstown

Carl Wellman, Washington University, St. Louis

INDEX

Individual(s)
  civic identity of (*see* Liberalism)
  closed groups and, 6–7, 91–93, 204, 211
  concern for, 235–36, 237, 244, 246
  consent of, 238–39, 243, 257–58
  cultural rights of, 45–46, 48, 49, 50, 183, 222–23
  group-based rights and, 38
  liberty of, 36, 48–49, 51, 98, 204, 205, 206, 208, 209, 211, 212–13, 224, 226, 269, 274–76 (*see also* Freedom, basic liberties and)
  multiple cultural identities and, 50, 183, 184, 216–17
  ontological priority of, 44–45, 48, 50, 71–72
  rights of, 6–7, 36, 38, 45–48, 50–52, 71–75, 91–92, 97–98, 222, 236, 269, 275
  social identification of, 1, 2, 4–7, 11, 26, 39, 44, 45–46, 56–59, 97–98, 100, 107, 183, 276–78
Individualism
  collectivism and, 97–98, 99, 100–101
  theories of group rights and, 71–75, 97–99, 100–101
  theory of groups and, 1–2, 33, 36, 37, 40, 49, 50, 97, 99, 100–101
  See also Liberalism
Inequality. *See* Unequal treatment

Jews/Judaism
  Holocaust and, 111
  identity of, 107
  religious practice and, 260, 270
Jones, Peter, 126, 256
Justice
  communitarian view of, 219, 220–21
  compensatory, 159, 167, 275 (*see also*

Affirmative action; Unequal treatment)
  contractarianism and, 121, 162, 220, 275
  cultural, 46
  democratic procedures and, 159, 161–62, 163–65, 220, 221
  distributive, 120–21, 122, 146–47, 158, 159, 160–77 (*see also* Affirmative action, equality of opportunity and)
  as fairness, 117, 120–21, 123, 152
  freedom and, 46
  least advantaged and, 160, 164, 167, 220
  Pareto efficiency and, 163, 167
  policy-making and, 165–66
  Rawls on, 160–62, 167, 170–71, 220–22 (*see also* Justice, as fairness)
  as reciprocity, 117, 121–22, 123, 167, 172–80 (*see also* Obligation(s))
  social, 33, 39, 42, 50, 69, 146–47, 159
  unjust arrangements and, 166–70
  utility and, 162 (*see also* Utility)

Kant, Immanuel, 148
Kelley, Dean, 249
Klosko, George, 259
Kymlicka, Will, 49, 50, 96–97, 98, 100–107, 109, 185, 203–4, 209, 210, 211, 217, 222–24, 236–37, 241–42, 244, 267–70, 271, 273, 275, 278

Larmore, Charles, 213, 254
Lee, Steven, 117
Leedes, Gary, 257
Legal theory
  Critical Legal Studies and, 100
  legal positivism and, 34–35
  natural law theory and, 34–35, 257
  sources thesis and, 35

Liberalism
autonomy and, 145, 151, 172, 203,
205, 214, 236, 248, 250–51, 255,
267–69, 275–78
civic identity and, 184–85
group rights and, 222–24, 242, 248,
251
harm principle and, 138, 144, 153–54
metaphysical distinguished from
political, 186–87
multiculturalism, pluralism, and, 215,
219, 220–24
privacy and, 144, 153
procedural form of, 213
reform movements and, 137, 152–55
religion and, 249–51, 253, 267–78 (*see
also* Religion)
social contract (*see* Political
legitimacy)
toleration and, 267–68
value neutrality and, 140–44, 145,
152–55, 186, 203, 212, 213–14, 224,
248–51
See also Democracy; Individualism
Libertarianism
concern for persons and, 235, 243, 244
democratic decision-making and,
153–54
groups and, 210
property rights and, 154, 210
welfare liberalism and, 243
See also Liberalism
Locke, John, 162, 252, 253, 273
Lyons, David, 33

MacCormick, Neil, 19, 28, 32
Macedo, Stephen, 254
Madison, James, 129, 254, 257, 258
Margalit, Avishai, 49, 224
Martin, Rex, 120
Marx, Karl, 59, 162, 167

Maximin Principle, 160. *See also* Justice,
Rawls on
May, Larry, 24, 27, 74–75
McCloskey, H. J., 28
McConnell, Michael, 254, 270, 271
McDonald, Michael, 26, 49
McGregor, Joan, 119
Mead, G. H., 3–5
Melden, A. I., 29
Meyers, Diana, 276–77
Mill, J. S., 12, 21, 30–31, 141, 146, 211,
212
Minorities, 26–27, 36, 39
cultural identity of, 46–47, 51, 52–53,
59–60, 96, 97, 102–7, 215–17, 275,
276–78
democratic systems and, 43, 96,
117–23, 215, 219–22, 229–25, 269
"national," 49–50
oppressed groups and, 47, 50–51,
63–64, 68–69, 102–7, 109–11, 216
(*see also* Affirmative action;
Unequal treatment)
persistent, 117–18, 124, 269
polyethnic, 269–70
stereotypes and, 62–63, 216
subminorities, 52–53
Moon, Donald, 186
Mormons/Mormonism, 211

Nagel, Thomas, 257–58
Native Americans, 119–20, 204, 209,
215–28, 260, 269, 271
citizenship and, 216–17
intercultural theory of, 216, 224–26
oppression of, 217–19
tribal identities of, 216, 217, 219
trust/treaty relations with United
States, 216, 218
See also Aboriginal/Native Peoples;
Groups, recognition of;